RADIOHEAD
AND THE RESISTANT CONCEPT ALBUM

RADIOHEAD
AND THE RESISTANT CONCEPT ALBUM

PROFILES IN POPULAR MUSIC

Glenn Gass & Jeffrey Magee, editors

HOW TO DISAPPEAR COMPLETELY

MARIANNE TATOM LETTS

INDIANA UNIVERSITY PRESS

Bloomington & Indianapolis

This book is a publication of

Indiana University Press
601 North Morton Street
Bloomington, Indiana 47404-3797 USA

www.iupress.indiana.edu

Telephone orders   800-842-6796
Fax orders   812-855-7931
Orders by e-mail   iuporder@indiana.edu

♾ The paper used in this publication
meets the minimum requirements of
the American National Standard for
Information Sciences—Permanence
of Paper for Printed Library
Materials, ANSI Z39.48-1992.

Manufactured in the United
States of America

Library of Congress Cataloging-
in-Publication Data

Letts, Marianne Tatom, 1970-
 Radiohead and the resistant concept
album : how to disappear completely
/ Marianne Tatom Letts.
     p. cm. — (Profiles in popular music)
 Includes bibliographical references
(p.   ), discography (p.   ), and index.
 ISBN 978-0-253-35570-6 (cloth : alk. paper)
 — ISBN 978-0-253-22272-5 (pbk. : alk. paper)
1. Radiohead (Musical group)—Criticism
and interpretation. 2. Rock music—
England—History and criticism. I. Title.
 ML421.R25L48 2010
 782.42166092'2—dc22
                                      2010018678

1   2   3   4   5   15   14   13   12   11   10

"Just because you feel it doesn't mean it's there."

RADIOHEAD, "THERE THERE" (HAIL TO THE THIEF)

CONTENTS

ACKNOWLEDGMENTS

My heartfelt thanks go to the many people who helped me during the process of completing this manuscript: Jane Behnken, my patient editor at Indiana University Press; Jeff Magee, series editor; Kevin Holm-Hudson, Dai Griffiths, and an anonymous reviewer, for their insightful comments; various people who read drafts along the way—Jim Buhler, Andrew Dell'Antonio, David Neumeyer, Byron Almén, Fred Maus, Mark Spicer—and those who offered comments at the Society for Music Theory, American Musicological Society, International Association for the Study of Popular Music, and Experience Music Project conferences; copyeditor extraordinaire Emma Young; managing editor Miki Bird; project editor Brian Herrmann; indexer Megan Giller; prog enthusiasts Bryan Sale and Steve Bonham; Nick Sibicky and Christine Amos Linial for Finale assistance; the Flightpath coffeehouse; Ruth Tatom, Marian Tatom, Richard Letts, Marmite, Esme, Tallulah; and dance friends both near and far.

It is helpful but not absolutely necessary for the reader to have a basic grounding in musical notation in order to understand the musical examples presented throughout this book. A number of fine introductory texts exist, including Stefan Kostka and Dorothy Payne's *Tonal Harmony*, 6th ed. (New York: McGraw-Hill, 2008). Because harmonic progression in most popular music functions in a different way than in Western art music (Bach, Mozart, and the like), any background knowledge will more assist the reader in understanding how Radiohead's music differs from the norm rather than in mapping conventional harmonic analysis onto it. More useful than trying to analyze a series of chords in a song as being in a particular key is exploring the idea of overall harmonic motion, of harmonic emphasis and resolution or lack thereof. Heinrich Schenker famously analyzed the music of "great" (dead, white, male) Western composers, pointing out that all "great" music proceeded from tonic (I) to dominant (V) and back again. Pop music uses different parameters for "greatness," including lyrics, orchestration, and even the personality of the artist. Walter Everett has famously used elements of Schenkerian analysis to look at the music of pop/rock artists, including Radiohead, but any "greatness" ascribed to such bands has little or nothing to do with their music's ability to be mapped onto a large-scale I–V–I progression.[1]

Although the tools used in conventional Schenkerian analysis are particular to a certain style of music, mainly that of the high classical period, they can still be somewhat helpful in examining the structure of other kinds of music. In brief, a piece of music can be reduced to two main lines, or voices (not to be confused with the human voice), generally referred to as soprano (higher) and bass (lower). Looking at how these two lines relate to each other can help map out the harmonic motion of a piece. In example 3.4, for instance, which shows the harmonic motion in "Everything in Its Right Place," the bass line moves stepwise, up a minor third from C to E-flat. Because the F in the soprano (here the actual voice) sounds discordant against the E-flat in the bass (producing a minor ninth), it can be connected instead with the bass's C, which shows that it is meant to go with that note. This "reduction" of the song shows what the listener might pay attention to and prioritizes some pitches over others. The reduction in example 3.7 serves as a guide to the song "How to Disappear Completely." The notes chosen are important structurally and show such elements as the harmonic ambiguity between the D and F-sharp, and the minor third (A to F-sharp) motive that appears in the voice, guitar, bass, and strings over the course of the song. Boxes indicate sounds that seem to exist out of time, or that have a faster harmonic rhythm than the other notes indicated. A true Schenkerian analysis would privilege a single I–V–I movement over the course of the entire piece,[2] but such a reading is not true to the pop idiom (or the artist's intent) and does not reflect the average listener's experience with the song.

Equally important for understanding structure in popular music is terminology such as verse, chorus, bridge, intro, outro, riff, groove, and hook. Definitions of the first several terms are given according to those set out by Everett, John Covach, and others:[3]

VERSE section of lyrics that usually comes right after the introduction; lyrics change each time; a song may have several verses

CHORUS lyrics that reoccur throughout the song and reaffirm the tonic and/or the song title or main message

BRIDGE a contrasting, transition section usually in a different key than the tonic

INTRO chords or riff that introduce the song, usually without lyrics

OUTRO chords or riff played after the last verse or chorus, may contain words that fade out

Thus, a simple mapping of a well-known song, the Beatles' "She Loves You," along these lines would result in the following structure:

Intro/chorus: She loves you, yeah yeah yeah . . .
Verse 1: You think you lost your love . . .
Bridge: She says she loves you . . .
Chorus (same as intro): She loves you, yeah yeah yeah . . .
Verse 2: She said you hurt her so . . .
Bridge: She says she loves you . . .
Chorus: She loves you, yeah yeah yeah . . .
Verse 3: You know it's up to you . . .
Bridge: She says she loves you . . .
Chorus: She loves you, yeah yeah yeah . . .
Bridge 2: With a love like that . . .
Outro: Yeah yeah yeah . . .

Mark Spicer's definitions of "riff" and "groove," and Richard Middleton's definition of "hook," are given as follows:

RIFF "a distinctive melodic-rhythmic idea—usually longer than a motive but not large enough to constitute a full phrase—which is frequently . . . sounded over and over again in the manner of an ostinato"[4]

GROOVE "the tapestry of riffs . . . that work together to create the distinctive rhythmic/harmonic backdrop which identifies a song."[5] Timothy Hughes adds that "groove" can refer also to the "various backdrops that support different parts of the song," and specifically to "a figure . . . designed to be repeated."[6]

HOOK a "repeated phrase" or "riff structure" that provides a structure of repetition "against which variation can take place." This repetition "offer[s] a route through the song to both producer and listener."[7] If it is short or catchy enough, a song's chorus can also function as a hook by providing something familiar for listeners to hold on to.

A famous example of a riff or hook would be the opening guitar melody to the Rolling Stones' "Satisfaction," whereas the groove would refer to the interaction of that riff with the syncopated vocal melody, the underlying bass and drums, etc.

Some of the additional terms most commonly used in this volume are:

ACCUMULATIVE GROOVE a gradual coalescing of the musical instruments toward a distinctive, interlocking rhythm

ARPEGGIO the notes of a chord played in succession rather than simultaneously (e.g., C, E, G, C for a C-major chord)

CADENCE harmonic motion in Western art music toward a resting point, such as V–I or IV–I; gives the sense of completion of a phrase

HALF-CADENCE harmonic motion in Western art music that rests at a non-final point, as in I–V; sounds incomplete

DOMINANT V chord (e.g., G-major chord in the key of C major; G is the fifth scale degree)

GLISSANDO notes played rapidly up or down the scale in stepwise motion

KEY scale around which a musical phrase is based; a key in Western art music includes seven diatonic pitches built on a tonic note

KEY AREA an area of harmonic emphasis, which may be for only part of a phrase or an entire musical work

MODULATE to move from one musical key to another

MOTIVE distinctive, reoccurring melodic phrase that often signifies a character or emotion

PITCH musical note

RESOLVE to move from a discordant harmony to a consonant one (e.g., the dissonance created by a minor seventh above the root of the V^7 chord generally resolves down a half-step to create a consonance in the next chord, typically I)

ROOT note that a chord is built upon (e.g., C is the root of the chord spelled C–E–G; C major)

SCALE in Western art music, seven diatonic pitches built on a tonic note

SCALE DEGREE the number corresponding to the distance a note in the scale is from the tonic (e.g., in C major, D is the second scale degree, E is the third, and so on)

SUPERTONIC the note or chord just above the tonic (e.g., in C major, D is the supertonic pitch)

SYNCOPATION shifting the normal accent by stressing other beats (e.g., in $\frac{4}{4}$, the normal accent is on beats 1, 2, 3, and 4; syncopation might involve accenting the off-beats instead)

TESSITURA the range of pitches for a given instrument or musical composition (e.g., a flute has a higher tessitura than a tuba)

TEXT-PAINTING technique used to illustrate words in the music (e.g., a verse about running up the stairs might use a quick, ascending melody)

TONIC the note underlying the major key area; the root of the I chord (e.g., in C major, C is the tonic)

VOCALESE singing on nonsense syllables (ooh, ah) rather than actual words; scat singing in jazz music is a type of vocalese

By having a basic understanding of both traditional musical notation and those terms endemic to popular music, the reader can understand both how Radiohead's music is structured and how it "resists" those musical conventions.

RADIOHEAD
AND THE RESISTANT CONCEPT ALBUM

Popular music of recent decades has emphasized the individual's isolation in modern society. Bands that address the anxieties provoked by contemporary culture are the darlings of critics, and music about alienation has, ironically, proven to have a strong market worldwide. The hero-worship that successful artists experience can spill over into their self-perception, creating most commonly either an overblown sense of their own importance or an ambivalent attitude toward their success. Some artists (such as Sting, Bono, and Peter Gabriel) embrace the opportunity to use their music as a platform to address such global issues as deforestation or third-world debt. Others (most drastically Kurt Cobain, but also the Manic Street Preachers' Richey Edwards, Alice in Chains' Layne Staley, and more recently Amy Winehouse) collapse under the pressure, unable to come to terms with the audience's refusal to believe that, as the Moody Blues said, "I'm Just a Singer in a Rock and Roll Band."

Radiohead has been perceived by audiences, critics, and scholars alike as one of the most important bands in popular music today. Though the band's seven studio albums to date have dealt extensively with aspects of alienation in a society of mass consumption, the band has also reaped the benefits of enormous success within this culture. The band repeatedly articulates an anxiety about being consumed, both literally and figuratively, yet it continues to produce goods for mass consumption. While decrying the effects of modern technology,

Radiohead takes full advantage of its promotional abilities, reaching listeners through not only conventional CDs, but also internet downloads, peer-to-peer file-sharing networks, chatbots, and an archive of continually updated and redesigned websites. In 2007 the band shook up the music industry by releasing the album *In Rainbows* initially as a download for which fans could specify the amount they wanted to pay, starting at nothing at all. Radiohead did eventually release the album as an actual CD as well, thus having it both ways and possibly earning even more money along with all the publicity. Although the releases of *Kid A* and *Amnesiac* in 2000 and 2001, respectively, were not such drastic leaps in a financial sense, at the time they represented a bold lashing out against commercialism and the record industry. The goal of this book is twofold: to examine in detail Radiohead's "experimental" concept albums, *Kid A* and *Amnesiac*, and to investigate the band's ambivalence and resistance toward its own success, as manifested in the vanishing subject on these two albums.

In order to comprehend Radiohead's position within and attitude toward capitalism, it is helpful to understand how contemporary theorists think about the formation of subjectivity (that is, individual consciousness and identity) in the modern capitalist system. Critical theory compares the "values" of modern society (freedom of the individual and equality for all) to the practices that often result from that system (social inequality and the subjugation of the individual by the government and/or economic forces). This critique can be expanded to include the wasting of resources that could be used to improve the environment and life in it, e.g., using technology to destroy nature rather than to conserve it. Critical theorists simultaneously comment on the modern condition of alienation and seek to combat it by working toward a more democratic and socially egalitarian society. The industrialized Western civilization is based on technological advances that purport to make life easier for humankind. Yet this system at its worst turns modern life instead into a machine dominated by governmental and economic forces, which reduces individual humans to mere drones. Capitalism, ostensibly a system of buying and selling goods, has the capacity to destroy political consciousness, turning everything into a commodity and giving every person in society a price. When everything and everyone can be bought and sold, then any motivation or tendency toward political activism is suppressed. The domination of nature (and thus of humankind) is a central aspect of Western civilization, which works toward bringing all of nature under the control of the human subject—who in the process is himself swallowed up by forces beyond his control. Theodor Adorno states:

> For since the overwhelming objectivity of historical movement in its present phase consists so far only in the dissolution of the subject, without yet giving rise to a new one, individual experience necessarily bases itself on the old subject, now historically condemned, which is still for-itself, but no longer in-itself. The subject still feels sure of its autonomy, but the nullity demonstrated to subjects by the concentration camp is already overtaking the form of subjectivity itself.[1]

In other words, the subject—that is, the human being—may still feel autonomous, but his thoughts and actions are in reality nullified by the societal forces that work to repress him. He may think he is acting of his own accord, but he is actually functioning under the influence of the conditions in which he lives. His actions and his very opinions are shaped and even dictated by market forces. He is told what and how to consume.

Adorno further states that popular culture makes people lazy because of the easy access to pleasure through the commodity; that is, anything that can be bought or sold. In the capitalist system, anything can be assigned a market value and owned by virtue of paying for it, be it food, clothing, shelter, or a pop star—thus, all of these things take on the form of the commodity. In contrast to real needs such as freedom and happiness, which are more difficult to satisfy on a mass level, culture creates false needs that can be more easily satisfied through capitalism. When people can buy pleasure on the cheap, they are able to ignore the appalling conditions in which they live and work. If they can relax with a TV dinner and a cold beer in front of a reality show after a long day of pushing paper or flipping burgers, then the needs created by mass culture have been satisfied with the consumer goods of mass culture, a cycle that effectively distracts citizens from any need to think about the higher aims of freedom or creativity. Frederic Jameson writes: "What has happened is that aesthetic production today has become integrated into commodity production generally: the frantic economic urgency of producing fresh waves of ever more novel-seeming goods (from clothing to aeroplanes), at ever greater rates of turnover, now assigns an increasingly essential structural function and position to aesthetic innovation and experimentation."[2] Savvy producers continually reinvent their products so that the urge to consume is perpetually renewed. Scarcely has the latest winner of *American Idol* been crowned than the audience is being primed to watch the next season—with even more appalling first-round auditions, even more scathing criticism by the judges, and even more praise heaped on the heads of the newest talent. As long as the audience receives ever-new talent (and can buy the iTunes release the day after an episode), they stay satisfied.

The success of bands that express alienation from and frustration with modern culture is ironic within this culture of commodification. With enough marketing skill, people can be convinced to buy the music of bands that articulate a resistance against commercialism yet still reap the monetary rewards of the capitalist system. Audiences are urged to conform by buying nonconformist music, T-shirts, and the like. By pushing products that purport to resist the mainstream, artists (and the companies behind them) create an insider culture of resistance that is actually united through its conformity to capitalism. Radiohead is not the only band that exists in this dichotomy between complaining about capitalism and benefiting from it, but their albums *Kid A* and *Amnesiac* present an interesting case study within the culture of anxiety created by life in the twenty-first century.

ANYONE CAN PLAY GUITAR: A BRIEF
HISTORY OF RADIOHEAD

Radiohead was formed by brothers Jonny and Colin Greenwood with their friends Thom Yorke, Phil Selway, and Ed O'Brien at the exclusive Abingdon School in Oxford, England. Various members had played together in other bands, but the present lineup had solidified by 1986. The five musicians were encouraged at Abingdon to learn to play instruments; they even practiced for a time at the school, though their sound was not particularly appreciated by the conservative faculty and students. Even after members of the band graduated and went off to college, the group still practiced together on weekends and played occasional gigs. Remarkably, even with the coming and going of members, the band managed to maintain its creative energy. Guitarist Ed O'Brien stated in 1997 that "there was never any question that we weren't going to do it. . . . Looking back on it, what was amazing was the commitment. Ten years ago, we talked about it. We knew we wanted to do this."[3]

The members of Radiohead have varying amounts of formal musical training. As a classically trained violist, guitarist Jonny Greenwood has the most, having played in the Thames Valley Youth Orchestra and later holding a composer-in-residence appointment at BBC Radio 3 and scoring the soundtrack to the films *Bodysong* (2003) and *There Will Be Blood* (2007).[4] The band's English public school background led some in the music press to take the attitude that Radiohead had not "paid their dues," and that their lack of professional experience before being signed by a major label meant they were somehow not qualified to produce music at that level. Dai Griffiths has noted that the band members' experience at public school might have influenced their "profound sense of being cut off from the rest of ordinary society," which they have expressed in their music throughout their career. Griffith states, however, that "the particular discourse of class is not available [to Radiohead] since of course in educational terms the band members were pretty solid beneficiaries of the capitalist system."[5] William Stone likewise observes:

> Some see the struggle of bands to avoid losing their honesty, their integrity, their souls in the heart of the corporate machine as being one of the great spectator sports of the late Twentieth Century. . . . Radiohead had to make a decision. Would they release their records on Parlophone straight and risk accusations of being nothing more than capitalist whores . . . ? Or would they release through some new label set up by the major to fake indie credibility? To their eternal credit they said it like it was—major they were, major they would be.[6]

This early effort toward major-label success would later turn to ambivalence toward the mainstream record industry as the band members found that they needed to subvert popular and audience expectations to remain true to their musical goals.

Radiohead exhibited fairly steady stylistic growth from their first album, *Pablo Honey* (1993), through *The Bends* (1995) and *OK Computer*

(1997), adding increasingly complex layers of production effects to an essentially guitar-driven sound. *Pablo Honey*'s success was due in large part to the single "Creep," which reached number 4 on the *Billboard* charts for Modern Rock Tracks of 1993, and ranked number 1 or 2 in various *Rolling Stone, Melody Maker,* and *New Musical Express* (NME) polls for that year.[7] (When "Creep" was initially released in the U.K., it reached only number 78 on the charts, but its rerelease after success in the U.S. charted at number 7. The single "Anyone Can Play Guitar" from the same album peaked at number 32 on the U.K. charts.[8]) Touring in support of one single wore the band members down. Jonny Greenwood stated in *Q* magazine that "We joined this band to write songs and be musicians, but we spent a year being jukeboxes instead. We felt in a creative stasis because we couldn't release anything new."[9] After the tepid reception of the album's other singles (the third being "Stop Whispering"), some in the industry predicted that Radiohead would be simply a one-hit wonder, but instead the band's popularity increased immensely over the period that saw the reception of *The Bends* and *OK Computer.*

During the recording sessions for *The Bends,* the band felt enormous pressure to try to duplicate the success of "Creep." Jonny Greenwood stated: "We were playing like paranoid little mice in cages. We were scared of our instruments, scared of every note not being right." According to bassist Colin Greenwood, the band tried to record the album's prospective singles first, but he thought in retrospect that they "might have done better to have completed the LP and chosen the singles to be taken from it later." The experience of trying to predict which songs would sell most successfully would influence the band's later attitude toward the music industry that resulted in the single-less *Kid A.* Radiohead had been called a "band to watch out for" by *Melody Maker* and NME in 1993,[10] and two years later *The Bends* marked what Martin Clarke called "the start of a remarkable growth in commercial success and critical applause that transformed Radiohead from a band that was highly revered into one that was being talked of as a historically classic group." This sentiment was echoed throughout the music press. *NME* stated that "Radiohead's new stuff appears to be all but classic," and "*The Bends* will be one of, and quite possibly *the*, indie rock album of the year [1995]." *Melody Maker* described the album as a "powerful, bruised and desperate record of frightening intensity . . . almost unbearably, brilliantly, physically tortured by the facts of being human."[11] *The Bends* has also been described as "the depressives' soundtrack to the nineties," a characterization that singer Thom Yorke has countered with statements such as "I did not write this album for people to slash their fucking wrists to" and *"The Bends* isn't my confessional."[12] The "culture of despair" prevalent in the years surrounding *The Bends'* release, which had given rise to the popularity of grunge bands like Nirvana and culminated in Kurt Cobain's suicide in 1994, might well have contributed to the album's popularity. Stone states: "[T]here was an entire generation of people with no heroes, no prospects, no faith in government or religion. Deafened and poisoned by corporate lies and pollution, they watched helplessly as the world was systematically deprived of any means of natural regeneration. . . . They had no real reason to stay alive."[13]

Despite the depressed cultural environment that may have helped boost Radiohead's sales, the press heaped accolades on the band. After the release of the single "Lucky" for the compilation album *Help!* (later included on *OK Computer*), which raised money for the charity War Child to benefit victims of war in the former Yugoslavia, *Melody Maker* wrote that "Radiohead are no longer capable of anything other than brilliance."[14] Stone states that "the beginning of 1996 saw Radiohead take their place at the very top of British Music."[15] The band's next album, *OK Computer,* was recognized as Album of the Year (1997) by *Q* magazine and *NME*, and the band garnered Band of the Year accolades from *Rolling Stone* and *Spin*, as well as receiving a Grammy for the Best Alternative Music Performance for the album.[16] (Radiohead would also later win the Grammy for Best Alternative Music Album for *Kid A* in 2001 and *In Rainbows* in 2009, and would be nominated in the same category for *Amnesiac* in 2002 and *Hail to the Thief* in 2004.) In addition to receiving critical acclaim, *OK Computer* drew comparisons with the art/prog rock albums of the 1970s, a sign that in addition to having widespread appeal the band was being perceived as more serious or intellectual than the typical pop-rock group. This marked its difference from such bands as Nirvana and Oasis, which consciously aligned themselves with the working class. Radiohead's English public school background and classical musical training also undoubtedly furthered the comparison to progressive rock, as did the fact that all the members of the band had attended university, and four of the five had graduated. (Jonny Greenwood dropped out of college after only a few weeks, by which time Radiohead was being courted by Capitol/EMI.[17]) Griffiths notes certain of the album's musical elements as being typical of "public schoolboy music"—rhythmic complexity, sustained ostinato, quasi-modal harmony, common-note progressions (pivot tones, or moving from one key to another by way of a pitch that both keys have in common), electronic music as background, and pitch/tonal continuity—and compares the band to Genesis, an earlier group of "public schoolboys" known for taking themselves more seriously than the average pop band.[18]

"Progressive rock" can be very loosely defined as music based in the rock tradition that contains elements from the realm of art music, such as long, structured songs; dynamics and expression; virtuosity; non-rock instrumentation; and often theatricality. Kevin Holm-Hudson points out that progressive rock should not be stereotyped as simply a fusion of classical music and rock, as is often the case.[19] Although progressive (or prog) rock and art rock have often been conflated, Holm-Hudson notes that art rock, in contrast to prog, "implies a certain sophistication, or even irony, without being explicit in its classical positioning."[20] Thus the work of an artist such as David Bowie might be considered art rock but not prog, because of his alignment with the world of visual art and his music's lack of classical form or instrumentation. Bill Martin offers a working definition of progressive rock that includes the characteristics "visionary and experimental," "played . . . on instruments typically associated with rock . . . and with the history of rock music itself as background," "played . . . by musicians who have consummate instrumental and compositional skills," and "expressive of romantic and prophetic aspects of that [English] culture."[21] As Edward Macan notes, the term "progressive rock" was originally applied to psychedelic music of the mid- to late 1960s in order to distinguish it from the non-psychedelic music that preceded it.[22] Critics and scholars writing about Radiohead have used the terms "art rock" and "progressive rock" interchangeably; however, it is less important to try to distinguish whether Radiohead is more closely aligned with art rock or prog than simply to note that the band's music has often been interpreted within the more general art/prog rock genre.

Radiohead had drawn comparisons to progressive rock well before *OK Computer*'s release. *Melody Maker* had asked in its review of *The Bends*, "Are Radiohead the spirit of prog-rock reborn?"[23] Some of the more obvious parallels between Radiohead's *OK Computer* and the progressive rock genre were the band's experimentation with the Moog and Mellotron—instruments used heavily by bands such as the Moody Blues, Genesis, and Emerson, Lake, and Palmer—and the use of hypermetric complexity in cross-rhythms and time signatures, common in the music of bands such as Yes and King Crimson. But the association also stemmed from the album's musically unified depiction of man's alienation in modern society. The lyrics and subject matter of *OK Computer* can be linked to such classic prog rock albums as Pink Floyd's *The Wall* (1979) and *Animals* (1977) and Jethro Tull's *Aqualung* (1971) and *Thick as a Brick* (1972). Holm-Hudson notes that *OK Computer*'s comparisons with *Dark Side of the Moon* (1973), another classic of the prog rock era, stem from "the continuity of its transitions between songs more than any perceived similarities in musical style." He further states that "'post-progressive' groups such as . . . Radiohead also draw upon selective aspects of vintage progressive rock, even as they actively seek to distance themselves from associations with the genre."[24]

Given Radiohead's art-college experience in addition to the band members' English public school background and classical training, it is certainly possible that their influences reach beyond the progressive rock era to encompass visual arts, theater, film, literature, and even the Romantic song cycle. Many of the original prog rock artists also came from an English art-school background, so it may be that the members of Radiohead came to similar notions about album construction by virtue of coming of age in a comparable environment rather than by having consciously set out to imitate their forebears in popular music. There is an evolution of visual imagery over the course of Radiohead's albums[25] tending toward a *Gesamtkunstwerk*, a complete artwork encompassing a unification of elements, visual as well as musical/lyrical. It is difficult to know whether Radiohead was being influenced by similar "packages" from the progressive world (examples begin with the Beatles' *Sgt. Pepper* and Frank Zappa's *Freak Out*, and continue on to any number of prog rock albums) or whether Radiohead had something more like Wagner's *Ring* cycle in mind. Regardless of the band members' true influences, critics and audiences alike have compared Radiohead's albums to art/prog rock, and it is that comparison to which the band members have reacted in many of their public comments.

The negative reaction that many people had to the "progressive" label after its 1970s heyday persisted in some critiques of *OK Computer* as well as in the band's reaction to the term. Clarke states that the "only real [negative] criticism of *OK Computer* was that it was redolent of that great seventies monster, 'prog-rock,' which conjured up images of flared trousers, pompous album artwork, soloist self-indulgence and gargantuan synthesizers." Colin Greenwood was reportedly "horrified" by *Rolling Stone*'s description of *OK Computer* as a "stunning art-rock tour de force," saying "What a ghastly thought. That makes it sound like Rick Wakeman and his Knights of the Round Table on Ice."[26] (Keyboardist Rick Wakeman of Yes famously staged his *The Myths of King Arthur and His Knights of the Round Table* as an Ice Capades show in the 1970s. Wakeman offered his opinion on Radiohead in 2001: "Sorry, guys, you're as prog as they come."[27]) Part of the negative reaction to the original era of progressive rock was the perception of its betrayal of rock's "authenticity" (another sticky term) by appropriating the trappings of the "establishment" represented by Western art music. Style traits borrowed from the classical realm included the use of orchestration, multi-movement works, instrumental virtuosity, and spoken or sung poetry. The ongoing negative perception of progressive rock can be seen in Chuck Klosterman's tongue-in-cheek definition of what constitutes "prog in 2005":

> An artist can be referred to as "kind of proggy" if he or she does at least two of the following things: writes long songs, writes songs with solos, writes songs about mythical creatures, writes songs that girls hate, . . . consistently declines interview requests, claims to be working on a rock opera, claims to have already released a rock opera, . . . refuses to appear in his or her own videos, . . . uses laser technology in any capacity. . . .[28]

Clarke cites *OK Computer*'s "enormous scope, its artwork, and its dense subject matter" as some less polarizing or negatively received elements of progressive rock.[29] Mark Spicer notes that Radiohead's "penchant for innovative formal structures and unique sonic landscapes" has also garnered comparisons to progressive rock, although he points out that their music actually sounds quite different from bands of the original progressive era.[30] Allan F. Moore and Anwar Ibrahim also observe that although Radiohead's style has "progressed" throughout its recordings, from "simple" to "more difficult/complex" (from a straightforward, guitar-heavy sound to one that incorporates layers of production and electronic effects), the band's style is not "progressive" in the sense of the 1970s genre.[31] Despite these caveats, Q magazine's special issue on "Pink Floyd & the Story of Prog Rock" listed OK Computer as number 10 on the list of "40 Cosmic Rock Albums," which includes albums by such art-rock dinosaurs as Genesis and the Nice (the number-one spot went to Dark Side of the Moon).[32] After OK Computer, Radiohead's style developed into one that stretched the limits even of prog rock's highbrow inaccessibility. The band's 2000/2001 albums, Kid A and Amnesiac, can be treated as versions of the defining art-object of the prog rock tradition, the concept album, but as entities that resist that tradition rather than aligning themselves with it. Regardless of whether the band itself set out to create a concept album with either work, their stylistic alignment with progressive rock and the unified approach that each album represents make the idea of the concept album a prime approach for understanding them.

AMBITION MAKES YOU LOOK PRETTY UGLY: COMMENTS ON THE CONCEPT ALBUM

Many albums of the post-Beatles period have been viewed not as loosely organized collections of radio singles, but rather as artistic utterances that develop deeper insights over the course of the song sequence. Prior to the Sgt. Pepper era, albums were generally released in support of one or two singles, with throwaway "filler" songs making up the rest of the material. Singles normally had an "A-side," which would receive the most radio airplay, and a "B-side," which had less commercial appeal.[33] B-sides are no longer necessarily seen as having less appeal; in fact, many bands, from the 1980s to the present, have capitalized on their fans' desire to possess all of their music by compiling collections of B-side material and offering it for sale. Knowledge of this (formerly) rarer material is sometimes taken as the mark of an insider, or a true fan. And of course the continued mining of the recording vaults for "new" older material generates additional income for the artist or, in the case of someone like Jimi Hendrix or Janis Joplin, for his or her estate. Thus is commodification possible even beyond the grave.

Many recording artists and producers still put together their albums in support of singles, positioning the songs intended for radio or virtual release prominently on their CDs in order to "hook" the listener as early as possible, generally on the first or second track. For many albums, however, particularly those by artists who aspire to be taken seriously to some degree in the adult- or indie-listener market, the song sequence is no longer an indifferent organizational aspect, but a prime location of meaning and significance, unfolding the actions or adventures of a protagonist. Regardless of whether an album's song sequence forms as cohesive a narrative as a novel or film, the listener can be tempted—even encouraged—to look for a similar development of meaning, particularly when a singer assumes a dramatic persona to guide the listener through the album's events, such as Bono's "Fly" or David Bowie's "Ziggy Stardust." When this persona is present, it can be understood as the representation of the subject, or protagonist, embodied in the voice, the place at which the singer and subject seem to coincide and produce an element of stability in the overall discourse. Although the singer's identity should not be strictly mapped onto that of the album's subject, the singer does embody the subject (by literally giving him a voice) in a way that makes it easy for the listener to conflate the two, or to confuse the singer's biography with that of the fictional protagonist. An artist such as Bowie could have been in danger of being pigeonholed as one of his many stage/album characters. Precisely because he has continually reinvented himself, however, he has managed to transform, chameleon-like, from one persona to the next with no loss in artistic integrity. A more modern example of persona versus voice is the Decemberists' live performance of their concept album *The Hazards of Love* (2009), in which various singers assume the parts of characters over the course of the narrative; the band members do not act out the action, but they sing the roles as they play their musical instruments.

If the listener regards musical events as dramatic actions, then she may attribute such actions to musical "agents" in the form of the voice, an instrument, or a melodic or rhythmic gesture.[34] Although much of the scholarly work on musical agents has addressed classical music, the temptation to assign intention or action to a voice, instrument, or motive is even greater in popular music, because of its attendant lyrics and the often-dramatic stage personae of its performers. If the listener identifies a collaboration among the various musical agents disclosed over the course of an album, whether such agents are presented as actual characters or simply as instrumental motives, she may perceive a unified subject and consequently experience the work as having a more cohesive form than any random collection of songs, even if they share a common lyrical theme. An album, and particularly a "concept album," may also produce the appearance of unity by presenting an explicit narrative of subject formation, as in the Who's *Tommy* (1969); a broad lyrical and/or musical theme, as in the Moody Blues' *Days of Future Passed* (1968) or Jethro Tull's *Aqualung*; or a reoccurring musical motive, as in Pink Floyd's *The Wall.* The term "concept album" is not well defined. Both scholarly articles and mainstream music reviews generally treat the term as self-evident, trusting that most people know what a concept album is without needing it defined. Beyond any apparent intent on the part of the artist to draw an album together into a coherent whole through its musical or lyrical content, *any* album is to some extent unified the same way a deejay's playlist is, simply by virtue of its sequence of tracks. A listener intent on listening to an album as a whole instead of in piecemeal three-minute chunks defined by the tracks can always, by being sufficiently clever, turn the running order into a mark of cohesion, constructing her own "concept" in the form of a narrative or at least a consistent theme. In this sense, as producer Ken Scott has said, "a concept album is in the eye/ear of the beholder."[35]

The most explicit version of the concept album is one tied to a stage or film musical, which connects a series of songs to a visual narrative. Whereas the songs of most musicals are written for a given plot and are meant to be sung by specific characters, other musicals weave a narrative around pre-existing material. Some examples of the latter are *Mamma Mia!* (musical 1999, film 2008, both based on the songs of ABBA) and, more whimsically, the film *Yellow Submarine*

(1968), which arranges the songs of the Beatles so they form a narrative that maps neatly onto Joseph Campbell's hero's journey.[36] Several new songs were commissioned for *Yellow Submarine* (including "Hey Bulldog" and "It's All Too Much"), but because these new songs do not have the pre-existing album associations for listeners, they have less dramatic impact. Some albums are brought to the stage or screen with their running order largely intact, such as *Tommy* and *The Wall*, and the more recent production of Green Day's *American Idiot* (which interjects B-side material as well as songs from their 2009 release *21st Century Breakdown*). Other musical productions are less clever in their use of pre-existing songs, and their lack of a compelling narrative may detract from their reception and appeal (such as the so-called "jukebox musicals" *The Times They Are A-Changin'*, using the songs of Bob Dylan, and *Movin' Out*, using the songs of Billy Joel).[37]

Grove Music Online defines "album" somewhat narrowly, as "a collection of songs organized around one central theme," which may be "unified by one pivotal idea" or "built around a narrative sequence."[38] Other sources define "concept album" more broadly:

· "an LP intended to be integrated on a set theme"[39]
· the "practice of tying a series of songs together by using both a reoccurring melodic theme and a program—that is, a unifying idea or concept which is developed in the lyrics of the individual songs"[40]
· the process of "taking the album itself as the level at which the music, production, cover art, and so on come together as a complete work of art"[41]
· "the texts of a Romantic rock aesthetic . . . [that] proved forerunners of a new social and economic sensibility in rock" (with regard to progressive rock)[42]
· and, rather vaguely, as simply an "'extended work' for rock."[43]

The concept album is "simultaneously a vehicle of artistic expression and a commercial commodity, a medium and a format";[44] any "concept" present may thus derive from the recording artist, the producer, the record company's marketing department, the listener, or any combination thereof.

The Beatles' *Sgt. Pepper* (1967) is still considered by many to be the first rock/pop concept album, although various albums released before it had attempted unification at different levels, from collections of diverse songs on a particular theme (going back even as far as Woody Guthrie's *Dust Bowl Ballads* [1940] and Frank Sinatra's *In the Wee Small Hours* [1954]) to more focused artistic statements (the Beach Boys' *Pet Sounds* [1966]). The time period surrounding *Sgt. Pepper* was rife with concept albums. Frank Zappa and the Mothers of Invention released their debut album *Freak Out!*—consisting of songs that all made satirical jabs at American popular culture—in 1966; *The Who Sell Out*, in which fake jingles for real products were interspersed among the more customary pop singles, came out in 1967[45]; and the Pretty Things' *S. F. Sorrow*—a song cycle based on a short story by the band's singer—was released in 1968. The Beatles' album is certainly the best known and most popular of these, and Moore observes that "*Sgt. Pepper* affords a looseness of perceptual clarity particularly through its lyrics, its images and the studio manipulation of its musical materials," suggesting that perhaps its status as a concept album stems from its perceived cultural importance and reception as much as from any inherent musical unity. Moore states also that *Sgt. Pepper*'s concept "in visual form is more easily assimilated than a thematic one."[46] That is, the perception of the album's unity comes from surface elements easily accessible to the casual listener, such as its cover packaging and song lyrics, rather than from those strictly musical unifying features commonly found in the art-music tradition, such as key relationships or tempos. Macan notes that

> prior to the late 1960s, the main purpose of an album cover in popular music was to show the performers. Significantly, *Sergeant Pepper* was the first rock music album sleeve that contained the lyrics to all of the album's songs. Clearly, the Beatles intended this first concept album to be a *Gesamtkunstwerk* (a "unified" or "complete art work") in which music, words, and visual art are all combined to convey a specific concept or program.[47]

By presenting the album's material as a stage show, complete with crowd noise and the introduction of a (fictional) singer, the Beatles were effectively staging a theater piece or a virtual concert experience. Studio wizardry such as stereophonic sound might also have helped "place" the listener with regard to the music, creating the sense of be-ing at a live performance (an ironic act, given the album's extensive overdubbing that could not be reproduced live—a contributing factor in the Beatles' decision to retire from live performance). In addition, the album cover and inner gatefold photograph showed the Beatles in costume (with instruments) as Sgt. Pepper's band, and the original sleeve included a page of cutouts such as a Sgt. Pepper mustache and badges. David O. Montgomery agrees that *Sgt. Pepper's* packaging as well as the order and content of its musical tracks brought greater coherence to the work, resulting in a total listening experience at the album level, but as William J. Schafer points out, the individual tracks themselves were "still built on the familiar pop-single pattern."[48]

The notion of individual songs being complete apart from the al-bum does not necessarily run counter to the idea of the concept album; even progressive rock masterpieces still retained the odd radio-friendly single (e.g., Emerson, Lake, and Palmer's "Lucky Man" from the band's self-titled first album [1970], or Yes's "Roundabout" from *Fragile* [1972]). When compared with a musical work from the symphonic realm (pre-sumably the ideal of "high art" to which the concept album aspires), however, the idea of excerpting an individual movement for radio play becomes much less palatable. Conversely, Roy Shuker states that *Sgt. Pepper's* treatment as a concept album stems from "its musical cohe-sion rather than any thematic [that is, deriving from the fictional char-acters described in the lyrics and packaging] unity."[49] Shuker seems here to be referring to the overall experimental and orchestrated style of the album, which marked a departure for the Beatles from their earlier work. If we discount the "White Album" (*The Beatles*, 1968) for a moment, *Sgt. Pepper* sounds like a logical stylistic link between *Re-volver* (1966) and *Abbey Road* (1969). Certainly *Sgt. Pepper's* cohesion is emphasized by its packaging, which implies a narrative coherence, and by the fact that no promotional singles were released from it. Lis-teners were therefore virtually forced to consider the album as a whole (a new prospect at the time), so again the concept album seems to be a function of commerce; that is, embodying a form of commodity. By not releasing any singles, not only did the Beatles "force" listeners to consider *Sgt. Pepper* in its entirety, but listeners were also "forced" to buy it as a whole. They could still listen to the album's tracks as individual "songs"; it had just become impossible to acquire them that way. Moore states that *Sgt. Pepper* represented "an early endeavor for rock to build a unity greater than that of the individual, self-contained utterance,"[50] that is, a cohesion beyond the level of the song, marking also a shift from the usual album format of what Shuker calls "a collection of heterogeneous songs" to a "narrative work with a single theme, in which individual songs segue into one another."[51]

Since *Sgt. Pepper*, many questions have arisen about how to define the form, characteristics, and significance of the concept album. James Borders expresses one important point of view in his analysis of Frank Zappa's *Freak Out!*, which he calls a "song cycle with a unifying sociological theme," stating that "the sequence of related songs that became known as the 'concept album' had revealed itself a literary rather than a musical form."[52] The *Grove* entry for "song cycle" offers the following definition and commentary:

> A group of individually complete songs designed as a unit . . . , for solo or ensemble voices with or without instrumental accompaniment. . . . They may be as brief as two songs . . . or as long as 30 or more. . . . The coherence regarded as a necessary attribute of song cycles may derive from the text (a single poet; a story line; a central theme or topic such as love or nature; a unifying mood; poetic form or genre, as in a sonnet or ballad cycle) or from musical procedures (tonal schemes; reoccurring motifs, passages or entire songs; formal structures); these features may appear singly or in combination.[53]

This definition can be applied to the concept album as well. Its coherence may derive solely from the lyrics (composed by the band collectively, by any of its members, or by an external source; an extra layer of coherence can be added by the singer's adoption of a dramatic persona—such as "Tommy"—other than simply the leader of the band), from reoccurring musical elements or orchestration (particularly if the latter is marked as distinct from the band's overall style as defined over the course of several albums), or from a combination of the two.

In addition to Borders, other music scholars have also discussed album-length works as song cycles: groups of songs on a particular topic meant to be performed together. Spicer, for instance, has analyzed

Genesis's "Supper's Ready" (1972) as a narrative song cycle, unified by reoccurring musical motives and key relationships, and as a prototype for the band's later album *The Lamb Lies Down on Broadway* (1974).[54] Peter Kaminsky has discussed Paul Simon's album *Still Crazy After All These Years* (1975) as a song cycle, noting especially its "unified text narrative" and "pattern completion and association," which together subsume the unifying strategies of motives, harmonic progressions, and key successions.[55] Both Shaugn O'Donnell and Holm-Hudson have examined *Dark Side of the Moon*, the former stressing its "tonal and motivic coherence" that make it the "'quintessential' concept album," as well as a song cycle, and the latter exploring its unifying "cinematic" elements such as "fades, dissolves, direct cuts, montage," and the "use of continuous segues from song to song to facilitate an unbroken trip."[56]

Some scholars, like Borders, see the "concept" of an album as literary; others prefer to focus on musical cohesion as the true source of relevance for the album. Shuker conflates the terms "concept album" and "rock opera," stating that both are "unified by a theme, which can be instrumental, compositional, narrative, or lyrical."[57] *Grove* suggests that rock operas "grew out of 'concept albums,' LPs with a theme, in the mid-1960s, and hence are really closer to the song cycles of the classical tradition than to opera." One way of distinguishing rock operas from concept albums is that rock operas, like regular operas, have characters, whereas concept albums tend to have only lyrical subjects, who express their thoughts and feelings in the first person. *Grove* notes that concept albums in America have tended to be singer/songwriter-based, and thus more reflective, more the utterance of a lyrical "I," akin to the traditional song cycle with its acutely personal lyrics.[58] Some of the classic British concept albums, by contrast, explore broad sociological themes or futuristic scenarios.

When we consider the sociological importance of poet/musicians such as Bob Dylan, Donovan, Leonard Cohen, and various other folksingers and protest poets of the 1960s, it seems logical that the concept album would emerge from the relevance of such lyrics to society, making the music relevant by default as the carrier of that lyrical meaning. The *Grove* entry for "pop" further notes that the "concept album" may be unified by its appeal to "social criticism," as in the case of Marvin Gaye's *What's Going On* (1971), a means of unification also used in

Jethro Tull's *Thick as a Brick* and *Aqualung* and the Kinks' *The Village Green Preservation Society* (1968).[59] Montgomery notes that Schafer has linked the concept album to the "themes, social concerns, and aesthetics of the counterculture."[60] That is, the experimentation present on many concept albums, both musically (longer songs, new electronic instruments) and lyrically (fantastic themes, outer-space imagery), was in part a reaction to the mind-expanding activities and societal rebellion of the youth counterculture during the Vietnam era and afterward. The aspirations of bettering society by loosening its restrictions found voice not only in the popular music of the time, but also in the popular literature (e.g., science-fiction works such as Robert Heinlein's *Stranger in a Strange Land* [1962]).

As much as many elements of the concept album make sense in a musical and historical context, the development of the format presented popular audiences with surprises and sometimes challenges. Given rock music's beginnings as a medium for dance, particularly with the nonsensical lyrics of many early singles ("Be-Bop-a-Lula," "Shimmy Shimmy Ko-Ko Bop," etc.), the concept album's new emphasis on lyrical unification could be read as a betrayal of the rock genre (recall that this was in fact one criticism of progressive rock). However, it could also be said that lyrics, evolving in prominence and complexity in early rock, simply provided an easier—or at least less esoteric—means of presenting a unified topic than writing songs in related keys or developing a musical motive over several three-minute songs.

Moore relates the concept album to the ideals of progressive rock in the 1970s, building on *Sgt. Pepper*'s appeal to unity at the album level (through packaging, characters, and a simulated stage performance) and articulating a "desire to establish a degree of aesthetic [that is, musical] unity greater than that of the individual song,"[61] though a direct correlation between the concept album and progressive rock should not be inferred.[62] Martin states that

> if this term ["concept album"] refers to albums that have thematic unity and development throughout, then in reality there are probably fewer concept albums than one might at first think. *Pet Sounds* and *Sergeant Pepper's* do not qualify according to this criterion; of the major albums of progressive rock, only a relative handful can truly be considered concept albums in the thematic sense. . . . However, if instead we stretch

the definition a bit, to where the album *is* the concept, then it is clear that progressive rock is entirely a music of concept albums.[63]

That is, if the "concept" becomes the album-length work itself, rather than a collection of disparate songs, then a genre that consists largely of album-length artistic statements can be logically linked to the idea of the concept album.

Macan also draws a parallel between progressive rock and classical music, including such common traits as the "continuous use of tone colors drawn from symphonic or church music, the employment of lengthy sectional forms such as the song cycle or the multimovement suite, and the preoccupation with dazzling metrical and instrumental virtuosity."[64] These traits could stem from the musical training and experience of the musicians involved in progressive rock, which tended to be more classically based than that of the typical "bar band"; it could also be that these musicians were attempting to align themselves with the art-music tradition in order to be taken more seriously. Macan further states that the very definition of the term "progressive rock" is derived from this relationship: "a style that sought to expand the boundaries of rock on both a stylistic basis (via the use of longer and more involved structural formats) and on a conceptual basis (via the treatment of epic subject matter), mainly through the appropriation of elements associated with classical music."[65] *Grove* notes that "nearly all the first examples [of the concept album] were British, reflecting the greater tendency on the part of art-school educated British rockers to aspire to high art in their emulations of the American vernacular."[66] That is, many British bands were taking an American art form, rock-and-roll music, and repackaging it back to American audiences as some kind of "highbrow" (but not too highbrow) listening experience.

Moore notes that Jethro Tull's *Thick as a Brick* and *A Passion Play* (1973) were both "considered concept albums in that they played unbroken from beginning to end, with a musical and lyrical continuity sufficiently strong to lead from one quasi-song into the next . . . although exactly what the 'concept' was remained rather obscure."[67] In the process, the band eroded song boundaries so that the songs could be incorporated into a larger text; in a sense this is a means of controlling the listener, a way of listening *for* the listener by prescribing the terms of listening. If an entire album side were made up of one continuous track (or groove, on an LP), in which songs faded in and out, the listener would be hard-pressed to excerpt a particular "single" to play. Moore points out that "[d]espite the fact that very few classical pieces attempt to achieve a sense of unity across spans in excess of half an hour, there remains a widespread assumption that concept albums are intended to do so, playing in an uninterrupted fashion."[68] The unifying aspect of performability is also common to the early concept albums; Pink Floyd had been performing *Dark Side of the Moon* live as a "complete piece" well before its recording,[69] and the Who made the nine-minute "mini-opera" "A Quick One While He's Away" a staple of their live set long after its release.[70] Pink Floyd and the Who also famously gave many live performances of at least lengthy portions of their concept albums *The Wall* and *Tommy*, respectively. In such cases, the songs can be read as deriving their meaning through their context within a larger work, rather than the album-length work attaining coherence through an overarching unity forged between individual songs.

A crowning challenge in defining what constitutes a concept album is deciding what it is *not*. Although a concept album is ultimately in the eye of the beholder, at some level a concept album should exhibit an intent toward cohesion on the part of the songwriter(s) or band, and this cohesion must come from an artistic level deeper than that of, say, a record company releasing a compilation album of songs by various artists on a theme chosen by someone other than the original artists (say, *Today's Country Christmas* [2007]). The recording artist's message may be interpreted by the listener to a greater or lesser degree, but it seems a stretch to call any album a concept album simply by virtue of being able to assign a narrative to its songs. If this were the case, then any random shuffling of tracks and subsequent creation of a playlist could be compiled and burned into its own "concept album." On the other hand, a musical artist's denial of whether a given recording is a concept album should not necessarily be taken at face value. Composers are somewhat notorious for resisting the interpretation of their work by outside analysts. Particularly in the case of Radiohead, when part of the band's marketing strategy is toward resistance, any claims on the part of the artist toward the product should be regarded with skepticism, if not outright suspicion. And when the negative reputation of concept albums in progressive rock is brought into the equation, it becomes clearer why certain (especially modern) bands might deny any link to that musical genre, while still producing albums that are conceptual at some level.

A beginning taxonomy of the different types of concept album might look something like this:

TABLE 1.1. Taxonomy of the Concept Album

I. Narrative (akin to novel, film, stage musical)
  A. Plot
    1. Explicit
      a. Timeless/mythic ("once upon a time")
      b. Flashback/flashforward (non-chronological)
    2. Implied
      a. Constructed by the listener with little effort (causal relationships between events)
  B. Characters
    1. Protagonist
      a. Sympathetic
      b. Anti-hero
    2. Aspects of one character's psyche
    3. Singer as protagonist or actor (see thematic/lyrical below)

II. Thematic (collections of songs)
  A. Music
    1. Recurring motives that comment on action
    2. Orchestration/instrumentation (strings, winds, electronica)
    3. Genres (classical, folk, rock)
    4. Broad themes denoted by instruments or motives (brass choir as heroic, acoustic guitar as simple and pure)
    5. Key/mode associations (one key or closely related keys; major/minor modes)
  B. Lyrics
    1. Songs on a given topic (death, environmental concerns)
    2. Sung by a character but not containing a narrative other than a stage show (emcee/host)
    3. May include key/mode associations (sad lyrics over minor music)

III. Resistant (unified but resists interpretation)
  A. Non-explicit plot/characters
    1. Doesn't carry through entire album (tenuously linked episodes)
    2. Protagonist dies or is completely absent
  B. Musical discontinuity
    1. Musical elements may contribute to dissolution of plot or failure of protagonist

C. Unclear "concept"
    1. Listener may be responsible for figuring out the concept
    2. Artist may deny that any concept is present
D. Lyrics
    1. Blur the action or intent rather than defining it

Concept albums can be broadly characterized as either narrative or thematic. Narrative albums are typified by having an explicit plot and characters, or at the very least a protagonist who undergoes some kind of trial or life journey. The plot may be cyclical, as in Joseph Campbell's hero's journey or Pink Floyd's *The Wall*. The story may be timeless or mythic rather than linear, or it may involve flashbacks or flashforwards. The characters may be imaginary or may exist only as aspects of the protagonist's psyche, as may the action. The protagonist might be unsympathetic, or might not triumph over adversity. The accompanying music often serves to propel the action along but may either support or challenge the protagonist; it may also function as a chorus commenting on the action or as a soundtrack to the subject's inner thoughts and feelings. *Tommy* and *The Wall* are classic narrative concept albums. In *Tommy*'s storyline, the protagonist is silenced after witnessing the murder of his mother's lover by his father, and then undergoes a series of abuses and life changes that ultimately turn him into a messianic figure. In the plot of *The Wall*, a protagonist retreats into his music after a series of losses and ultimately creates a barrier between himself and his friends, family, and audience. *The Wall*'s narrative is constructed as a cycle that repeats endlessly each time the album is played: the last song segues smoothly into the first, suggesting that the actions reoccur on a loop inside the protagonist's mind. The protagonist of a narrative concept album is normally heard as the lead singer, in some cases literally embodying him onstage (as in *Tommy*), although, as stated earlier, the events of a given album are unlikely to match exactly those of the singer's life.

The thematic concept album can be split into the categories of musical or lyrical. The lyrical concept album consists of a collection of songs on a given topic (setting aside the collections of songs by different artists on a specific topic, such as the aforementioned *Today's Country Christmas* and "cover" versions of tunes by a given songwriter, as in the 1991 album *I'm Your Fan*, on which various artists interpret the songs of Leonard Cohen). The lyrically thematic concept album may have strong links to the Romantic song cycle, in which several poems are set to a series of tunes that form a logical harmonic progression and may develop a musical motive, but this type of concept album might not include the tonal associations that would lead a series of songs through a sequence of actions supported by traditional harmonies and key relations. Examples are the Moody Blues' *Days of Future Passed,* which matches song titles to the times of day in an unnamed subject's life ("Tuesday Afternoon," "Nights in White Satin," etc.; the "classical" orchestration and interludes also mark the album's unity), and Nick Cave and the Bad Seeds' *Murder Ballads* (1996), a collection of songs about murder (the unifying musical elements stem from Cave's overall style rather than an album-specific artistic choice).

A musically thematic album may contain reoccurring motives that appear at crucial times in the plot or are transformed to reflect a change in the protagonist's attitude. The theme may change from major to minor, or may be truncated or extended, depending on the underlying action. Both *Tommy* and *The Wall* exhibit musical unity, the latter album to the point of overload and almost of parody, as the stepwise minor-third riff first heard in the lyrics "We don't need no . . . ," in "Another Brick in the Wall, Pt. 2," supersaturates the texture. Themes in a broader sense may exist as groups of instruments (woodwinds or brass) or as genres invoked as musical codes to comment on a given topic ("Tommy's Holiday Camp" uses a voice that sounds like a carnival barker and a rollicking band that sounds little like the Who on their other tracks). The album may play themes off each other or contrast them to make a larger point. An album's theme may comment on problems facing humanity or on universal truths rather than simply presenting a localized set of conflicts for a given protagonist to combat. Jethro Tull's *Aqualung* pits groups of acoustic/folk, rock, and blues/jazz instruments against each other to articulate the singer/songwriter's feelings on the problem of homelessness and man's inhumanity to man. Pink Floyd's *Animals* looks at the cruelties of capitalism through images inspired by George Orwell's *Animal Farm.*

Other concept albums in these categories are Pink Floyd's *Dark Side of the Moon* (thematic, with reoccurring lyrical and musical elements), Jethro Tull's *Songs from the Wood* and *Heavy Horses* (1977 and 1978; lyrically thematic, though the former also includes some acoustic musical elements that support its "pagan" lyrical theme), Liz Phair's *Exile in Guyville* (1999; lyrically thematic), Liars' *They Were Wrong, So We Drowned* (2004; thematic, with both lyrical and musical elements that relate to the overall theme of the witch trials), Green Day's *American Idiot* (2004; lyrically thematic), and the Decemberists' *The Hazards of Love* (narrative as well as lyrically and musically thematic).

Some concept albums attain their impression negatively, as it were, by consistently resisting one or another of the categories. "Resistant" albums are those that stretch the parameters of the traditionally defined concept album (a clearly articulated narrative, characters, or a musical/lyrical theme) while still conveying some kind of concept beyond a single sequence of organized tracks over the course of an album. The protagonist may expire before the end of the album or may be completely absent, and the musical elements may actively work to annihilate him or may supersede the voice's normally active role in the texture. In addition, it may be difficult or nearly impossible for the listener to discern the "concept" without being told it explicitly through album packaging, marketing, or statements by band members. All of these elements may also enhance and strengthen the concept album experience. Pink Floyd's *Wish You Were Here* (1975) achieves unity in part through its song titles ("Shine On You Crazy Diamond" parts I–V and VI–X) and musical motives, but it may also enrich the listener's experience to imagine that the album refers to the mental breakdown of former lead singer Syd Barrett, though this connection is not made explicit by the album itself. In a resistant concept album, the artist subverts expectations while still attempting to tie him- or herself to the form. Resistant concept albums, which are more a strategy than a type in the pure sense, include the Circus Devils' *The Harold Pig Memorial* (2002; the band is a side project of Guided By Voices' frontman Robert Pollard), which presents a wake for a dead biker in which he is reconstructed through his friends' memories; and the Radar Bros.' *And the Surrounding Mountains* (2002), which presents images of sacrifice and nature, loosely unified by references to family members ("You and the Father," "Sisters," "Uncles," "Mothers"). The important point to consider with regard to the overall art form is that a concept album need not be strictly narrative to present a cohesive "concept" to the listener, nor should she necessarily be looking for one.

Treating Radiohead's *Kid A* (2000) as a resistant concept album can help make sense of an otherwise baffling musical work. This analysis is, of course, only one way of viewing the album. Its very resistance to the conventional rock genre opens it up to a variety of interpretations. The album presents a challenge to cohesion in the sense of most popular music, as it does not have clear singles or even conventional verse/chorus construction on many of its songs. Despite what would normally be treated as shortcomings in pop/rock music, the album is remarkably unified through its packaging and its filtered sounds, electronic beats, and nihilistic lyrics. *Kid A* can be viewed through the lens of the concept album in order to examine ways in which it resists that tradition while still reinforcing it. On *Kid A*, the subject is gradually built up until the midpoint of the album and then self-destructs, only to receive and then abandon a second chance in the album's second half. This subject is then revived for Radiohead's follow-up recording, *Amnesiac* (2001), but encounters similar challenges in trying to create meaning from modern life. Singer Thom Yorke has stated that *Amnesiac* is "like getting into someone's attic, opening a chest and finding their notes from a journey that they've been on. . . . There's a story but no literal plot, so you have to keep picking out fragments. You know something really important has happened to this person that's ended up completely changing them, but you're never told exactly what it is."[71]

Kid A, given its cohesive packaging and unified overall lyrics, is clearly concerned with creating a subject. Nevertheless, it resists conventional notions of cohesion associated with the concept album, its subject neither a character with a narrative story nor an avatar of the lead singer. Instead, it offers a hopeless, self-negating subject who disintegrates at the moment of maximum articulation. The band's distinctive sense of alienation, explored throughout *Pablo Honey, The Bends*, and *OK Computer*, makes any centered sense of the singer-as-subject no longer possible. The song that marks the crisis point of *Kid A*, "How to Disappear Completely" (track four), provides a negative afterimage of a persona destroyed instead of the more customary moment of unification between singer and subject.

A review of the atmosphere surrounding Radiohead's previous album, *OK Computer,* will shed some light on why this type of nihilistic disintegration may have been appealing to the band members at the particular career point when they released *Kid A.*

THE RECEPTION OF **OK COMPUTER** AND **KID A**

To better position *Kid A*, it is important to look at the analysis and reception of its predecessor, *OK Computer* (1997), Radiohead's third album, which is not only the band's best-selling album to date but has retained its popularity long after its release. Reviewers have called *OK Computer* "the greatest album, like, ever," and "one of the most hysterically praised releases in rock history." It was voted "best album of all time" by *Q* magazine readers in 1998, and, significantly, again in 2001, after the release of *Kid A* and *Amnesiac*. In 2008 *OK Computer* was number 3 on *Q* magazine's 50 Best Ever British Albums, beating out the Beatles' *Revolver, Sgt. Pepper,* and *Abbey Road. OK Computer* was ranked number 1 on *Spin*'s Best Albums 1985–2005, not for being a document of its own decade, but because it "uncannily predicted our global culture of communal distress."[1] *Rolling Stone* gave *Kid A* the number 1 spot on its "100 Best Albums of the Decade" list, stating that "only 10 months into the century, Radiohead had made the decade's best album—by rebuilding rock itself, with a new set of basics and a bleak but potent humanity."[2]

OK Computer has also received a great deal of analytical attention from music scholars, many of whom have treated the work as a concept album, at least in part. James Doheny argues that the track sequence rather than just the subject makes this album a song cycle (that is, a "cohesive focused group of songs with an underlying theme") and compares it to Pink Floyd's *Dark Side of the Moon*.[3] *OK Computer*'s theme of technological alienation is articulated throughout such songs as "Karma Police," "Paranoid Android," and "Climbing Up the Walls." Doheny suggests that the album has both a "positive stream" and a "negative stream" that interlock and vie for supremacy; the positive stream loses strength as the negative gains it, and the negative stream wins out in the end, when the album ends on a weakly positive song ("The Tourist").[4] Nadine Hubbs likewise calls OK Computer a "concept album that immerses the listener in images of alienated life under techno/bureau/corporate hegemony. . . . [A] vivid flavor of alienation and disaffectedness . . . is built up by layer over the course of twelve album tracks." Rather than presenting a straightforward plot with characters, its lyrics are, Hubbs says, "already oblique in their written form" (that is, before any studio distortion) and "are often intelligible only in fragments." Because of Thom Yorke's treatment of the words as "vowel and consonant sounds . . . molded, shifted, stretched in shadings of the texture-color," the "audible effect of these songs [is] one approaching pure musicality." Hubbs also notes the alternating moods of the songs, but designates them as "violent embattlement" and "dreamy resignation" instead of positive and negative.[5]

Along with the label "concept album" have come the inevitable comparisons with progressive rock. Hubbs cites the evocation of "a state of alienation into which actual aliens figure . . . along with androids" as well as the "neo-prog-rock grandiosity" of "Paranoid Android,"[6] with its layers of vocal counterpoint. Edward Macan lists "rich vocal arrangements" as a characteristic of at least English progressive rock, further stating that they "can probably best be explained in the context of English music history," that is, as stemming from the medieval and early Renaissance periods of English vocal arranging.[7] Even prior to the album's release, Radiohead had been aware of the potential for comparisons with prog. During the tour before OK Computer, when the band was still working out the songs' arrangements, one of the members had stated after a performance of "Paranoid Android" (eventually the album's first single): "Ignore that. That was just a Pink Floyd cover."[8] Allan F. Moore and Anwar Ibrahim note that OK Computer "gain[ed] its 'age-defining' status through a combination of both musical and sonic exploration, with lyrics concerning the themes, simultaneously universal and personal, of alienation, information overload, and fear of an imminent new millennium. It is both a timely and a timeless record, unmistakably Radiohead but still managing to express sentiments shared by people in all walks of life."[9] Many of the prog rock traits of OK Computer seem more organic than cerebral, in contrast with the original progressive bands; for example, Radiohead uses the Mellotron as simply part of the musical texture, rather than showcasing it as a solo instrument, and the band's metric shifts are less frequent and demanding on the listener. The band also updates the practice of presenting spoken words. Instead of an eloquently intoned poem to introduce and conclude the album, something the Moody Blues, for example, used on most of their albums, Radiohead included "Fitter Happier," a series of phrases about the alienation of man's modern condition read by a computerized voice and marking a pause between the album's halves. This is actually an anti-progressive characteristic, as the words are stripped of expression rather than drenched in significance. (Compare the Romantic poeticism of "Cold-hearted orb that rules the night" with "Fitter, happier, more productive, comfortable, not drinking too much, regular exercise at the gym.") In addition, some of OK Computer's hypermetric complexity remains in the background of the texture and is not performed by the entire band, as in the guitar's repeated five-note phrase in the introduction to "Let Down," which coincides with the downbeat every five bars. Dai Griffiths comments that in this song, the listener "can achieve Zen Buddhist levels of concentration, by counting fives . . . with the guitar notes."[10] The album was created with elements of a somewhat archaic style, using an instrument that was once cutting-edge but now sounds dated, yet Radiohead nevertheless managed to make a musical statement that was perceived at the time as being very much an account of the present and a look toward the immediate future.

Griffiths views OK Computer as having a core of four songs (the sequence from "Let Down," track five, to "Electioneering," track eight) around which the rest of the album is built. ("Fitter Happier" appears as track seven.) Griffiths traces an "image trail" through the album's lyrics to build the case for it being a concept album, and also notes its musical continuity, though he states that OK Computer is ultimately a "diverse collection given greater unity by its context as an album,"[11] a description that would seem to apply to any album, concept or no.

Moore and Ibrahim compare *OK Computer*'s structure with that of *Pablo Honey*, stating that the newer album "works as a coherent whole in a similar but superior way . . . mainly due to the similarly slow pace at which its songs unfold" (presumably referring to unfolding at the song rather than the album level). The authors also note the "multisectional, multilayered" characteristics of the songs ("Paranoid Android" being the most obvious example), as well as the band's "lack of adherence to any existing stylistic conventions," which work to create "the impression that . . . the music is very much Radiohead's own."[12] *Q* magazine wrote after *OK Computer*'s release that "[n]ow Radiohead can definitely be ranked high among the world's great bands."[13] Rock critic James Delingpole went a step further in assessing the album's significance as a document of the future: "If *The Bends* was the best album of the 1990s, *OK Computer* is surely the finest of the 21st century."[14] Griffiths sees the album, rather than pointing toward the future, as capturing its own year of release: "*OK Computer* might in time be a focal point for historians of life at the close of the twentieth century. 'This is what was really going on.' You want to know what 1997 felt like? *OK Computer*: tracks six–eight ['Karma Police,' 'Fitter Happier,' 'Electioneering']. Pushed for time?—track seven ['Fitter Happier']."[15] *New Yorker* columnist Alex Ross agrees that the album encapsulated the time period, saying that the band "caught a wave of generational anxiety" and created an album that "pictured the onslaught of the information age and a young person's panicky embrace of it."[16] Doheny adds, "*OK Computer* is quite a short album by modern standards [at 53' 45"]—but feels like an age, in the most positive sense."[17] The perception of *OK Computer*'s historical importance has persevered: it has continued to rank high in "best album" polls for over a decade. Although popularity and historical importance do not necessarily coincide, the longevity of *OK Computer*'s appeal has undoubtedly contributed to the perception that it marks an important moment in musical history.

The members of Radiohead have discounted the overall significance of *OK Computer* and see less unity in it than the critics do. Drummer Phil Selway has complained about what Joseph Tate calls the "over-intellectualization of Radiohead's music by fans and critics alike": ". . . we don't want people twiddling their goatees over our stuff. What we do is pure escapism."[18] Jonny Greenwood has stated, "I think one album title and one computer voice [on 'Fitter Happier'] do not make a concept album. That's a bit of a red herring." Indeed, the band claims they did not intend the album to be what has been claimed on its behalf by both critics and fans—what Martin Clarke describes as a "concept piece about the age-old fear of the mechanized world being dehumanised by computers and technology."[19] Thom Yorke has said, "It's not really about computers. It was just the noise that was going on in my head for most of a year and a half of traveling and computers and television and just absorbing it all." Jonny Greenwood goes a step further in denying OK Computer's unity, stating that the album is "too much of a mess to sum up. It's too garbled and disjointed, and the title is only supposed to introduce you to the record." Mac Randall agrees with Greenwood about the album's lack of intentional meaning but says that even if the band did not "plan this album to be a Big Statement," it is still possible to discern themes, such as the "dehumanization of the modern world," the "power of technology," and the "presence of machines." In other words, the concept album is once again in the eye of the beholder. Other elements of OK Computer that Randall links to the earlier, "classic" (progressive-era) concept albums are the "epic sweep of the songs" and the use of the Mellotron, as well as Yorke's decision to write songs from the viewpoint of characters rather than as himself, even if the results were not apparent to the listener since these characters were not named on the album. Yorke has stated that "I didn't feel any need to exorcise things within myself this time. It wasn't digging deep inside, it was more of a journey outside and assuming the personalities of other people."[20] When the singer is the same person who wrote the song, or at least the lyrics, it is easy to conflate the two and assume an autobiographical statement. The combination of Yorke's authorial distance in the professedly less personal songs and the computerized voice and electronic instruments gave the album the potential to express broader perceptions, as it explored themes with collective, rather than just individual, meanings.

Despite the band's protests to the contrary, with OK Computer's release suddenly Radiohead seemed to be spokesmen for a generation of disaffected youth, what Ross calls the "poster boys for a certain kind of knowing alienation."[21] Yorke had stated before recording OK Computer that he realized he "could fall into the trap of thinking 'Oh my

God, I've got to supply another maudlin one' but . . . We're not trying
to prove anything and I think that's a good thing for Radiohead."[22] Ed
O'Brien has acknowledged a degree of musical exploration, of playing
with listeners' expectations, observing that "'Paranoid Android' is the
song we play to people when they want to know what the album's like,
'cos it should make them think, 'What the fuck is going to happen
on the rest of the album?'"[23] If listeners were confused by the musical
experimentation on OK Computer, they were in for a shock with the
band's next offering, Kid A.

I'M NOT HERE, THIS ISN'T HAPPENING: EXPERIENCING KID A

After the global success of OK Computer, Radiohead seemed "tantaliz-
ingly close to rock deification. According to conventional wisdom, one
more similar album, one more tour, would get them there for certain."[24]
Or at least some music critics thought so. Still, Radiohead faced an
artistic challenge: should the band duplicate its known formula for
success, or should it proceed in a new direction? According to Clarke,
Yorke was also having "deeply ambivalent feelings about the direction
of the group as a whole, and his role within it," including "consider-
ations about how to progress as a band and as a human being with any
integrity, in the face of the massive success that subsumed Radiohead
into the world of commerce."[25] This internal conflict would continue
to dog the band on subsequent albums, as they released fewer singles
and experimented with ways of letting the listener place a value (both
monetary and artistic) on their music instead of allowing the record
industry to assign one to it. Radiohead also began looking at ways to
leave a smaller environmental footprint on its tours, selling T-shirts
made from recycled plastic and encouraging concert attendees to car-
pool even to mainstream venues.[26]

After OK Computer, Yorke stated that he wanted to move beyond
a simple guitar-and-vocals formula and integrate wider influences into
the band's sound.[27] Even prior to that, in 1996, Yorke had said, "The
most important thing in our lives is trying to maintain enough control for us to carry on being creative."[28] Instead of recording material
designed to live up to the commercial success of its previous three

albums, the band, presumably with the support of its management, decided to next release an album with no promotional singles and fewer radio-friendly tunes than any of its previous work. As a comparison, *Pablo Honey* had spawned three singles ("Creep" [the only Radiohead single to have reached the Top 40 charts in the U.S.], "Anyone Can Play Guitar," and "Stop Whispering" [U.S. only]); and *The Bends* and *OK Computer* had yielded multiple singles each, roughly half of the twelve songs on each album (see Table 2.1). Radiohead would later return to releasing singles with *Amnesiac*, including "Pyramid Song" (U.K. 5) and "Knives Out" (U.K. 13). Zev Borow quoted the baffled reaction of a "Capitol Records insider" on first hearing *Kid A*: "[I]t's amazing, but weird, there aren't any radio singles, and they hate doing press. . . . Roy Lott [Capitol president] is going to shit." Phil Selway has stated that their record company had a similar initial reaction to *The Bends*, worrying unnecessarily that "there wasn't a single on it—and we ended up with five Top 30 hits from it!"[29]

Radiohead's ambivalence toward its previous commercial success, as well as the band's determination to explore its creativity rather than cave to industry demands, led to the production of *Kid A*, which commentators called an "eerily comforting blend of rock riffs, jazz chords, classical textures, and electronic noise"[30] that "[drew] a line under the band's previous output and completely re-imagine[d] what Radiohead were about in this post–*OK Computer* world."[31] This "re-imagining" involved leaving behind (for the most part) the conventional pop-single formula of singable verses and choruses as well as changing the guitar sound to a more keyboard-based one, a striking move for a band with three guitarists. Radiohead also began relying on studio manipulation and electronic sounds that were less easily reproducible outside the studio. Greg Hainge notes that these stylistic shifts "entirely reformulated the conception of what a band is."[32] Others felt that this change in style was simply the next logical step in the band's artistic progression; Erin Harde asserts that Radiohead began its evolution into its present (post–*Kid A*/*Amnesiac*) state with *OK Computer*.[33] Writing even before the release of *OK Computer*, William Stone had observed: "Utterly concerned with their own sound, problems and potential, they're too bloody-minded, too damn stubborn to suffer easy categorisation. As any scene-members, even the prime movers eventually discover

TABLE 2.1. Chart Positions of *The Bends* and *OK Computer* Singles

The Bends (1995)	"My Iron Lung"	UK 24	—
	"High and Dry"	UK 17	US 78
	"Fake Plastic Trees"	UK 20	—
	"Just"	UK 19	—
	"Street Spirit (Fade Out)"	UK 5	—
	"The Bends"	—	—
OK Computer (1997)	"Paranoid Android"	UK 3	—
	"Karma Police"	UK 8	—
	"Let Down"	—	—
	"No Surprises"	UK 4	—
	"Lucky"	UK 51	—

Sources: http://chartstats.com (U.K.); http://www.allmusic.com (U.S.); accessed 26 June 2010.

to their own immense discomfort, they either stand on their own or not at all."[34] The attempts at placing Radiohead and *Kid A* beyond classification, after the enthusiastic worldwide reception of *OK Computer*, seemed to exalt the band, to place it already in the company of such other uneasily categorized bands as the Beatles. The Fab Four have become the yardstick of greatness against which other bands are measured, as the iconic group that remained highly successful despite being innovative for their time. Yet ironically, the innovation that leads to exaltation can also incite antagonism when a band goes against the tried-and-true formula to create a product about which the marketplace feels ambivalent, and this can create ambivalence even in the artists themselves toward their own success. Sometimes, as in the case of John Lennon, this leads to the artist turning against his success and even deriding the mass audience for having created and sustained it. In the case of Radiohead, however, any sense of scorn seems to be directed at the record industry rather than at the audience.

The 1998 documentary of Radiohead's yearlong *OK Computer* tour, *Meeting People Is Easy*,[35] shows the band gradually being worn down. Although the band members always seem engaged onstage in the footage, the protracted promotional activities (interviews and radio spots) begin to numb them after they are asked the same questions over and over in different cities around the world. *Meeting People Is Easy* functions as the antithesis of the Beatles' *A Hard Day's Night* (1964), in which the young musicians exult in their new-found celebrity. Rather than engaging in witty banter with the press as the film Beatles do ("What do you call your hairstyle?" "Arthur."), the members of Radiohead instead apologize to the interviewers for being tired, rundown, and irritable (though still polite). Although the Beatles complain in the film about having seen nothing but "a train and a room, and a car and a room, and a room and a room" on their tour, they are able to escape from the entrapment of their fame for a little while, by playing cards on a train, going to a party, and (in Ringo's case) taking a walk by the river. Radiohead makes similar complaints about not even knowing which city they are in, or wishing they could go see the sights in the places in which they are performing, but ultimately they are resigned to the fact that "it's not what we're here for." The film grows increasingly claustrophobic until the final credits, when "Exit Music (for a Film)," which was composed for the movie *Romeo + Juliet*, is performed during what appears to be a sound check. The lyrics offer a chance for escape, but this attempt is likely to end in despair (for a fuller discussion of "Exit Music," see chapter 4). The mood of the band over the course of the *OK Computer* tour as captured in the documentary clearly foreshadows the retreat from commercialism that they would undertake with *Kid A*, after a three-year break.

Based on the buzz from fans and critics alike, advance sales sent *Kid A* soaring into the *Billboard* charts at number 1 (it reached number 1 on the U.K. charts as well[36]). The album sold 200,000 copies in its first week of release, more than four times what *OK Computer* had sold in its first week.[37] During the second week, however, *Kid A* dropped to number 10, and just two months after its release the album had fallen off the *Billboard* Top 100 altogether. The drastic fall in chart positions suggests that the album did not initially sell many copies beyond the band's dedicated core fan base. The initial reviews of *Kid A* were tepid, and the lack of singles for radio play limited the album's exposure to a wider audience. Even the reactions of hardcore fans were varied, with some stating that they appreciated the fact that Radiohead was striking out in a new, more innovative direction, but others complaining that they missed the old sound (and, no doubt, hit singles) of *The Bends* and *OK Computer*.[38] Early critical reaction similarly emphasized the peculiarity of *Kid A*, but for many this was a positive trait. *Q* magazine, for instance, called the album "about as experimental as a major rock record could get within the corporate straight-jacket [*sic*] that Radiohead despise."[39] *Billboard* said *Kid A* was "the first truly groundbreaking album of the 21st century"; *Spin* called it "a post-rock record"[40] and predicted that "fans will persevere and discover that *Kid A* is not only Radiohead's bravest album but its best one as well."[41] Douglas Wolk of the *Village Voice* perhaps summed up the album best: "It's . . . really different. And oblique oblique oblique: short, unsettled, deliberately shorn of easy hooks and clear lyrics and comfortable arrangements. Also incredibly beautiful."[42]

Critics inevitably drew comparisons between *Kid A* and the wildly successful *OK Computer*, observing that although the later album continued the same theme of alienation amid technology, its experimental sound made it less immediately accessible. How ironic that the greater use of technology underscores the theme of alienation amid technology by making that theme more difficult to discern! Michelle Goldberg noted that "while *Kid A* is a big stylistic departure for the band, it captures the same sense of vulnerability and paralysis in the face of frenzied, overwhelming change that coursed through *OK Computer*."[43] The alienation made explicit in *OK Computer* by such "wordy" songs as "Fitter Happier" was scribbled in shorthand on *Kid A*, the same fragile subject presented with far less transparent articulation. Wolk wrote that "if *OK Computer* was an 'about' file for a 20-gigabyte suicide note, *Kid A* feels like a handwritten letter from somebody who's spared his own life and wonders if he made the right decision."[44] Wolk's gendering the subject as male aligns it with the male singer, evoking the biases of such "classic" concept albums as the Who's *Tommy* and Pink Floyd's *The Wall*, for which each band staged performances of the album with the lead singer literally embodying the dramatic subject. Whereas *OK Computer*'s conflicts had been on the surface, the struggles in *Kid A* were masked by distorted vocals and baffling lyrics, hidden in a largely electronic texture; the album's indecipherable "handwriting" is apparently a result of the subject's own fragility. Despite *Kid A*'s initial lack of widespread acceptance, critics still understood the album as having the potential for far-reaching effects. Tim Footman noted that *Kid A* was "designed to be influential rather than popular, thought-provoking rather than loveable,"[45] suggesting that Radiohead had by this point bought into its own mythological status. If *OK Computer* had made a significant statement on the modern human condition without the band's intention, the theory went, Radiohead was now trying to purposefully replicate that importance with its new album. Much as the Beatles had with *Sgt. Pepper*, another "influential" album, Radiohead, by refusing to release any singles from *Kid A*, effectively demanded that the album be considered as a whole. Curtis White stated that rather than being self-indulgent and insisting on its own music-historical significance, Radiohead actually proved its "artistic and political health" by refusing to give in to the pressures of commodi-fication,[46] releasing an album whose importance would become clear only after its own time. Perhaps the band's artistic dues were finally being paid, or at least acknowledged, years after the beginning of their success.

Not all critics, however, were willing to accede to such intellectu-alism in their assessment of *Kid A*. *Melody Maker*, for instance, stated that the band had "created a monument of effect over content, a smoth-ery cataclysm of sound and fury signifying precisely f*** all [expletive masked in original quote]."[47] That is, whereas *OK Computer* could be widely received as an important artistic statement, *Kid A* was a mere vanity project. *Mojo* found the album lacking when compared with the band's other material: "*Kid A* is intriguing, eccentric, obviously a grower, but by Radiohead's standards it can't help but disappoint." Radiohead's own "standards" being purportedly noncommercial, of course, the band itself might have considered the album a success simply by eliciting the descriptors "intriguing" and "eccentric" from the reviewer. Other reviews declared that the band's experimentation had been a failure. *Sonicnet* wrote: "*Kid A* represents the first time in Radiohead's short history where their desire to do something different has outrun their ability to give their experiments a personal imprint. The problem with the album isn't that it's introspective, or obscure, or even that it's derivative . . . , but rather that the striking group personal-ity so well defined on the last two collections has seemed to evaporate."

This "striking group personality" had previously manifested itself as the straightforward, radio-ready full-band sound of songs with verse and chorus and guitar solos aplenty, all of which were mostly missing on *Kid A*. Arguably, the very departure from that sound was the band's attempt at making a "personal imprint." *Resonance* magazine agreed that the album suffered from its lack of clearly delineated material, calling *Kid A* "a record that might've been amazing if the band had only bothered to write some actual songs."[48] This comment can also be read as a criticism of what some saw as Radiohead's prog rock tendencies, if *Kid A* is viewed as containing larger musical moments than conventional pop singles.

Critics overall agreed that *Kid A* required some effort at interpretation, but they were divided on whether this was a reasonable request to make of the general listener. Comparing it with its immediate predecessor, *All Music Guide* declared that "*Kid A* is never as visionary or stunning as *OK Computer*, nor does it really repay the intensive time it demands."[49] This "intensive time" might have felt less of a burden, of course, had the band released promotional singles to saturate the airwaves, so that listeners could be eased into the album's sound by encountering it in public forums amid other, more conventional songs, rather than having to experience the album on its own, as a totality. David Fricke wrote: "If you're looking for instant joy and easy definition, you are swimming in the wrong soup," and called *Kid A* a "work of deliberately inky, almost irritating obsession."[50] Many perceived the band as trying to purposefully confuse the listener, rather than simply following its own muse. Andrew Goodwin stated: "The lyrics are a Rorschach test. What do you hear?"[51] The Rorschach test is a psychological evaluation tool consisting of ten inkblots on cards that the subject/patient has to examine and respond to. It is controversial because of its subjectivity and the fact that diagnosis is based on finding latent sense in apparently meaningless images. Thus the metaphor implies that Radiohead's music has no meaning beyond whatever the individual listener projects onto it. Since the band is the entity holding up the "cards," it acts as psychologist, with the power to simultaneously deny any intrinsic significance and pass judgment on whether the listener hears the "right" meaning. Along these lines, Nick Hornby wrote in the *New Yorker*:

You have to work at albums like *Kid A*. You have to sit at home night
after night and give yourself over to the paranoid millennial atmosphere
as you try to decipher elliptical snatches of lyrics and puzzle out how
the titles . . . might refer to the songs. . . . *Kid A* demands the patience of
the devoted; both patience and devotion become scarcer commodities
once you start picking up a paycheck. . . . The album is morbid proof
that this sort of self-indulgence results in a weird kind of anonymity,
rather than something distinctive and original.[52]

Although some critics complained that the band required listeners to work at making sense of *Kid A*, rather than simply presenting an
album that could be enjoyed at face value with no need to delve for
meaning, this is not necessarily a fair assessment of the band's artistic
intention. Recall that the perception of *OK Computer* as "important"
was not shared or promoted by the band members themselves, at least
at the time of its release, so although they may have intended *Kid A*
to be significant as an experimental piece of art music, and a step in
a more innovative direction, the general listener was not necessarily
intended to grasp any inherent "meaning" in order to enjoy the album.
Footman observed that even the much-lauded *OK Computer* "hadn't
been the sort of album to grab listeners by the ears and bellow 'love
me!' But this [*Kid A*] was uneasy listening and then some. In spades.
With a cherry on top."[53] *OK Computer* marked a moment in the band
members' output that propelled them, rightly or not, from being simply the creators of hit singles to message-bearers for a generation, and
its music had overcome the discomfort of the message (alienation
amid modern technology) to become a hit despite the band's insistence that it hadn't set out to make one. The music of *OK Computer*
amplified the message to the extent that the album was read as both
an important statement on modern life and a document for the future. Conversely, *Kid A* went so far in its musical experimentation that
any message, already encoded and obscure, would probably be lost to
most listeners because they were unlikely to put in the time needed to
retrieve it.

The band members themselves, in a reaction to the exploitative
oversaturation of the *OK Computer* tour as seen in *Meeting People Is
Easy*, appeared determined not to yield to the commercial pressure of

promoting *Kid A*, choosing to release several "antivideos" of anima-
tions set to snippets of the album's songs rather than participating
in the more conventional videos, singles, interviews, or tour. (These
"antivideos" were released in 2004 on a DVD collection, *The Most
Gigantic Lying Mouth of All Time*, which also contains short films
set to Radiohead's music that were originally meant to be screened
on radiohead.tv, the band's streaming website. They solicited films
through the website as well as producing some studio performances
of their own.[54]) Although Yorke has stated that he "can't really see the
difference between shooting a video and making a car advert," even
Radiohead's earlier "promotional" videos had resisted commodification, acting more like short films (some even in black-and-white) and
thus further linking the band with the high-art tradition (and, in the
process, with art/prog rock).[55] The band's record company, Capitol/
EMI, did launch a chatbot (GooglyMinotaur) to promote *Kid A*, and
both the band and Capitol/EMI encouraged fans to distribute the *Kid
A* material through the internet before the CD's official release. The
fact that *Kid A* was available in its entirety on the peer-to-peer file-
sharing network Napster did not appear to negatively affect its sales; in
fact, it may even have increased them.[56] Clarke states that Radiohead
had "always been a band with a social conscience, but being trapped
inside the commercial machine after *OK Computer* had reinforced
their ideals."[57] Releasing and distributing their material for free was
one way of thwarting the "commercial machine" that the band would
explore on a larger scale later. MTV and many other music websites
screened Radiohead's antivideo clips, which were also available on
the band's own website, itself a study in obfuscation (the band periodi-
cally redesigns the site but keeps old versions archived).[58] Rather than
presenting fans with easily navigable areas from which to glean data
(even such basic information as the release dates of new material or
biographical data on the band members), the site at the time of *Kid
A*'s release instead contained links labeled "waitingroom," "trapdoors,"
and "testspecimens." These links led the viewer through galleries of
cartoons and blurred photos of the band with implicitly politicized text
underneath: intriguing images and words, but no useful facts for anyone seeking concrete information on the band. Even on Radiohead's

current (2010) website little of the usual information is presented, although the site does list "links to other sites about Radiohead" run by fans around the world.[59]

The booklet enclosed in the *Kid A* CD jewel case continued the mystery generated by the band's website and antivideos, presenting computer-generated and -manipulated art rather than the more customary band photos. Hainge has noted the evolution in packaging over the course of Radiohead's albums, from conventional photos on *Pablo Honey* and *The Bends* to the increased use of artwork and puzzling snippets of text on the band's later albums. *Kid A* was the first Radiohead album not to include lyrics in its packaging (*Amnesiac* was also released without lyrics, but *Hail to the Thief* [2003] did include them).[60] The only human figures on the *Kid A* packaging appear in a photo in the middle of the booklet, in which a group of people (the "nuclear family"?) stands huddled together with their backs to the camera, staring at a wall of graffiti. This wall is covered with words and images that permeate the booklet's other pages. An additional booklet of handbills was concealed behind the back of the jewel case in the CD's initial pressing and was later made available for download through the band's website. The artwork is reminiscent of cartoonist R. Crumb, famous for his work with the Grateful Dead, another band with a countercultural message that still reaped enormous benefits from the capitalist culture, particularly through their tours and merchandising. This second, "secret" booklet presents some text that is recognizable as *Kid A*'s lyrics, but for the most part it merely serves to create, like the computer art, a feeling of desolation in a post-apocalyptic wasteland. By creating a companion "art project" in the form of the antivideos, website, and booklet art, Radiohead furthered the notion that *Kid A* is high art, to be taken on its own terms rather than the marketplace's. The band members seemed to be making the statement that they were above commerce and were simply releasing an album for its own sake, or for the sake of art. Given the earlier comparisons of Radiohead with progressive rock bands, it is interesting to compare this booklet with the faux-newspaper packaging of Jethro Tull's *Thick as a Brick*, an album that Bill Martin describes as a "great send-up of English pomposity, provinciality, and the class system."[61] The texts enclosed in both albums address capitalism, but Radiohead's does so only obliquely, by virtue of ignoring the terms under which the album was created and the reception it might face in the marketplace.

Despite *Kid A*'s apparent disregard for the workings of capitalism, foregrounded by its bewildering artwork, lack of promotional material, and experimental sound, Radiohead remained fully conscious of its place within the capitalist system and undoubtedly gave careful thought to how to position the album for maximum success within the "commercial machine." Yorke has stated that "what frightens me is the idea that what Radiohead do is basically packaged back to people in the form of entertainment, to play in their car stereos on the way to work . . . but then I should shut the fuck up because it's pop music and it's not anything more than that."[62] The frightening aspect of the packaging of any form of art—music, literature, etc.—is that it makes the artist him- or herself into a commodity, no better than the product itself, and no better than the corporate drones for which Radiohead and other bands appear to have such contempt. If a person's or group's creative goal is presumed to be an artistic statement that exists above and/or superfluous to the corporate culture that will ultimately receive and promote it, then packaging that statement to sell back to the consumer, in the process making money off the very people with whom the artist claims to identify (in Orwellian terms, the proles), is the ultimate irony. Yorke has underscored his consciousness of the band's place within the capitalist system with his declaration that "you're lying if you're pretending it's not a product, that you're not trying to sell something."[63] Obviously conscious of the hurdles involved in negotiating corporate culture, in this statement Yorke reveals the man behind the curtain, creating the smoke and mirrors of anticapitalism while still reaping benefit from the products' sales. Radiohead's highly successful marketing strategy appears to be centered around creating riddles for fans to try to solve. Ross states that "the records, the videos, the official website, even the T-shirts all cry out for interpretation."[64] By being deliberately obscure in its presentation, Radiohead creates a community of followers who gain insider status by sharing and debating the clues left behind by the band. In addition, by creating an air of mystery in the presentation of its product, as well as decrying the very system upon which its ultimate financial success depends, the band cleverly builds demand by aligning itself with its audience against the record industry and elevates its artwork above mere "pop music" into the realm of the intelligentsia; only the astute can interpret the music's true meaning, and attempting to do so initiates the listener into an insider network of people outside the mainstream. This "Gnostic" aesthetic has been linked to progressive rock;[65] however, instead of accepting that association, the band instead uses it as a kind of countercultural stance against capitalism itself.

MUSICAL ELEMENTS
IN **KID A**

The cold, alienating landscape envisioned in the artwork of *Kid A* can be viewed as the backdrop to its songs, or perhaps even as the literal space within which the album's subject dwells. The listener's impressions begin with the scratchy images and computer-generated artwork of the CD booklet, and upon diving in, she finds that the album requires several songs to form a complete musical and lyrical thought, let alone any kind of coherent subject. Just as different visual images are overlaid in the packaging, any overt meanings obscured, so too are the band's instruments distorted, filtered, and layered to build up the overall effect of bewilderment amid technology (an effect created, of course, by mastery of the actual studio technology by the musicians and producer Nigel Godrich). Although the lyrical themes of *Kid A* are similar to those of *OK Computer* (alienation as a reaction to the onslaught of technology), *Kid A* challenges Radiohead's earlier methods of narrative cohesion by forming a hopeless, self-negating subject who disintegrates at the midpoint of the album at the moment of his maximum articulation. The layering of the instruments occasionally coalesces to form an interlocking groove, which stabilizes the music but also lends the opportunity for the voice-as-subject to be treated as a combatant instead of an ally. Rather than being bound to the singer as on other "concept albums," the subject on *Kid A* is decentered and diffused among the instruments and is subsumed by them midway through the album, in "How to Disappear Completely" (track four).

Since we conceptualize this subject as human, it must be gendered. Thom Yorke's distinctive tenor is somewhat androgynous, and Radiohead can be seen as displaying an ambivalence toward gender (as discussed by Erin Harde[1]). Nevertheless, any androgyny in the band's musical presentation cannot erase the perception of the male voice of the singer, even when it is heavily filtered and disguised as on *Kid A*, so it seems easiest to refer to the subject also as male. Because of this, and in order to avoid the depersonalization implied by using "it," I will refer to the subject as "he" or "him" throughout my analysis, although I do not mean that there is any strict mapping of subject to singer. Any action performed by this subject remains ambiguous, and my descriptions should be taken as one listener's observation, rather than as statements of the intentions of the band.

Kid A presents a compelling challenge to interpreting or even discerning narrative personae. Not only is there no clear persona to guide or even ground the listener, but there is no main character (as in the Who's *Tommy* or Pink Floyd's *The Wall*), and no clear dramatic action. Rather than giving the listener an immediate sense of the singer-as-subject, the lyrics to the first three songs consist of puzzling statements ("yesterday I woke up sucking on a lemon," "I slipped away on a little white lie," "everyone has got the fear"). Carys Wyn Jones has discussed the difficulty of locating "the position of the singer" given the album's heavy filtering of the voice,[2] which leads to the destabilization and fragmentation of the subject, who dissolves completely into the instrumental background by track five, "Treefingers." Allan F. Moore and Anwar Ibrahim note that "[w]here *OK Computer* featured 12 highly inventive and original takes on the concept of a rock song, *Kid A* . . . saw Radiohead producing tracks that not only defied categorization as rock music but that, on occasion, also challenged perceived notions of '[pop] song.'"[3] Whereas Radiohead had been lauded for its earlier albums that, while innovative, still contained songs with the traditionally constructed verse, chorus, and guitar solos, critics and fans alike viewed the songs of *Kid A* not as a further (progressive in the generic sense) musical advance, but as something that threatened the very pop-music genre. Because *Kid A*'s songs do not, for the most part, stand on their own as three-minute pop "singles," each with a discrete narrative of its own (even one created by the verse/chorus construction), the listener is compelled to derive the album's meaning instead from the song sequence, which, rather than presenting a plot with characters, builds up a tentative subject gradually and then suddenly erases him. The voice and various other musical agents (piano, orchestra, etc.) typically work together to construct a complete musical subject, or a "unified utterance of the composer's voice," as Edward T. Cone puts it, but on *Kid A* these elements instead engage in a constant struggle for dominance.[4] Kevin J. H. Dettmar suggests that such conflict is a hallmark of Radiohead's style in general—"an almost epic battle between Thom Yorke's frail voice and the music which alternatively undergirds and overwhelms that voice."[5] Yorke's voice is more heavily filtered on *Kid A* than on the band's earlier albums, but its fragile, high tone has remained consistent across Radiohead's opus. In *Kid A*, this tendency of the voice to engage in a struggle with the other instruments is pushed to the breaking point: any attempt at a "unified utterance" by the band fractures apart, with all of the musical agents working actively *against* a coherent subject formation (which would normally be centered in the voice).

Musical sparring between the voice and instruments on *Kid A* can be parsed as the binary oppositions of vocal sense versus nonsense, and electronic versus "acoustic" (though not truly acoustic, since the sounds were recorded electronically; most of the sounds that seem acoustic at first hearing are actually sampled). Table 3.1 shows how some elements from the first five songs of *Kid A* fit into these categories. Sounds can appear in more than one category; for instance, all of the sampled "acoustic" sounds of "Kid A" could also appear in that category's binary opposition of electronic. If "music" (or sense, at the verbal level) is taken as a way of encoding social norms and codes into organized sound, then "noise" (or nonsense) is that which erupts and disturbs the order. The table shows how representative lyrics from these songs either support the category of sense or comment on the binary opposition of nonsense. In "Everything in Its Right Place" (a title that appears to firmly establish the boundaries of sense), the voice asks for clarification: "what was that you tried to say?" The lead vocal is attempting to interact with the sampled voice, split between the two channels and babbling nearly incoherently. The opening words of "Kid A"—"I slipped away on a little white lie"—cause the listener to begin to

TABLE 3.1. Binary Oppositions in the First Half of *Kid A*

Song	Voice: Sense	Voice: Nonsense	"Acoustic"	Electronic
"Everything in Its Right Place"	"What was that you tried to say?"	sampled voice split between channels	sampled voice is derived from live performance	sampled voice
"Kid A"	"I slipped away on a little white lie"	birth cry at end of song	blowing wind, marimbas, music box, and strings are all sampled	filtered voice
"The National Anthem"	"Everyone has got the fear"	vocal cries in coda	horn glissandi	ondes martenot, tape winding down
"How to Disappear Completely"	"I'm not here, this isn't happening"	"aahs"	acoustic guitar, strings, tambourine	
"Treefingers"		faint "aahs"		filtered guitars

mistrust the subject or would-be narrator. The birth cry at the end of the song further raises the anxiety level. This sound recalls the crying baby heard on *The Wall* before the track "The Thin Ice." Whereas that wail is soothed by the words that follow, "Momma loves her baby," the cry on *Kid A* is met with cold, synthesized chords and the sound of howling wind. In "The National Anthem," the voice comments on this mass anxiety—"everyone has got the fear"—then moves into vocalese near the end of the song. Finally, in "How to Disappear Completely," the voice decries its own existence, saying "I'm not here, this isn't happening" before devolving into wordless "aahs." "Treefingers" is absent a strong lead vocal or any words at all, the voice/subject being present only in the far distance of the musical texture. Nonsense/noise has triumphed for the time being.

As Yorke had desired, the band continued on *Kid A* and *Amnesiac* to enrich and expand their sound with different instruments beyond the conventional guitar, bass, and drums of rock music. This experimentation had shown up on *OK Computer* with the use of the Mellotron, an artifact of progressive rock that helped draw comparisons with that style. The ondes martenot, which represents a distinctive feature of Radiohead's style on *Kid A* as well as a further step in the band members' experimentation with orchestration, is likewise a throwback to the inclusion of new forms of technology in the "art music" of the twentieth century, a parallel that furthers Radiohead's association with "high art." The ondes martenot in particular brings to mind the work of Olivier Messiaen, for whom Jonny Greenwood has expressed admiration since his youth. Greenwood has further aligned himself with art music with his compositions for the BBC and on his film soundtracks.

In terms used by French economist and cultural theorist Jacques Attali, noise represents an ambiguous intrusion that disrupts the musical texture, yet it is also the means by which new order and meaning are created. When a network's existing codes cannot repress the attacking noise, the network will be destroyed and replaced by another that can organize the noise into a form that is culturally accepted. In lay terms, a societal structure might be threatened with revolutionary ideas that then become normalized into new cultural practices. This noise thus initiates a sacrificial crisis in order to "transcend the old violence and recreate a system of differences on another level of organization."[6]

Attali's theory deals with music in general historical terms, as one genre attacking an established one and then creating something new, but this process may also occur in microcosm, at the song or album level. Noise can emanate from an outside source, such as the sound effects of a music box, horn glissandi, or a tape winding down—which intrude beyond Radiohead's normal instrumentation of guitars, bass, drums, voice, and even keyboard—or from within—as when the voice moves into non-verbal utterances.

Dettmar discusses the battle between the voice and the other instruments on the albums *OK Computer*, *Kid A*, and *Amnesiac*, which he terms a "triptych which is not quite a trilogy," stating that "something of a closet drama is played out between the voice and the noise." He also mentions the band's exploration over these three albums of "whether the human voice can retain its authority and authenticity in the reign of Walter Benjamin's 'age of mechanical reproduction,' through the inhuman processing of human utterance." Dettmar observes that the intrusion of noise begins in the "big distorted guitar sounds" at the beginning of *OK Computer*, above which the singer struggles to be heard;[7] this battle is staged more dramatically on *Kid A* and *Amnesiac*, where the singer's words can barely be deciphered even when his voice is audible. The first half of *Kid A* can thus be understood, in Attali's terms, as a fracturing of the musical structure that builds to a crisis point at which the subject is purged by the voice's escape into a falsetto range above churning strings. The second half of the album then attempts to build a new structure by resurrecting the subject for a different series of songs, but the subject fails to negotiate his struggles successfully and abandons his attempt at the end of the album. In this failed attempt, which results in a suicide on the parting words "I will see you in the next life," the subject again escapes into falsetto, but this time the underlying strings support the voice. The pattern of disruption followed by new meaning is incomplete this time; Attali's transcendence of the old violence is the voice's falsetto escape, and the promised other level of organization is the "next life" to come, which does not occur on *Kid A* but may provide a blueprint, or at least a foretaste, of the band's next album.

The members of Radiohead are likely to have been conscious at some level of subverting these opposing categories of musical sound ("acoustic" versus electronic) when recording *Kid A*, even if their intent had more to do with expanding their tonal palette and subverting listener and industry expectations than with creating easily defined binary oppositions. Indeed, their artistic intent may have had more to do with blurring these categories. In speaking of the recording sessions that produced *Kid A* and *Amnesiac*, Jonny Greenwood commented that "a voice into a microphone onto a tape, onto a CD and through your speakers is all as illusory and as fake as any synthesizer. . . . But one is perceived as 'real,' the other somehow 'unreal.' It's the same with guitars versus samplers. It was just freeing to discard the notion of acoustic sounds being truer."[8] By questioning the perception of acoustic instruments as being somehow more "real" or "authentic" than electronic media, Greenwood further destabilizes the categories of acoustic and electronic. The electronic/filtered sounds of *Kid A* present an unfamiliar sonic space that might normally be represented as "unreal" (in the form of distorted and/or non-acoustic instruments) but here must be treated as the only space that exists for the subject/protagonist and thus as the only "real" space available to him. In yearning for the unattainable ideal of the unconstructed real that cannot exist apart from the produced studio album, the subject finds that the only way to reach this state is to "disappear completely." Rather than escaping into a "more real" sonic environment, however, the subject ends up in the gray nothing-space of "Treefingers"—another non-acoustic soundscape—as he cannot leave the sonic space of the album and must begin his journey anew on the album's second "side."[9] The subject's "suicide" at the end of the album thus becomes not an empowering act but instead the ultimate failure. When viewed in this way, *Kid A* makes sense as the expression of an attempted resolution to an existential crisis, a different kind of sense than a story with a plot and assorted characters.

HERE I'M ALLOWED EVERYTHING ALL OF THE TIME: SONG SEQUENCE AND STRUCTURE

Regardless of whether *Kid A* can be assigned a convincing traditional narrative, in which a series of actions and motivations are ascribed to a main character, it is certain that the band members put some thought

into the order of the songs so that the key structures would flow harmonically, or at least avoid harmonic disruption. James Doheny states
that Yorke worked on the song sequence of *OK Computer* for two weeks
after all the songs had been recorded, and it can be assumed that similar care was taken on *Kid A*, particularly since the band had recorded
over twenty songs from which to choose for both this album and *Amnesiac.*[10] Given the modal ambiguity of many pop songs, in which a
tonic note or key is not clearly defined, it is often misleading to force
these songs into a major or minor key, as the chord progressions do not
project a tonal center within functional Western harmony. Radiohead's
tendency to use pedal tones (a single sustained pitch, often the lowest
in a musical texture, played underneath the harmonic motion in the
other voices) and to oscillate between two chords related by a third
(A major to F-sharp minor, for instance; the roots A and F-sharp are
a third apart, and the chords built on those notes share the common
pitches A and C-sharp) further muddies the tonal waters.[11] Example
3.1 shows the general harmonic flow of *Kid A*'s song sequence; notes in
parentheses represent competing tonal centers rather than notes that
sound at the same time.

3.1. *Kid A*, general harmonic flow. Notes in parentheses
indicate competing tonal centers.

"Everything in Its Right Place" alternates between the keys of C
and F. "Kid A" is seemingly in F, one of the keys of the previous song.
The transcribed piano/vocal/guitar score presents a bracketed F above
the first measure,[12] perhaps to indicate the song's suggested harmonic
emphasis rather than an absolute one. Although many rock musicians
find transcribed scores to be perfectly adequate for learning parts to

these tunes, the published score in rock music does have its limitations, particularly when the music is as complex and layered as Radiohead's. Transcriptions should perhaps be taken as no more than a general road map to what is really going on in the recording. In reference to pop music, Allan F. Moore has stated that the "only thing we have approaching an authoritative score [in pop music] is . . . the recording itself."[13] With that caveat, "The National Anthem" is in D; "How to Disappear Completely" shifts between the tonal centers D and F-sharp (related by a major third and sharing the pitches F-sharp and A); and "Treefingers," the midpoint of the album, is centered around F-sharp. "Optimistic" returns to D, which could be heard as a dominant (V chord) to the G of the next song, "In Limbo." "Idioteque" alternates between the tonal centers of G and E-flat (related by a major third and sharing the pitches G and B-flat). "Morning Bell" is in A, the upper-neighbor (step above) tone to G, and "Motion Picture Soundtrack" finally "resolves" to G in a high voice with harp and choir accompaniment (suggesting a dramatically forced resolution), though the harmony does not present a G-major chord until the coda after the main song has faded out. The ultimate resolution is thus beyond the scope of the actual song.

Reducing the album to a single overall harmonic progression is too pat a solution when the songs are examined more closely, however. Rather than a single large progression leading to a G-major chord, the album can be grouped into sets of three songs each, plus a separate song that finishes off the album, as seen in example 3.2. The songs in

"Everything in Its Right Place,"   "How to Disappear Completely,"   "In Limbo," "Idioteque,"   "Motion Picture Soundtrack"
"Kid A," "The National Anthem"   "Treefingers," "Optimistic"   "Morning Bell"   (track 10)
(tracks 1-3)   (tracks 4-6)   (tracks 7-9)

3.2. *Kid* A, song groupings

each group are linked by lyrics or style and are supported by harmonic underpinnings. Each grouping also forms an unfolding dialectic triad, with a thesis, an antithesis, and a synthesis (though often a weak one). At a microcosmic level, each group can be seen as presenting a stable structure (some less so than others), then an attacking noise intrusion, and finally a new structure that integrates the noise. The first series ("Everything," "Kid A," and "The National Anthem") builds up the emerging subject of the album, and the ambiguous F of the first two songs is followed by a clear statement in D in the third song. Before the subject even appears, the stage is set for "everything" to be "in its right place." When the subject "Kid A" emerges in the title track, however, he finds the world a difficult place. The third song, "The National Anthem," forcibly integrates the subject into a society of alienation. The harmonic structure may be more stable, but the subject must pay the price of living in a culture in which "everyone has got the fear."

The next group of three songs ("How to Disappear Completely," "Treefingers," and "Optimistic") articulates, destroys, and then reconstitutes the subject; the F-sharp of the middle song mediates between the D/F-sharp of the first song and the D of the third song by virtue of being present in each of the tonal centers, whether as a root or as a third over the D. The subject is finally given a full, undistorted voice with real verses and a chorus in "How to Disappear Completely," but he immediately loses his voice again in the violent musical texture and then becomes merely a ghost figure in the ambient landscape of "Treefingers." The subject then reappears as a more pessimistic entity in "Optimistic," grudgingly existing only because he has failed to erase himself. Again, harmonic stability has come at the cost of the subject's comfort or happiness.

The third group of songs presents the renewed subject's continuing struggles with modern life, through "Idioteque" and "In Limbo"; this group concludes with the wakeup call of "Morning Bell," which shows that the subject is still unsuccessful in his second incarnation. The tonal center of the third song, A, lifts the G of the first two songs to a higher pitch level. Normally when a song modulates up a step (as from G to A), it provides a brightening effect, but here the effect is merely temporary as the song's chromatic-third harmonic progression (A to C-sharp) is disjunct and jarring, ultimately causing more anxiety for both the subject and the listener. The album's final song ("Motion Picture Soundtrack") ends with the subject's second, "real" "death" (as opposed to the existential-crisis-as-death in "How to Disappear Completely") and provides a forced resolution and coda after a moment of silence (providing a reminder that the music, and thus the world, continues to exist even in the subject's absence). The music that reenters after the subject's parting shot as he attempts again to erase himself shows that the subject is indeed gone. The subject's death is finally confirmed by the music that exists without his voice, even the muted vocalese that had been present on "Treefingers." Despite the heavenly sounds of flowing harp chords, there is no cause for rejoicing over the subject reaching his goal. His victory is a hollow one; the world and soundscape would have existed without him regardless, so his death is of no consequence. This nihilistic reading is supported by the album that came next, *Amnesiac*, but even without *Amnesiac* to color our feelings about *Kid A* we can surmise that the subject's cynicism extends to the world around him, which had never supported him anyway.

An additional musical link occurs between the song that signifies the first "death" and the one that reconstitutes the subject. Example 3.3 shows how the closing notes of "How to Disappear Completely"

"Aah..." (track 4: 5:22 to 5:34)　　　　　　"Ooh..." (track 6: 0:00 to 0:10)

3.3. Ending of "How to Disappear Completely" and opening of "Optimistic"

(A–F-sharp) reappear in the opening notes of "Optimistic" (A–B–F-sharp) after the interlude of "Treefingers," illustrating that the subject is essentially picking up where he left off, after his unsuccessful suicide attempt. The victimized subject of "How to Disappear Completely" is presented in "Optimistic" with the opportunity for a fresh outlook on life; the anguished "aahs" of the earlier song have been transformed into soothing "oohs." The subject's negative attitude is still present; however, it has now been turned outward toward society.

The songs of *Kid A* are also tied together, if not wholly unified, by lyrics. Rather than constructing a clear narrative, or even a straightforward articulation of the subject's feelings, the words merely drop clues about the subject's state of mind and his reaction to his environment. Each half of the album presents similar lyrics, which provide a bridge across the subject's first death. The statement "I slipped away on a little white lie" in "Kid A" is echoed in "Motion Picture Soundtrack," the

album's final song, as "they fed us on little white lies," a comment perhaps on the paranoid environment surrounding the album's recording
sessions. The statement of denial in "How to Disappear Completely,"
track four, that "this isn't happening" is countered in "Idioteque," track
eight, as "this *is* really happening" (italics added), as the subject tries
to come to grips with his reality. Rather than trying to negate himself
in order to escape to some imagined ideal state of being, the subject
tries in the latter song to force himself to accept a harsh and unwanted
reality. The Orwellian reference in "Optimistic" ("living on an animal
farm") can be linked to the dystopian command "stop sending letters,
letters always get burned" in "Motion Picture Soundtrack." The "dinosaurs roaming the earth" mentioned in "Optimistic" are recalled in
the apocalyptic warning of the "ice age coming" in "Idioteque." The
calmly uttered observation "rats and children follow me out of town"
and the command "c'mon kids" in "Kid A" return as the hysterical
stutter "women and children first" and "the first of the children" in
"Idioteque," as the subject must face up to his fate instead of trying
to escape it. The words "laugh until my head comes off" in "Idioteque" indicate that even a moment of levity has dire consequences in
Radiohead's post-apocalyptic wasteland. As expressed here, laughter
negates reason when the convulsing body literally loses its head. The
lyric also recalls the "heads on sticks" in "Kid A," which have already
been separated from their bodies and must rely on "ventriloquists" to
choose and articulate their message. (The "heads on sticks" could also
relate to the "talking heads" of TV, which speak the messages of their
governing corporations, filtered through the politics of the networks.
This imagery can be contrasted with Radiohead's own internet broadcast channel, radiohead.tv, which sent out its own "message"—surreal,
nonsensical images—to the masses. Which is the more nonsensical:
the rantings of Glenn Beck or Bill O'Reilly, or the antivideos and cartoon bears of radiohead.tv?)

The more specific musical elements of *Kid A* can help locate dramatic action, or at the very least develop a clearer idea of the album's
subject. As discussed earlier, the album's first three songs gradually
build up the shaky picture of an unwilling pseudo-protagonist defined
in negative space by his reactions to the world around him. The subject's instability makes it easier for noise (whether from an internal

or external source) to eventually devour him. The first three songs of *Kid A* toy with the conventional song construction of verse/chorus but present nonsensical, fragmented lyrics in distorted tones rather than a logical, singable melody. The three guitars customarily associated with Radiohead are heavily filtered and mostly unrecognizable. "Noise" thus exists both as altered versions of Radiohead's usual instrumentation and as the sound effects and synthesized strings that constantly interrupt the musical texture.

"EVERYTHING IN ITS RIGHT PLACE"

Despite its title, "Everything in Its Right Place," track one, presents a musical scenario in which expectations of resolution are continually frustrated. The song's long musical introduction (a repeated keyboard riff) gives it a prelude quality, as though its purpose is to merely hint at what is to come later rather than to present a clear statement of the album's thesis. The anticipatory feel of "Everything" should not be misconstrued as serving the more conventional purpose of an overture (as in *Tommy* or any number of Broadway productions), which introduces musical themes that will be developed later. The sections of the song can be labeled as chorus, verse, chorus, verse, and coda (see table 3.2), departing from the more customary order of verse, chorus, bridge, verse, and chorus.[14] Because the statement "everything in its right place" reoccurs throughout the song, it is more accurately labeled as the chorus even though it comes before the verse in the song. Each "verse" ("yesterday I woke up sucking on a lemon" and "there are two colors in my head") presents a single observation rather than rhyming lines as in a more conventional verse. The lack of a bridge or other transition material further suggests a static state rather than any forward motion, which foreshadows the feel of the rest of the album.[15] The song is in $\frac{10}{4}$ meter (represented in the published guitar/keyboard transcription as alternating measures of $\frac{4}{4}$ and $\frac{6}{4}$), with the bass drum providing a quarter-note pulse. This large metric grouping produces a suspended feeling in the music that is extended by the voice's slow melody being somewhat disconnected from the meter. A pedal C sounds throughout the song, regardless of the chords (variously C major, D-flat major, E-flat major, and F major). Although the voice's initial statement in-

TABLE 3.2. Structure of "Everything in Its Right Place"

Intro (7 mm.)	C–D-flat–C/E-flat motive established in keyboard
0:35 A/Chorus (4 + 4 mm.) "Everything…"	F–C–F in voice over E-flat–F–C–D-flat–E-flat in keyboard (which "resolves" incorrectly by leaping down a minor seventh to match the voice) C–B-flat–D-flat–C in voice over E-flat in bass (moves to C with voice, then goes back to motive)
1:14 b/Verse 1 (4 mm.) "Yesterday I woke up…"	Pedal C in voice over D-flat in bass (moves C–E-flat–D-flat); bass resolves to C to match voice, then both move to E-flat and F (bass motive continues)
1:37 A/Chorus (4 + 4 mm.) "Everything…"	Same as above
2:12 b/Verse 2 (8 mm.) "There are two colors…"	Voice and keyboard have same rhythm; keyboard moves to E-flat major when voice finally drops out; pedal C of keyboard is gone
2:55 A'/Coda (15 mm.; fades out) "Everything…"	Keyboard motive repeats over and over; voice is absent until babble comes in with the pedal C

troduces the melodic motion F–C–F, the C should not be construed as serving a true dominant (V-chord) function to the F as it might in traditional Western art music, as the harmony does not emphasize a clear "tonic" chord with a cadence at the end of a phrase.[16] Apart from presenting the stepwise motion of major chords, the harmonic function remains unsettled. This vague harmonic motion belies the song's title; everything is *not* in its right place.

The intrusion of a sampled voice threatens the tenuous stability of the initial keyboard motive. This voice babbles nonsensically in alternating speakers; in one channel the voice breaks up lyrics that are heard slightly later ("yesterday I woke up sucking on a lemon," a lyric that Tim Footman observes could be an analogy for *Kid A*'s "whole listening experience—it hurts like hell, but it probably does you some kind of good"[17]). In the other channel, the voice announces the album title, or possibly a lead character (0:16), though again the subject is too nebulous to be a true protagonist: "Kid A." An undistorted voice then

enters in the middle of the speakers with the word "everything" (0:34).
At first blush the lead vocals, perceived as "acoustic" in nature (as
Jonny Greenwood has stated, this is a technically faulty if predictable
perception), seem to represent something like unadulterated "nature,"
as well as music, and the babbling vocals "technology," as well as noise.
The relationship grows more complicated as we realize that one voice
has been created from the other: the main vocal (derived from live
performance) has been spliced and rearranged into the babbling one.[18]
Mark B. N. Hansen states that "Everything in Its Right Place" alludes
to Yorke's breakdown on Radiohead's yearlong *OK Computer* tour, his
main symptom being an inability to speak. Hansen further states that
this loss of speech triggered the band's "complex deterritorializations"
of the voice and "its instrumental avatar, the guitar,"[19] which would
manifest on *Kid A* and *Amnesiac*. Though guitars are present on *Kid
A*, as on Radiohead's previous albums, they are heavily filtered and
function as a background texture rather than as the more traditional
lead/solo instruments. The noise element produces disharmony here
by turning one of the musical elements (the voice) back on itself by
reconfiguring it, and suggests the domination of the "false" (spliced)
voice over the "true" (live) one, just as the production of a music album
itself represents the triumph of human technology over organic sound.

While the voice and keyboard in "Everything" seem to be battling
each other to determine the key, the keyboard seems even to be battling itself. The opening keyboard statement is in C major but keeps
moving to C minor by way of a D-flat-major chord that leads to E-flat,
a tone that changes the mode from C major to C minor. The harmonic
ambiguity is obvious from the opening keyboard descent (A-flat, G, C),
which includes the dominant (G) and tonic for C but also borrows A-flat
from C minor. Over this initial keyboard statement comes the voice's
F-C alternation over an E-flat in the bass line (throughout this section,
"bass line" refers to the lowest-sounding series of pitches, here played
by the keyboard), creating a major-ninth dissonance between the F and
E-flat. The bass then moves down a minor seventh, from E-flat to F,
before returning to the C–D-flat–E-flat motive again under the voice's
sustained F. This minor-seventh leap in the bass anticipates the minor-
seventh dissonance created by the voice's D-flat over the bass's E-flat on

the emphasized word "right," as well as the major-seventh dissonance of the voice's repeated C over the bass's D-flat in the verse beginning "yesterday." The vocal melody presents a pseudo-dominant/tonic (F–C–F) relationship on the word "everything" that sounds stable on its own. The bass's relationship to the voice, however, is forced and an ill fit. As the phrase continues with the words "in its right place," the voice moves to D-flat on the word "right," implying that all is *not* right with the musical space in which the ensemble is moving. The voice stresses this D-flat, as though to concede that something is amiss. The minor-seventh dissonance formed by the voice's D-flat over the bass's E-flat does at least resolve "correctly," when the voice moves down a half-step to C for the word "place." (In conventional Western harmony, the minor-seventh interval found in the V^7 chord [say, E-flat to D-flat in a chord containing the members E-flat, G, B-flat, D-flat] typically resolves down to the third of the next chord, the I [say, A-flat, C, E-flat, with a half-step fall from D-flat to C], and this provides a satisfactory resolution. Although the harmonic motion is different, the resolution of dissonances in "Everything" recalls that element of Western harmony.) The bass's C comes in half a beat before the voice's C, to anticipate this resolution or perhaps guide the voice to it (see example 3.4). This C creates the impression of a dominant when taken with the

3.4. "Everything in Its Right Place," chorus

voice's opening F-C. Rather than resting on this tentative resolution for long, however, the bass simply reiterates the C–D-flat–E-flat motive while the voice continues to hold its C. The first verse of the song (1:14) adds an echo to the keyboard and to the lead vocals for the undistorted lyrics "yesterday I woke up sucking on a lemon." The melody is stagnant, repeating the C over the C–D-flat–E-flat movement in the bass until the final statement of "on a lemon," when the voice sings E-flat–F as the bass moves to F to take up its original motive again.

The form in the second verse (2:12) mutates slightly so that each lyrical idea is repeated twice. The statement "there are two colors in my head" implies that the subject is aware of a fracture. These "two colors" are reproduced sonically in the battle for dominance between F and C, the split between the speaker channels, and a division between what appears to be a rational "conscious" voice and a babbling subconscious. The rational voice attempts to interact with the babbling one, asking "What *is* that you tried to say? What *was* that you tried to say?" (italics added), but it receives only nonsense in return. The move from present to past tense suggests action taking place in the present rather than an event that has already taken place outside the song, constructing a sense of time as experienced by the subject that is internal to the album and not based on the way the song was actually recorded. As the main voice asks for clarification, the babble strives for coherence but achieves only the static back-and-forth motion of a major second (F to E-flat). The melody grows slightly more complex, mimicking the bass line. The repetition of "tried to say" implies an attempt at closure, the main voice growing stronger as it moves back to F and the babble recedes into the background. The main voice tries to overcome the babble by simply drowning it out, but the babble triumphs in the end, cutting off the coda statement of "everything" (3:36) as the main voice moves from one channel to the other. The now-babbling main voice is itself cut off by the keyboard at the end of the song and descends into garbled synthesized sounds, thus being absorbed into the musical texture. This struggle for dominance between the music and noise elements grows increasingly violent over the course of the next several songs, until the midpoint of the album. The split between music and noise evident in the songs can be mapped onto a split between rational and irrational thinking, which produces a schizophrenia, literally a "shattered mind," in the subject. This dichotomy can also be mapped onto the split between the reproduction of a given sound (say, the distorted voice) and the source of that sound (Yorke's own voice), which R. Murray Schafer has described as "schizophonia."[20]

"KID A"

The second song on the album, the title track "Kid A," continues to blur the categories of "acoustic" and electronic, presenting the synthesized sound of wind blowing and a slow keyboard pattern that sounds like a music box being wound. A counter-rhythm on a marimba-like keyboard (0:28) enters and alternates between channels, along with occasional percussive tapping reminiscent of a typewriter. The song feels like technology trying to replicate natural sounds, recalling the blurry distinction between computer- and hand-drawn art in the CD's booklets. When the voice finally enters, at 1:02, it is distorted and mechanized, as though flattened through a radio transmission. Doheny notes that "the character, the 'spirit' perhaps, of Thom's voice, has been electronically superimposed on the 'artificial' pitches of the onde [sic]."[21] This superimposition makes it possible for the "real" singer to absolve himself of any responsibility for meaning; Yorke has stated in reference to the song "Kid A" that "the lyrics are absolutely brutal and horrible and I wouldn't be able to sing them straight. But talking them and having them vocodered . . . so that I wasn't even responsible for the melody . . . that was great, it felt like you're not answerable to this thing."[22] Thus technology creates a schizophrenia (or schizo*phonia*) between the singer and the subject, as well as furthering the fragmentation of the subject himself with impenetrable lyrics and foggy harmonies. The aural incomprehensibility of the lyrics recasts the main vocal as nonsense and maps it onto the category of noise.

"Kid A" presents five short lyrical segments: two verses, a chorus, a wordless bridge (distinguished by its musical dissimilarity with the surrounding sections), and a final verse. The verses have approximately the same melody, and the chorus keeps the same instrumentation but expands the vocal melody. Rather than reoccurring between verses, the chorus simply repeats the same lyrics four times in a row. The bridge section presents radically different orchestration but then segues easily into the final verse. The lyrics of the first verse speak to the challenge between reality and falsehood, or the conflict between acoustic authenticity and technological artifice that underscores the ambiguity of the subject's identity: "I slipped away, I slipped on a little white lie." The second verse (1:36) brings the voice and drums to the forefront and adds a second voice in nasal harmony, shifting to the collective first person for the words "we got heads on sticks, you got ventriloquists," which evoke the image of puppets whose voices originate from an unknown outside source. It is unclear who "we" and "you" are: the distinction could be made between band and listener, between parts of the subject's psyche (perhaps the schizophrenic "two colors in my head" from the previous song), between the band plus its fans and some other entity (such as multinational corporations or big government), or between the protagonist/subject and someone or something else.[23] Despite the implied rivalry, the image suggests a shared effort, as the "heads on sticks" held by one side cannot have a voice without the "ventriloquists" of the other. This collaboration speaks to the very experience of listening to Radiohead's album, though the band's part in the partnership was played out in the creation of the album in the studio.

The opening "music box" motive of "Kid A" presents an interlocking pitch collection that changes the harmony over the course of each measure and produces a diatonic fog of constantly thickening and thinning layers of harmonic ambiguity. This background harmony grows more intricate when the synthesized marimba comes in (0:28). The "marimba" provides a slower series of parallel tenths (parallel in that the same interval is present in each chord; parallel tenths are essentially the same as first-inversion chords, in which the third of a chord rather than the root is played by the lowest voice; thus, an F-major chord in first inversion would have A in the bass rather than F), which clashes with the preexisting music-box melody. First-inversion and second-inversion (chords with the fifth in the bass) chords are less harmonically stable than root-position chords. Although the marimba's pattern is harmonically unstable, it does provide an anchoring riff as well as a syncopated counter-rhythm to the music-box chords (evenly spaced quarter notes). When the marimba's series of parallel tenths is coupled with the underlying music-box sound, up to six adjacent pitches of the F-major diatonic collection are present at any given time, as shown in example 3.5. The notes in this example are unmetered, and the dotted lines indicate a move to the next beat.

These chord clusters sound less discordant than they might if all the notes were played by the same instrument, but their effect is to arrest the song's harmonic motion (and also to make it chordally indifferent, inasmuch as so many pitches are present at any one time) while still building up a sonic background over which the voice can enter. The distorted voice presents yet a third, unrelated melody, which fits

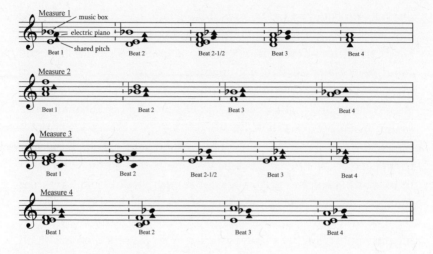

3.5. "Kid A," introduction

more closely (though uneasily) with the marimba than with the music box. Although the marimba riff remains the same, the voice slots into different chords in the pattern each time. The vocal line does emphasize members of the F-major triad (F, A, and C), but it does not present a strong F until the chorus (2:10). Even then the voice ends on C, which would be heard as the fifth scale degree (if not the dominant V chord) in the context of the key of F. For what passes as the chorus—the four-times-repeated statement "standing in the shadows at the end of my bed"—a bass guitar is added to the sound, and the drums grow much louder. Near the end of the chorus (2:44), the bass enters with a rhythmic motive on B-flat and C (a major-second interval that recalls the move from E-flat to F by the babbling voice in "Everything in Its Right Place"). This riff repeats at the end of the final verse and is similar to the one that begins the next song, "The National Anthem" (see example 3.6).

In the bridge section of "Kid A," about three-fourths of the way through the song at 3:06, a synthesized-string interlude presents a C^{13} chord (a diatonic triad with additional notes stacked above the root of C; the published score omits the third and ninth, with the result of C, G, B-flat, F, and A being played together), saturating the texture, a kind of reversion to the unorganized sound existing in nature. Although stacked non-chord tones are often used to enhance a dominant chord before it moves to the tonic chord (C^{13} would be V^{13} in F major), their addition here continues the destabilization of any true tonal center. Whereas the presence of strings normally humanizes or "sweetens" a musical texture (a famous example being Phil Spector's work on the Beatles' "The Long and Winding Road"), their synthesized representation here appears unnatural and almost sinister, foreshadowing the use of strings as noise in "How to Disappear Completely." The music-box motive returns under the strings (3:18), and the voice sings the final verse (3:52), again focusing on C and A rather than on the expected tonal center of F. The strings fade out as the singer begins the last verse, but they seem to be simply lying in wait to capture the voice, as they immediately rise in the mix again. The lyrics of the final verse, "rats and children follow me out of town," could refer to Radiohead's feeling toward its audience, that they will follow the band naively as though it were a magical Pied Piper. The Pied Piper of legend lured away children only after the people of Hamlin failed to pay him for ridding their town of rats. Footman notes that "[t]he Piper is a clear precursor to the Rock Star As Messiah idea exploited so brilliantly by Bowie and with which Thom Yorke is profoundly uneasy."[24] The singer's halfhearted delivery of the closing words "c'mon kids" suggests that he is reluctant to lead the children (or his audience) away. The drums and bass rise in the texture again, with the music box still in the background under the increasingly encroaching strings, again emphasizing C. The C that had battled for dominance in the previous song, "Everything in Its Right Place," has finally triumphed here, though only after being abandoned by (or cutting off) the voice. (The resolution does not last long, however, as the next interval heard, between the C in the bass and strings at the end of "Kid A" and the F-sharp in the bass at the beginning of "The National Anthem," is a tritone, traditionally the least harmonious interval.) The strings fade out under an anguished vocal cry (4:24), which blends into high keyboard effects that are abruptly cut off by the next song, "The National Anthem." Although the voice itself falls under the "nonsense" heading this time, it is again defeated by the non-vocal sounds. Technology has again triumphed over nature, albeit a faux nature since all the sounds are synthetic.

"THE NATIONAL ANTHEM"

The third song on *Kid A*, "The National Anthem," possesses a sense of irony while still expressing the subject's feelings of alienation. A traditional national anthem is composed to unite and instill pride in a nation's people, but Radiohead's "The National Anthem" instead articulates the terror that many feel, even (or especially) in a crowd of citizens: "everyone is so near, everyone has got the fear, it's holding on." Despite (or perhaps because of) the proximity of the crowd, the subject still feels alone, perhaps even more so because of this stifling press of humanity. This condition recalls David Riesman's observation in his classic sociological analysis *The Lonely Crowd* that "Caught between social character and rigid social institutions, the individual and his potentialities have little scope. . . . Modern industrial society has driven great numbers of people into anomie, and produced a wan conformity in others, but the very developments which have done this have also opened up hitherto undreamed-of possibilities for autonomy."[25] The subject here is being pressured to conform to a "national" standard but finds that everyone around him is connected only by a "wan conformity" of fear and alienation. His failure to conform ultimately produces an existential despair at the thought of the human condition. "The National Anthem" begins with an aggressive bass line that repeats relentlessly throughout the entire song (see example 3.6). The drums fade in and out as though the drummer is reconsidering his participation. The bass seems determined to make up for its limited motive at the end of "Kid A" and articulates a new version of the motive that stretches a major third to F-sharp, F-natural, and then E, but ends on D each time. This collapsing of the intervals within the new motive, from a major third (F-sharp to D) to a minor third (F-natural to D) and then a major second (E to D), underscores the claustrophobic feel of the lyrics. The voice's final A that is heard in "Kid A" on the words "c'mon kids" returns in the ondes martenot melody of "The National Anthem" that comes in after the bass riff has been established. Whereas the A in "Kid A" had been articulated (spoken/sung) at a low volume, the initial A in "The National Anthem" is two octaves higher and much more dominant in the texture.

One of the hallmarks of Radiohead's musical style is a strong "groove." Dai Griffiths has noted Radiohead's striking and complex

"Kid A," bass riff (track 2: 4:09-4:26)

"The National Anthem," bass riff (track 3, beginning at 0:22)

"The National Anthem," horn riff (track 3, beginning at 2:39)

"Kid A," bass riff (track 2: 4:09-4:26)

"The National Anthem," bass riff (track 3, beginning at 0:22)

"The National Anthem," horn riff (track 3, beginning at 2:39)

3.6. Comparison of "Kid A" bass riff and "The National Anthem" bass and horn riffs

"layering of the guitars and drums" on *OK Computer*,[26] and Ross has stressed the importance of the band's interlocking sound: "Take away any one element—Selway's flickering rhythmic grid, for example, fierce in execution and trippy in effect—and Radiohead are a different band."[27] Mark Spicer has discussed Radiohead's use of an "accumulative beginning" for *Amnesiac*'s opening track, "Packt Like Sardines in a Crushd Tin Box," in which "the addition of each new component seems to be a deliberate attempt to surprise the listener . . . so that when the groove ultimately does crystallize it sounds as if it has 'emerged' out of a state of rhythmic, metric, and tonal confusion."[28] Because the rhetoric of music theory (and of all good analytical writing) is toward clarity, and should thus be able to explain moments of musical uncertainty or ambiguity, it is tempting to read this accumulation of sounds as emergence out of disorder, mastery won over the confusion of the song itself. Given Radiohead's tendency toward ambiguity and creating deliberate puzzles for the listener, however, the band's use of the accumulative groove is unlikely to be an act of disclosure in moving from confusion to clarity; rather, the band is more likely to strip off one veil only to reveal an even more opaque one. The band plays with the technique of accumulation (and with listener expectations) on "The National Anthem" by having instruments drop out and reenter after the groove has been established, lending emphasis to the voice. Any momentary clarity achieved by the groove once all the instruments have coalesced is immediately dispersed by part of it dropping back out, so that the listener is unsettled once again. As shown in table 3.3, the song can be divided into the large sections of intro, verse, and outro. The verse repeats at 2:18, but for convenience the two verses are not divided in the table. The outro begins at 3:43, when the horns hold a sustained pitch and all the rhythm instruments except the bass drop out. Entrances throughout the song are indicated by X, and exits by O. The voice, for example, enters for the first time at 1:36 and exits at 1:57.

As the singer says "everyone" at the beginning of each verse, the instruments drop out as though they are making way for him; ironically, "everyone" abandons the subject as he sings the very word. The musical texture is built up by the guitar and by vocal babbling (evocative of *Sgt. Pepper*'s crowd noise); this babbling reoccurs when the lead vocal drops out later in the song, at 4:00 in the outro. Slight feedback behind the vocal line emphasizes the synthesized element, and the voice is limited to the same major-third (D to F-sharp) range of the bass riff. Rather than contracting the melody as the bass does, however, the voice extends it upward and stepwise, from D to E and then to F-sharp. As the vocalist sings "it's holding on" (1:57), he grows more hysterical, as though he himself is barely holding on or is struggling to keep the song together. His change of the top note in the pattern, from F-sharp to F-natural, lends a sinister bent to the melody. His "aahs" on a high A and G-sharp near the end of the song (3:52) foreshadow the "aahs" in "How to Disappear Completely" that signify the subject's dissolution in

TABLE 3.3. The Accumulative Groove in "The National Anthem"

(X = entrance; O = exit; (X) = still sounding)

Intro: CD timings	0:02	0:09	0:13	0:23	0:25	0:39	0:46	0:49	0:53	1:01	1:04	1:17
Bass	X											
Drums			X	O	X							
Ondes martenot (melody)				X								X
Horns												
Noise (babble, ondes, or electric guitar)		X	O			X	O	X	O	X	O	

Verse: CD timings	1:36	1:57	2:18	2:21	2:26	2:27	2:35	2:36	2:39	3:20	3:21	3:30	3:31	3:41	3:42
Voice	X	O	X						O	X	O	X	O	X	O
Bass	(X)														
Drums	(X)		O	X											
Ondes martenot (melody)		X	O						X						
Horns									X						
Noise (babble, ondes, or electric guitar)		X	O		X	O	X	O	X						

TABLE 3.3. *(continued)*

(X = entrance; O = exit; (X) = still sounding)

Outro: CD timings	3:43	3:53	4:00	4:50	4:53	5:11	5:30	5:46
Voice		X	O					
Bass	(X)							
Drums	O		X	O	X	O		
Ondes martenot (melody)	O					O		
Horns	X						O	
Noise (orchestral snippet; tape winding down)							X	O

the noise of the strings and guitar. Footman notes that "The National Anthem" is "threatening music, harnessing the incendiary rage of free jazz to what's supposed to be a pop song."[29] In the second verse, the "natural" sound of what Colin Greenwood has referred to as Charles Mingus-style horns[30] challenges the technological supremacy of the ondes martenot, filtered voice, and keyboard effects heard thus far on the album. Greenwood's allusion to Mingus apparently refers just to the sound of the instruments, but we might also consider Mingus's tendency to present several distinct lines at once, so that although the surface seems cacophonous, each line is credible on its own. The horns begin a rhythmic minor-seventh riff (2:39; see example 3.6) that recalls the incessant bass line as well as the earlier bass riff of "Kid A," with free improvisation by a trumpet and saxophone representing babble or nonsense over it.

This horn riff never "resolves," in the sense that the top note of a minor-seventh interval "should" descend stepwise to the note below (as it did in "Everything" with the voice's resolution from D-flat to C over the piano's E-flat), but rather serves as a confining frame from which the higher sounds try to escape.[31] In effect, the other instruments seem to be closing in on the voice, furthering the subject's paranoia. After several increasingly desperate repetitions of the lyrics "holding on," on the motive F–E–D, the rational voice leaves us at 3:42 with the bass, isolated horns, and vocal cries evocative of the earlier ondes martenot melody. Noise consumes the texture in the end, when the horns let loose with screeching glissandi. The horns are cut off by a snatch of orchestral melody reminiscent of Edward Elgar's music (5:31), an ironic commentary on English nationalism since Elgar's music has been so strongly associated with the old Empire way of thinking and the days of colonialism when Britons proudly—and accurately—claimed that the sun never set on the British Empire. Radiohead, by contrast, espouses a worldview based on free trade and cooperative solutions to problems such as global warming. This melody is distorted to sound like a tape being wound down, as though to represent the failure of technology's use in society, or to indicate that music, too, is but a representation, ultimately a reproduction that is only as convincing as the technology that made it possible.

"HOW TO DISAPPEAR COMPLETELY"

After a brief pause, a discordant string harmony begins to play, then a strummed acoustic guitar opens the next song, "How to Disappear Completely (and Never Be Found)." A single high B-flat string tone is left to sound above the guitar, a subtle yet dissonant noise over the alternating D-major and F-sharp-minor chords (a third-related pivot, as well as the same pitch boundaries of the bass and vocal lines of "The National Anthem"). This B-flat can be heard above the melody until the beginning of the chorus (1:37). The alternating chords and the pentatonic bass line (F-sharp, A, B, E, C-sharp) present a harmonic ambiguity upon which the noise can readily encroach. (A pentatonic pitch collection has five pitches, generally spaced as three in stepwise succession, here A, B, and C-sharp, followed by two more separated by a step, here E and F-sharp; the tones between the two-note and three-note collections are absent.)

Example 3.7 presents a reduction of "How to Disappear Completely" that shows how the musical elements interact with the noise.[32] Three lines are represented: the voice, the guitar/bass, and the elements of "noise" such as electric guitar, strings, and horns. The label-

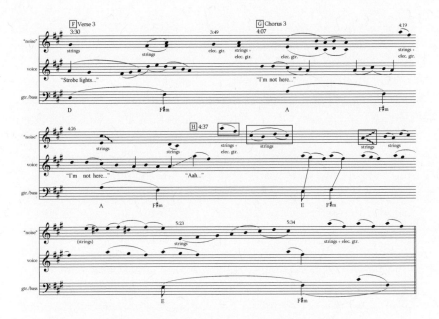

3.7. "How to Disappear Completely," reduction. Example courtesy of Mark Spicer and John Covach, eds., *Sounding Out Pop: Analytical Essays in Popular Music*, © The University of Michigan Press, 2010.

ing of these instruments as noise does not refer to their being out of tune, but rather to their disruption of the more stable elements of the voice, guitar, and bass. These noise intrusions are represented on the top staff of the example, with boxes indicating repeating notes or patterns that exist out of time from the other elements. Notes with stems on the heads indicate structurally important pitches (such as the F-sharp in the bass at the beginning of the example) or pitches to which a musical line is leading (such as the A in the opening words "that there"). A note with a stem and a flag, such as the E in the bass on the last line of the example, shows that while structurally important, the pitch functions mainly to lead to the next pitch, the stemmed F-sharp. Curved lines, or slurs, show the direction of a given melody and group some pitches together (either stepwise, as in the string notes at 5:23 on the last line of the example, or by minor third, as in the A to F-sharp interval that permeates all of the voices). The song can be broken into intro, verse one, chorus one, verse two, chorus two, verse three, and an extended chorus three that ends the song. The song builds up to a crisis at which the noise that has been threatening the musical texture over the entire album forces the structure to the breaking point.

Although "How to Disappear Completely" presents the most complete depiction of the subject thus far, with its coherent lyrics, clear verse/chorus structure, and relatively undistorted tones, the singer denies his existence from the very outset, in the opening line "that there, that's not me." In a sense, the singer is speaking of his recorded voice from outside the song, calling to mind Attali's notion of reproduction, in which the original is displaced by its copy: "people originally intended to use the record to preserve the performance, and today the performance is only successful as a simulacrum of the record."[33] Tate notes the literalness of the song's statement: the band is not present while the listener is experiencing the music, and the "performance" not only is not happening as the album plays, but in fact may have never taken place, given that modern recording sessions generally involve the musicians recording their parts separately.[34] The lyrics describe a dreamlike vision that contrasts with the claustrophobia evoked in "The National Anthem": "I go where I please, I walk through walls, I float down the Liffey [a river in Dublin[35]]." The song "How to Disappear Completely" was written in 1997 and performed on tour the next year;[36] its performance in the documentary *Meeting People Is Easy* evokes the disconnect between the public persona of being on the concert stage and the singer's own reality as a private individual. Jones has noted the "schism . . . between Thom Yorke the icon and Thom Yorke who experiences mundane, everyday life,"[37] one that surely exists to some extent in every public figure. Yorke's use of "other voices" (that is, filtered ones) elsewhere on *Kid A* is "a way of saying, 'obviously it isn't me,'"[38] but again, to some extent the recording of any artist's voice disconnects that voice by separating it from the body that performs it.

Yorke has stated that "How to Disappear Completely" refers to a dream in which he was flying around Dublin.[39] He has spoken elsewhere about a dream he had the night of a concert in Dublin with 33,000 people in attendance: "It was sheer blind terror. My most distinctive memory of the whole year was the dream I had that night: I was running down the Liffey, stark bollock naked, being pursued by a huge tidal wave."[40] Regardless of whether this dream is the same one that inspired "How to Disappear Completely," the river in the song represents an attempt at escape, and the vocal line reflects this imagery by growing progressively more disembodied as the song progresses. The bass line presents a "two against three" feel (dotted quarter notes that can be heard in $\frac{6}{8}$ rather than in the $\frac{3}{4}$ meter of the vocal line) against the "fast three" feel ($\frac{3}{4}$) of the guitar's rhythmic pattern, which also contributes to the feeling of being out of time. The A to F-sharp minor-third interval dominates the texture, stated by the electric guitar before the voice comes in and eventually moving to the other instruments. This interval has a wistful, keening feel that recalls the opening intervals of the Moody Blues' "Tuesday Afternoon" from the classic concept album *Days of Future Passed*. On that song, however, the orchestral forces work with the singer (and acoustic guitar) rather than against him as in "How to Disappear Completely." The vocal line begins with a minor third ("that there," 0:41) but immediately adds a major one ("not me," 0:51), alternating between a major and minor sound and suggesting an ambiguity in the singer's mood (if major is equated with happy and minor with sad, then what do we make of a rapid alternation between the two?). The guitar's minor third returns at the end of the first verse (1:30) and at the end of the second and third lines of the chorus ("this isn't happening" and "I'm not here," respectively).

In the second verse (2:14), the singer contradicts his earlier assertion of non-existence: "in a little while, I'll be gone." That is, he *is* here now, although he will be leaving shortly. The drums and tambourine enter the texture at the beginning of the verse, and the strings reenter during this section, following the vocal line's dynamics to swell or subside. In the next chorus (2:51), the singer's claim that "this isn't happening" starts to ring hollow, as ascending and descending scalar patterns (spanning B to F-sharp) played by synthesized horns begin to pepper the texture along with more intrusive minor thirds. The singer can no longer deny the reality of the noise intrusion. As the strings and electric guitar struggle for dominance in the third verse (3:30), the singer describes the crisis point in terms of cataclysmic scenes of the concert stage and the outdoors (or technology and nature): "strobe lights and blown speakers, fireworks and hurricanes." The singer grows yet more insistent in the final chorus (4:07), holding out the ends of phrases and almost overenunciating. He denies his existence ("I'm not here") one more time just before his death throes, when he transcends the violent texture and climbs into a higher tessitura with anguished "aahs" (4:37) claiming the minor-third interval as his own. At first the strings support him, but as he holds out a G-sharp (4:56), the note that fills in the gap in the minor third between A and F-sharp, the strings grow discordant and finally leave the voice hanging precariously alone. When the strings return, they proclaim the minor-third interval in unison with the electric guitar from 5:33 until the end. The forces have been joined, but the truce has come only with the elimination of the voice. As Cone has stated, musical accompaniment "symbolically suggests both the impingement of the outer world on the individual represented by the vocal persona, and the subconscious reaction of the individual to this impingement."[41] Thus the violence expressed in the musical battle between voice and strings can represent not only external forces working on the subject, but the subject's own subconscious bubbling up and spilling over as a reaction to the events of the world. Within the context of this album, the subject himself is unable to cope with the soul-draining alienation of modern society and longs for release.

"TREEFINGERS"

After repeatedly proclaiming that "I'm not here, this isn't happening," the tenuous subject of *Kid A* does disappear, nearly completely, in the next song. "Treefingers" marks the space between the two halves of the album, neither the end of side one nor the beginning of side two. It is an imaginary dividing point between the "A" and "B" sides of the nonexistent vinyl album, a space where nothing happens and yet everything does. In that sense, the track is the very sound of an ambivalence under erasure: neither A nor B, neither dead nor alive, neither music nor noise. The subject has erased himself at the end of "How to Disappear Completely" and will not appear again until "Optimistic," the simulacrum of a side-two single. In "Treefingers," the subject has lost all words, reverting to a pre-verbal state, and his voice is present only in stray "aahs" heard in the distance of the ambient texture. The instrumental forces that had previously battled are absent from this song as well; the only sounds present are New Age–style filtered guitars, which change tones quite slowly.[42] Rather than representing a literal beyond-death experience, the absence of the subject in the technological soundscape of "Treefingers" suggests that a constructed "real" or "nature" exists apart from and is thus superior to the subject. Not only does technology triumph over nature, it forms a new, human-made "nature" that absorbs and subjugates the subject. Yet this background "nature" consists in the end solely of technology. Radiohead understands that culture is at its root technological, that is, a human intervention into nature, and that nature as such appears only in the way that culture manages its "other." Art is in a sense that which both conceals and reveals the technology that makes society possible. It is impossible to escape technology into a nature that exists outside technology, and we become acutely aware of this fact when technology fails. In the course of a "normal" concept album, the protagonist's death would end the musical journey; here, however, since the subject has been diffused and undefined for so long, the background of instruments filtered by technology becomes the force that drives the album forward. "Protagonist" is perhaps too strong a label for this subject, who is unnamed and in danger of shattering apart at any moment. Because of the continued existence of the stage on which the dramatic action has taken place, represented by the electronic instruments, the album's final judgment does not have to occur upon the death of the voice-as-subject; instead, the subject can be revived and given a second chance.[43]

Jonny Greenwood's Messiaen influence is evident in his chord choices in "Treefingers," in subtler ways than his use of the ondes martenot. The series of tonally unstable chords with added sixths and ninths (intervals above the root, usually abbreviated as "add6" or "add9"; see example 3.8) in "Treefingers" moves very slowly and produces a lan-

track 5: 0:00   0:16   0:22   0:37

3.8. "Treefingers," chords

guorous rather than a dizzying effect. The chords in the introduction move from F-sharp major add6 to E major add6 to B major add9 to C-sharp major add9; each chord is sustained for up to sixteen seconds, an eternity in pop music. This series of chords is repeated, and the rest of the song continues to emphasize F-sharp major add6. The chords alternate slowly between E-major and F-sharp-major chords, and then move to B major add9 for several seconds before returning to F-sharp major add6. A descent from F-sharp to E to D-sharp then returns again to F-sharp add6, moving up to G-sharp add6 and then finally back to F-sharp add6 for the end. Taken together, this progression forms the pitch collection B, C-sharp, D-sharp, E, E-sharp, F-sharp, G-sharp, and A-sharp. This collection is symmetrical (the intervals in the series E-sharp–F-sharp–G-sharp–A-sharp are the inversion of B–C-sharp–D-sharp–E; that is, the intervals in the first series are half-step, whole step, whole step, and in the second are whole step, whole step, half-step) and can thus be conceptually linked to Messiaen's modes of limited transposition.[44]

The position of "Treefingers" halfway through *Kid A* saps what little momentum had developed over the first four songs. After experiencing a dichotomy between nature and the ego over the first four songs on the album, the subject now attempts to quell his internal struggle, which takes form as an attempt to domesticate his inner anxieties as music. Failing to be kept at bay, his inner demons erupt as noise, sporadically until "How to Disappear Completely" and then taking over the texture. This eruption of noise dislocates the subject, ungrounding him for "Treefingers." The new musical space that results seems amorphous, musically flat. It is almost a reversion to nature, that is, music before the subject has placed his mark upon it. Yet it is also the ground on which the subject can reinvent himself. And this subject *must* rediscover himself—his *self*—to complete the form of the commodity: only half the album has yet been played. The pause between album halves is a trace of the physical act of turning over an LP. The irony of course is that there is no album to turn, nor a band actually present; the hiatus is completely imaginary, though real. This pause also plays with the idea that vinyl is more real, more authentic, than the CD, whose shiny, reflective surface returns the narcissistic image of the listening subject rather than the enigmatic hole of despair of the vinyl album. Here, the tropes are inverted, and the pause calls to mind that very place of desolation. How should that blank space be filled in?

"Treefingers" can also be read as playing out, in microcosm, the allegory of the band's own dilemma, which is worked through in *Kid A* and *Amnesiac*. Just as the subject takes his leave from the "music" to regroup between "death" and his seemingly empty reconstitution, so the band took a long (three-year) break before moving in a new direction with the studio sessions that precipitated these two albums.[45] While

"Treefingers" thus maps onto the break between the still "commercial" *OK Computer* and the "experimental" *Kid A*, it also maps onto the six-month break between *Kid A* and *Amnesiac*. If the first half of *Kid A* presents a baffling series of experimental songs, and the second half returns to a somewhat more commercial sound, then *Amnesiac* may be expected to function as a "commercial" savior for the experimental *Kid A*. Thus, *Kid A*'s first half is to its second half as *Kid A* as a whole is to *Amnesiac*.

Kid A first half : *Kid A* second half :: *Kid A* : *Amnesiac*

In this analogy, "Treefingers" anticipates on a lower level the band's brief hiatus, that period of reflection between *Kid A* and *Amnesiac* during which Radiohead reacted to *Kid A*'s reception and produced *Amnesiac*.[46] The subject that expires on the first half of *Kid A* is revived for the album's second half, and would be resurrected yet again for *Amnesiac*. The precariousness of this subject who moves back and forth across the threshold of death can thus be read as an allegory of Radiohead's own feelings toward their success. The subject is conflicted about his very existence. The members of Radiohead were likewise conflicted about whether and how to proceed within the mainstream music industry, torn between continually reproducing their old, successful sound and forging ahead with new musical ideas that might not have been received favorably by fans or critics. Given the enormous pressure under which the members of Radiohead found themselves after the *OK Computer* tour, trying to push themselves artistically while satisfying market demands after the success of their previous two albums, one can guess that they might literally have wanted to "disappear completely and never be found." In this sense, the studio sessions that produced *Kid A* and *Amnesiac* represent the band members' attempt to reclaim their artistic voice from the "ventriloquist" critics, fans, or music-industry executives who wanted to dictate the band's message. Radiohead's own experience of artistic commodification within the market culture of popular music shapes *Kid A*'s critique of the conditions of alienation and repression under which the subject lives in postindustrial society.[47]

Radiohead had championed Naomi Klein's book *No Logo* in their online blog prior to *Kid A*'s release, and the band purportedly even considered calling the album *No Logo* to underscore their anti-corporate stance.[48] *No Logo* offers an examination of the abominable conditions under which market goods are produced in developing countries, in which allowances are made for the producers but not for the workers or consumers. Klein discusses the separate tax status for export processing zones (EPZs) in communist countries. These EPZs ignore the mistreatment of their workers, and the working conditions may even have served as a lyrical inspiration for "How to Disappear Completely": as Klein writes, "this is *definitely* not really happening, *certainly* not here where the government in power maintains that capital is the devil and workers reign supreme" (italics in original, presumably indicating sarcasm).[49] Yet ironically enough, Radiohead's own situation is perilously close to that of the countries that Klein berates. Like the government and the media, the band makes money off the populace whom it exhorts to reclaim power. In a sense the audience does have the power, since the sale of CDs—the profits that accrue—bestows the ability of the band to "speak" through promotional appearances on the radio and television channels controlled by international corporations. Yet Radiohead, too, benefits financially from its relationship with capital. The band creates a product that it hopes its audience will consume, while simultaneously telling them that the society that urges such consumption is corrupt and oppressive. In this way, Radiohead thrives within the very system it purports to seek to destroy. The failure of the subject on *Kid A* to master the noise of technology, to transform it into compelling music, thus becomes a critique, an allegory for the band's inability to escape the clutches of the capitalist record industry and the commodity culture that it underwrites. Just as the human voice is unable to overcome the electronic instruments manifesting as noise on the first half of *Kid A*, so too is the subject unable to cope with the demands of living in modern society, and likewise is Radiohead unable to thrive outside the very corporate music industry it claims to despise.

THE SECOND
DEATH OF **KID A**

After the gray nothing-space of "Treefingers," the nebulous subject of *Kid A* is resuscitated and given a new chance at life, in what passes for a second-side single, "Optimistic." The second half of *Kid A* forms something of an opposition with the first, yet the mood created by the tentative sound of the songs leading up to "Treefingers" sets the stage for the rest of the album. The subject returns to a concrete form and existence, but although he has been reborn, he is now but a hollow, cynical shell. Consequently, the self-doubt and negativity expressed in the earlier songs are turned outward into a scathing, almost psychotic critique of the modern world. Radiohead's pessimism over the possibility of escaping the very public consumption they had courted as a struggling rock band manifests as false hopefulness in "Optimistic." With this puffed-up pseudo-single, Radiohead almost seems to be mocking the demand to create another hit in the "old style." The industry itself was apparently unsure what to make of this song. Some radio stations even purportedly promoted "Optimistic" as a single, in spite of the fact that it was never officially released as such. Yet the song presents a subject as jaded as the members of Radiohead appeared to be, preferring instead to make provocative comments and let listeners puzzle out whatever meaning the song might contain for themselves. Coupled with *Kid A*'s reluctant subject, the political and anti-corporate messages sent, not only by the song itself but particularly by the band's resistant marketing strategy, create a sort of cognitive dissonance. Although the band seems to be appealing to people to stand united as individuals (a return to the "together yet alone" message of "The National Anthem"), it repeatedly abandons them without a leader, as in the voiceless "Treefingers." This refusal to lead makes the subsequent upbeat message of "Optimistic" sound even more hollow, just as big business and government proffer only empty slogans for the masses, a literal "Electioneering" (track eight on OK Computer).[1] Although the band often points out that the mainstream political messages of the media lack substance, Radiohead's own substance here can be expressed only by negation in the album's obscure lyrics.

Part of the appeal of "Optimistic" as a single comes from its placement in the album's song sequence, a stark contrast to the surface formlessness of "Treefingers" that precedes it. This placement is remarkable in itself, as a single customarily appears quite early in an album's track listing. David O. Montgomery explains that the LP and single traditionally have had a symbiotic relationship: "An LP . . . could be released to capitalize on the strength of a successful single, while additional singles could be drawn from the LP for simultaneous or future release." Furthermore, "the single, from which clear profits were made, was also the leading form of advertising for the LP which, because of the nature of the material, yielded still further singles."[2] Thus a single could be released to herald the album on which it would appear, and upon the single's success (and the increased sales of the album), further singles could be selected for release, perpetuating the cycle of sales. (Today, this cycle is perpetuated in part by the continual reissuing of "classic" albums with new bonus tracks and enhanced sound due to technological advances since the original album's release.) Presumably, the more singles with which listeners are familiar from radio airplay or, today, iTunes or internet radio stations such as Pandora or Folk Alley, the greater the likelihood that they will buy the complete album. Noted producer George Martin provided the following rule of thumb for assembling an album: "Always make side one strong, for obvious commercial reasons. . . . Another principle . . . when assembling an album was always to go out a side strongly, placing the weaker material towards the end but then going out with a bang."[3] The rules for ordering an album's songs probably derive from live performance; just as an artist wants to make a good first and last impression on the audience, so too the strength of an album's first side can dictate whether the listener ever makes it to side two. Ending the second side "with a bang" leaves the listener with good feelings toward the band, leaves her wanting more, and so encourages future consumption of the recording artist's other products. In the old LP format, for an album's main single not to appear until side two would have been unusual and probably frowned upon by a record company's marketing department (although exceptions do exist, including Paul Simon's "You Can Call Me Al" [*Graceland*, 1986] and Sinéad O'Connor's "Nothing Compares 2 U" [*I Do Not Want What I Haven't Got*, 1990], each of which appears on the second side of the album).[4] In addition, if listeners had purchased the album on the strength of the single heard on the radio, as was dictated by the marketing, then they would expect to hear something familiar immediately, rather than several tracks later and possibly after turning the record over.

Given that the listeners of *Kid A* have not received a single over halfway through the CD, and thus have had little so far to hold on to, the album requires the appearance of a single at this point. The apparently dead subject and the confused and imperiled listener both need a point of orientation. Even the empty form of a simple, conventional pop song would be a relief. As James Doheny has stated, "Any fans who found the first half of *Kid A* intrinsically baffling must have been profoundly relieved by 'Optimistic.'"[5] Radiohead was well known even before *Kid A* for its uncomfortable lyrics detailing man's alienation within society, but up until *Kid A* the band's songs had only spoken of alienation without enacting it directly. At the very least, the band's earlier albums had followed a more or less conventional structure of verse and chorus, but with *Kid A*, alienation takes form directly, absent the trappings of pop artifice. When "Optimistic" appears, these trappings of artifice are revealed for what they are: false and sloganistic. Yet this revelation does not open only onto emptiness: Doheny also points out that this song marks the first on the album to deal "explicitly with . . . political issues,"[6] that is, those of capitalism and modern society rather than just the subject's own existential crisis. In a sense, the clearer subject matter, though still bleak, is comforting because we are no longer confronted with the embarrassment of the subject's death wish.

The subject may well be feeling just as nihilistic, but he is decrying the modern human condition rather than expressing a personal angst.

"OPTIMISTIC"

The lyrics of "Optimistic" detail evolution as a dead-end process within the capitalist machine ("this one just crawled out of the swamp . . . fodder for the animals living on an animal farm"). The subject's reaction to the failure of his attempted "death" on side one puts emotional distance between the listener and himself but also encourages the listener to side with him on more universal issues. Rather than making baffled statements about the unreality of his situation, as on *Kid A*'s first half, the subject now makes harsh, visceral statements about modern life that feel hyper-real by contrast: "flies are buzzing around my head, vultures circling the dead." The subject has failed to actually die, but in a spiritual sense he is already dead, trapped within the cogs of society.[7] It is tempting to say that the subject has lost his humanity in the act of attempted self-negation; as a product of the modern world, however, perhaps he never had any humanity to lose. Despite (or because of) his status as a drone in a dog-eat-dog society, the subject lacks empathy toward others suffering from the same conditions of oppression. After detailing the horrific conditions of flies, vultures, and dead bodies in verse one (0:42), he makes the careless statement that it is "not my problem" (1:01), then seems willing to offer assistance ("I'd really like to help you, man," 2:57) but immediately makes the snide observation "nervous, messed-up marionette, floating around on a prison ship" (3:09), indicating a laissez-faire reluctance to help the less fortunate. The subject, like many street pedestrians walking past the homeless who line the sidewalks, is looking out for himself first even while recognizing society's ills. The song's catchy chorus/hook[8] (1:06)—"if you try the best you can, the best you can is good enough"—seems to be an afterthought. Despite the band's purported efforts not to market itself, a single has emerged after all, complete with a singable chorus containing a hollow slogan for those depressed and disenchanted by their daily lives. As long as people "try the best they can," they can muddle through modern existence, not thinking too much about anyone else's problems. The hook also provides the only tangible, vaguely positive link with the title of the song. Although on the surface the chorus seems positive and encouraging, its placement after the lyrics "living on an animal farm" and "floating around on a prison ship" makes it sound sarcastic and insincere.

As Doheny observes, both "Optimistic" and OK Computer's "Electioneering" appear about halfway through their respective albums. Both songs come after a song that breaks the album's momentum: "Electioneering" after the computer-voiced "Fitter Happier" and "Optimistic" after the wordless "Treefingers." However, as table 4.1 shows, OK Computer had presented four both potential and actual singles by the time "Electioneering" appeared. The table also shows the track listings and single placements of several of Radiohead's other albums. Pablo Honey and The Bends reflect the old practice of placing singles early on each side of an LP, but OK Computer distributes the singles more evenly, reflecting the different format of the CD, which was commonplace by the time of OK Computer's release. (The singles on Hail to the Thief, the follow-up to Amnesiac, are spaced evenly throughout the tracks, similar to OK Computer.) Whereas Kid A dispenses with "real" singles altogether, Amnesiac returns to the formula of a second single appearing halfway through the tracks. Had there been a single on Kid A prior to "Optimistic," the placement of "Optimistic" would have been akin to that of Amnesiac's second single, "Knives Out." Thus, although "Optimistic" occupies the traditional placement of a second-side single, Kid A itself lacks the other necessary trappings: at least one strong single, if not two or three, on the first half of the album, followed by "filler" or weaker songs leading up to the aural/physical break of turning the LP over and encountering another single as the first song on the second side. Instead, Kid A has presented only one real "song" with verse and chorus up to this point, and that at track four, "How to Disappear Completely," much later than it would have appeared in the old LP format. "Optimistic" thus represents a mere shell of a "single" after the rest of the album's form has been stripped away. After his failed attempt at death, the subject reemerges in "Optimistic" in what is traditionally a strong position, the second-side single, but this placement still fails to create that sense of an authoritative voice for the album found in Radiohead's other work. Rather than presenting a clear protagonist from the first song onward, the album has gradually built

TABLE 4.1. Song Placement on Radiohead Albums (singles are in bold)

Track	Pablo Honey (1993)	The Bends (1995)	OK Computer (1997)	Kid A (2000)	Amnesiac (2001)
1	"You"	"Planet Telex"	**"Airbag"**	"Everything in Its Right Place"	"Packt Like Sardines in a Crushd Tin Box"
2	**"Creep"**	**"The Bends"**	**"Paranoid Android"**	"Kid A"	**"Pyramid Song"**
3	"How Do You?"	**"High and Dry"**	"Subterranean Homesick Alien"	"The National Anthem"	"Pulk/Pull Revolving Doors"
4	"Stop Whispering"	"Fake Plastic Trees"	"Exit Music (for a Film)"	"How to Disappear Completely"	"You and Whose Army?"
5	"Thinking about You"	"Bones"	**"Let Down"**	"Treefingers"	"I Might Be Wrong"
6	**"Anyone Can Play Guitar"**	"Nice Dream"	**"Karma Police"**	"Optimistic"	**"Knives Out"**
7	"Ripcord"	**"Just"**	"Fitter Happier"	"In Limbo"	"Amnesiac/Morning Bell"
8	"Vegetable"	**"My Iron Lung"**	"Electioneering"	"Idioteque"	"Dollars & Cents"
9	"Prove Yourself"	"Bullet Proof . . . I Wish I Was"	"Climbing Up the Walls"	"Morning Bell"	"Hunting Bears"
10	"I Can't"	"Black Star"	**"No Surprises"**	"Motion Picture Soundtrack"	"Like Spinning Plates"
11	"Lurgee"	"Sulk"	**"Lucky"**		"Life in a Glass House"
12	"Blow Out"	**"Street Spirit (Fade Out)"**	"The Tourist"		
13	"Creep" (radio version)[1]				

Note:

1. The radio version of "Creep" changes the lyrics "you're so fucking special" to "you're so very special."

TABLE 4.2. Album Placement of "Electioneering" versus "Optimistic"

OK Computer	Kid A
"Karma Police"	"How to Disappear Completely"
"phew, for a minute there, I lost myself"	"I'm not here, this isn't happening"
"Fitter Happier"	"Treefingers"
spoken-word, no vocal melody	no lyrics, wordless "aahs"
	in background
"Electioneering"	"Optimistic"
guitar intro, verse, chorus,	verse, chorus, verse, chorus,
verse, chorus, guitar outro	bridge, verse, chorus, coda

up a shaky subject whose disappearance is almost inconsequential, and whose reemergence is startling.

Examining "Optimistic" and "Electioneering" in terms of the songs immediately before and after them does yield several similarities, as shown in table 4.2. Each song comes after an atypical break in the flow of the album: "Optimistic" follows the ambient "Treefingers," and "Electioneering" comes after "Fitter Happier," in which a computer-generated voice intones a description of the perfect conformist lifestyle ("an empowered and informed member of society").[9] On OK Computer, this midpoint pause had occurred after "Karma Police," which ends with the repeated words "phew, for a minute there, I lost myself" (2:46).[10] Here, the singer-as-subject is playing an active role, conscious of having slipped into a reverie (or paranoid episode), and of wanting to return to reality instead of negating the self. Dai Griffiths discusses the "phew" that ends "Karma Police" as an exclamation that embodies the subject, a sigh of relief: "What's happening is a genuine thing: the knowledge of karma police (whatever that is, or they are) has got so bad that as a solitary individual the singer has lost his sense of self. . . . You could imagine saying 'Phew!' all the way from small things like a small faint brought on by physical exertion, through a momentary sense of stress getting the better of oneself, to some dreadful political suppression."[11] (This return to bodily reality experienced on the earlier album also occurs on Amnesiac in the sharp intake of breath at the beginning of "You and Whose Army?" and the squeaking guitar strings on "Hunting Bears," each of which makes the listener conscious of the person generating the sound in the recording studio.) On *Kid A*, conversely, rather than being bodily present, the subject up until this point has been active only in trying to make himself "disappear completely" (and even then, his activity is confined to trying to convince himself that he is "not here," that he is not identical to the self, the lyrical "I"). His reemergence after the words "I'm not here, this isn't happening," is structurally similar to the reappearance of *OK Computer*'s subject after the statement "I lost myself" in "Karma Police." Whereas "Treefingers" has no lyrics, "Fitter Happier" by contrast is "all lyrics" and no vocal melody.[12] Each song presents an interruption to the flow of its respective album, although *Kid A*'s narrative (or lack thereof) is markedly different, and less commercially directed, than that of *OK Computer*.

The structure of "Electioneering," the beginning of *OK Computer*'s second half, is verse one, chorus, verse two, chorus, bookended by a long intro/outro instrumental section dominated by guitars. The song sounds "live" and raucous, a stark contrast to the preceding computer-generated "Fitter Happier." The key moves from D minor to C major and then A minor, and the voice emphasizes scale degrees one and five in D (D and A, which both sound over an A-minor chord) at the midpoint and end of each section. Lyrically, the verse divides into a rhymed couplet and then the sloganistic "I trust I can rely on your vote" (0:55). Each rhyme of the couplet ends on A minor, and the "slogan" ends on D minor. The chorus of "Electioneering" presents a counterpoint between the lead voice and a lower voice in unison with the guitar. As shown in example 4.1, the lead voice moves C–G–F–E

4.1. "Electioneering," chorus

(which is discordant with the D-minor accompaniment) before finally coming to rest on D, while the lower voice moves upward and stepwise from D to end on A (beginning at 1:03). These voices moving in opposition are recalled in the chorus of "Optimistic" in the form of a rapidly ascending guitar against a descending bass under a fairly static vocal line. The formal structure of "Electioneering" is simpler than that of "Optimistic" and demonstrates the band's earlier, guitar-driven style. In each song, the verse goes straight into the chorus, which feels like a relief after the anxiety generated by the verse. *OK Computer*'s song sequence moves next to the creepy "Climbing Up the Walls,"[13] and then includes two more singles before the album ends.

On *Kid A*, "Optimistic" starts with renewed energy and follows a fairly traditional structure (verse one, chorus, verse two, chorus, bridge, verse three, chorus, and coda). As shown in example 4.2, the song begins

"Aah..."   "Ooh..."
"How to Disappear Completely"   "Optimistic"

4.2. "How to Disappear Completely" and "Optimistic," vocalese

with an echo of the vocalese that appeared at the end of "How to Disappear Completely." The smooth, wordless "oohs" at the beginning of "Optimistic" are transformed into more plaintive "aahs" near the end (3:57), returning to "oohs" in a coda (4:22) that revives the melody from the intro.[14] The vocal line in both the verse and chorus of "Optimistic" is static and echoes the rhythm of the drums and guitar. A loud, rough guitar line underscores the vocals; the heavy-handedness of the guitar after its previous absence gives the impression of an awkward attempt at belatedly producing a "single" in line with the band's earlier material. Here, the guitar becomes an uncomfortable signifier of Radiohead's old (and seemingly abandoned) style, playing against the singer's ambivalent delivery. Despite this purported "single" status of "Optimistic," which might imply a typical Radiohead harmonic progression, the verse is based in D major but begins and ends on the supertonic (E, the ii chord) rather than on the more stable tonic (D, the I chord). A more accurate way of reading the progression is as neighbor tones to D. Harmonic progressions unconventional to traditional music theory are not unusual in popular music, but until *Kid A*, Radiohead's music had not presented such a stark dichotomy between the instrumental lines and the vocals; in "Optimistic," the vocal line often does not fit into the accompanying chords at all. The midpoint of verse one lands on an A over an E-minor V_2^4 chord (that is, an E-minor-seventh chord in third inversion; the A is discordant because it falls between two pitches being sounded in the chord, G and B-flat) on the word "crumb" (0:52), and the verse ends on a D over the same chord (the D is the seventh of the E-minor chord) on the word "some" (1:04). In each case, the accompanying chords move to a D-major chord only after the vocal ends, presenting a resolution too late. These chords thus function more to start the next line than to finish the previous one.

The chorus of "Optimistic" (1:07) at first seems more conventional at the harmonic level. The bass presents a descending progression against an ascending statement in the electric guitar, recalling the two voices of "Electioneering," and the two lines meet with a harmonious major third at the end of the last line. The vocal line leaps a fifth between the end of the verse and the start of the chorus, making the slogan "try the best you can" pop out of the texture. The voice briefly holds out a 4–3 suspension over a D chord at the midpoint of the chorus ("can," 1:11), but then returns to the static verse melody and ends on the same D over an E-minor V_2^4 chord as before, on the word "enough" (1:16). The conventional overall verse/chorus structure furthers the illusion of a "single"; however, the third verse ends prematurely (3:15), without a rhyme for the first half. The voice breaks off after the phrase beginning "nervous messed-up marionette" and is subsumed by feedback, as though the image of the marionette on the prison ship is too horrifying to proceed with another lyric. Society's cruelties that have manifested as technology have apparently overcome the subject once again. The melody of the third verse is a third above the melody of verses one and two but remains static. This higher, somewhat shrill-sounding melody ends, without resolution, on E. The underlying chords finish the progression from E minor seventh to D major as before, then the final chorus begins. The "optimism" of the final chorus seems even more false after the imagery of the aborted third verse. This final chorus ends with the repeated phrase "dinosaurs roaming the earth" (3:40) on the transposed vocal descent (A–G-sharp–F-sharp, here transposed to F–E–D) of "How to Disappear Completely." The last statement adds an E-flat to the descent, emphasizing the word "earth," and then moves to "aahs" on the earlier F–E–D for several repetitions. The "oohs" that return in the coda bring an optimism that sounds even more forced, as though the singer is determined to end on a soothing, positive note, with a veneer of calm, despite the appalling imagery he has just related in the lyrics. "Optimistic" ends with an instrumental vamp (4:52) on the neighbor tones to D (the pattern goes D–C–E–D) that segues into a hammering rhythm also focused around D, which then falls into the spiraling triplet feel of the next song, "In Limbo."

"IN LIMBO"

After the momentary coherence of "Optimistic," the album returns here to its earlier method of disorientation: as on "Kid A," the voice is buried deep in the mix, creating a swirling eddy of sounds. The subject now appears humanized, singing "I'm on your side," but nevertheless falls through "trapdoors that open, I spiral down." The subject does not seem to mind this peril, however, dreamily asserting that "I'm lost at sea, don't bother me, I've lost my way." This stance, a resignation at his condition as well as a warning not to bother him, contradicts his earlier beckoning to the listener/audience in "Kid A" ("c'mon kids") but furthers his attempts to cast off the role of leader. "In Limbo" begins with quiet babbling: "I'm the first in the Irish Sea, another message I can't read." These words are, ironically enough, incomprehensible in their non-written form (and are not included in the album's packaging, though the published guitar/keyboard transcription and various fan websites list them); the song ends with the same words muttered under vocal howls that are eventually distorted and then dissolve into feedback. The vocalized "aahs" ("How to Disappear Completely") and "ooh/aah/oohs" ("Optimistic") reemerge at the end of "In Limbo," distorted into a sustained "aagh" (2:56) over the sound of throbbing machinery; the subject is in the process of being ground down like the students being fed into the meat grinder in the film *Pink Floyd: The*

Wall (1982). The peaceful "Liffey" of "How to Disappear Completely" has here been transformed into the raging "Irish Sea." The voice's return to babble and its final reversion to howling might thus be read as a primal cry from the subject's subconscious against the condition of modern humanity, a theme that has been growing more and more articulate over the course of the album. The clearest lyrics in "In Limbo" are those that proclaim the subject's helplessness ("I'm lost at sea"). These comprehensible lyrics could be taken as being sung by a different persona than the one muttering, in which case the howling at the end of the song could be a cry for help from a drowning man, unheeded by the persona who "can't read" the message. The refusal to hear such a clear message hearkens back to the coldhearted proclamation in "Optimistic" that it's "not my problem." The two voices mark a return to the schizophrenic split within the subject, a divide that has existed since the "two colors in my head" of "Everything in Its Right Place."

4.3. "In Limbo," contracting triplet progression

As example 4.3 shows, "In Limbo" begins with a contracting triplet progression, which moves from a perfect fifth (D to A) to a perfect fourth (A to E) to a minor third (E to G) to a major second (G to F) and finally to a minor third (F to the D that begins the triplets) to begin the progression anew. The bass line in the example shows the pitches that sound at the beginning of each triplet. The triplet feel evokes the song "Nice Dream" from *The Bends*, although that song does not contain the cross-rhythms used here. Moreover, the conventional- or classical-sounding triplets of "Nice Dream" seem cheerful, outlining major chords, but the triplets of "In Limbo" simply "spiral down" (as the vocals say) into negativity, despite their actual upward-reaching melody. As example 4.4 shows, the triplet progression of "In Limbo"

4.4. "In Limbo"

is transposed up a step, to a pattern beginning on C, and changes slightly for the beginning of the verse. With this transposition, the meter changes from $\frac{6}{4}$ to $\frac{4}{4}$, and the progression contracts from six triplets to five. As the pattern finishes on a C^6 chord (first inversion, with a sustained E in the bass), the voice emphasizes the pitches F-sharp and G, and the words "I spiral down" (0:51) end with a leap of a major sixth that illustrates this physical drop. The triplets begin again as the voice sustains its last pitch. Here, the voice and the guitar are, if not working together, at least providing enough space for each other to articulate the musical phrase.

4.5. "In Limbo," rhythmic interaction of guitar and voice

Example 4.5 shows the voice's interaction with the spiraling guitar line. Over the triplet figure in the guitar, the voice sings a square, syncopated $\frac{4}{4}$ riff that gives the sense of struggling against the eddy of music: "I'm lost at sea . . . I spiral down . . ." Even after being reconstituted for the second half of the album, the subject appears to still be battling for his existence. His acknowledgment of this struggle foreshadows his eventual "second death" by choice, at the end of the album. The original contracting triplet progression centered around D minor in $\frac{6}{4}$ returns for the final chorus, in which the voice sings a distorted melody that emphasizes G and B-flat. No longer maintaining the false optimism of the previous song, the lyrics "you're living in a fantasy world" ring out in the chorus (1:01), standing more as a bitter existential comment about abject denial than as a wish to escape the world. The world, it seems, is obscured by fantasy, and only a glimpse of that world can be caught behind the "optimistic" screen constructed by the forces of capitalism. The subject knows that any attempt at escape beyond the soundscape of the album is impossible for him to achieve. The outro returns to the C-minor progression in $\frac{4}{4}$ for the words "I can't read" (2:34), which are howled on a sustained high G. A background vocal repeats the words that began the song, "another message I can't read." Here, the subject makes us understand that *every* message, not just the one mentioned at the beginning of the song, is one that he cannot read. Similarly, the opaque lyrics over the course of the entire album obscure any message the band is trying to send to the listener, with the result that the message becomes ambivalence itself, and interpreting *Kid A* becomes a metaphor for surviving in modern society. The cacophony of the triplet progression, the background vocals, and the howl is gradually ground down to a quiet, stuttering tone on G that constitutes a reversion to pure sound.

"IDIOTEQUE"

"Idioteque," track eight, begins with heavy drums that serve as a ghost of the bass riff in "The National Anthem"; just as the subject has been reconstituted but still barely exists, so too the earlier musical elements have begun to reemerge as shades of their former selves. The quickly changing keyboard chord clusters (lasting four beats each but changing on the second half of the fourth beat of each measure, which produces a forward-moving feel due to the syncopation) present an animated contrast to the languorous chords of "Treefingers."[15] The harmonic motion, in contrast to the rhythm, is static, as the chords simply reiterate different inversions of an E-flat-major-seventh chord, in third inversion (D in the bass), second inversion (B-flat in the bass), first inversion (G in the bass), and root position (E-flat in the bass), respectively. The upper and lower voices expand outward with each new inversion, so that the chord spacing is widest at the end of the pattern. Having the root (E-flat) in the bass at the end of the vocal line makes the music sound

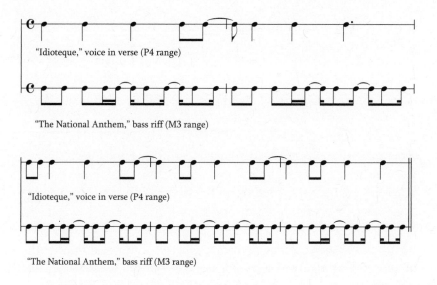

"Idioteque," voice in verse (P4 range)

"The National Anthem," bass riff (M3 range)

"Idioteque," voice in verse (P4 range)

"The National Anthem," bass riff (M3 range)

4.6. "Idioteque," vocal line, and "The National Anthem," bass line

more stable, even under the jittery melody of the verse. The rhythm of the drums at the beginning of "Idioteque" surges into the vocals; as example 4.6 shows, the rhythm of the vocal line is essentially identical to that of the bass line in "The National Anthem," although the voice sings the rhythm at half the speed.

Rather than being destroyed by the musical elements, as in "How to Disappear Completely," the voice-as-subject in "Idioteque" is now possessed by them. Just as the bass line of "The National Anthem" had been confined to a major third, the vocal line of "Idioteque" is now confined to a perfect fourth. The song makes use of the accumulative groove (see table 4.3), and the keyboards drop out as the vocalist sings "we're not scaremongering, this *is* really happening" (2:09, italics added), an explicit refutation of the denial expressed in "How to Disappear Completely" that "this isn't happening." The band again plays with listener expectations by having instruments drop out at surprising moments in the song, so that any comfort derived from the coalescence of the accumulative groove is immediately undermined. Of all the songs on *Kid A*, "Idioteque" relates most closely to the post-apocalyptic images of the CD booklet art, with such lyrics as "Who's in a bunker . . . ? Women and children first . . . ice age coming . . . throw it on the

TABLE 4.3. The Accumulative Groove in "Idioteque"

(X = entrance; O = exit)

CD timings	Intro			Verse 1	Chorus	Verse 2	Chorus		Outro		
	0:00	0:12	0:38	0:59	1:34	1:52	2:35	3:10	4:05	4:19	4:49
Drums	X										
Sound effects	X					O	X				
Keyboards		X	O	X		O	X	O	X		O
Voice				X			O			X	O

fire." This apocalypse has never happened in the world outside the album, and is thus an analogue for a suicide that has not yet happened either. Just as the subject is no better off after his attempted demise at the end of side one, so too are we in a sense no better off than if the apocalypse had actually happened, to the extent that we do nothing about changing the world in which we live to avert disaster, no matter how dire the warnings become. Panic over a would-be apocalypse leads only to the condition of fatigue over the world's condition and apathy toward trying to effect actual change. The subject's jadedness at the end of the album, on "Motion Picture Soundtrack," is the inevitable reaction to his hysteria here.

The other lyrics of "Idioteque" also recall the album's earlier songs: the lines "here I'm allowed everything all of the time" (1:34) and "take the money and run" (2:30) evoke the capitalist message of "Optimistic"; and the chant "the first of the children" in the background at the end of the song (4:18) brings to mind the "rats and children" following the protagonist in "Kid A." Though it seems at first that these children will be safe in the bunker, as they are going in "first," they may well be less safe in the end, as the bunker will only produce a fear that will make them prisoners of their condition, analogous to the individual in modern society. Tim Footman links the phrase "the first of the children" instead to the "slaughters of the first-born in the Bible,"[16] which were a consequence of the Egyptian pharaoh's refusal to release the Israelites from slavery, a tale showing parallels to the Pied Piper's taking of the children after the residents of Hamlin reneged on their payment for ridding the town of rats. This reading, which links the muttered aside "c'mon kids" in "Kid A" to the hysterical stuttering "the first of the children" in "Idioteque," reinforces the subject's growing agency over the course of the album. Whereas before he had been a reluctant and half-formed leader, now he is fully present and reacting violently to the imagined destruction around him. This reaction furthers the split in his personality. The lyric "I laugh until my head comes off" (1:08) illustrates this split musically by adding a second voice, split between channels just after this lyric. The next line, "I swallow till I burst," shows that the excess of being allowed "everything all of the time" can lead to self-destruction through overabundance. This imagery could also relate to the drowning man in the Irish Sea of "In Limbo," or it may refer to the hazards of taking Ecstasy on the dance floor, which can lead to hyponatremia, or "water intoxication," caused by an imbalance of electrolytes in the body after drinking too much water. The song's heavy dance beat and the -eque suffix in the title, a play on "discotheque" (no doubt having the European meaning of "dance club" rather than the 1970s-specific American meaning) as well as "idiotic" (perhaps a glimpse of the world behind the screen after the hollowness of "Optimistic"), make this at least a plausible explanation. The title also plays on the word "idiolect," the individual's unique way of using language, which ties notions of individuality and discursive formation to "idiocy" and the dance of the "mindless" body after its head falls off. In this way, the title "Idioteque" suggests an idiotic (and ideological) fragmentation of the subject along the fault line of the mind/body split, a schizophrenia of the body as well as the mind.

Circling a tentative tonic, the singsong, stuttering vocal line of "Idioteque" recalls that of "Optimistic." The chorus (1:34) marks a change to a connected melodic line that feels somewhat false, akin to the sloganistic chorus of "Optimistic." Whereas the verse of each song is speechlike and confined to a narrow range, each chorus moves to a higher, more songlike melody to articulate the song's "slogan" ("the best you can is good enough" in "Optimistic"; "here I'm allowed everything all of the time" in "Idioteque"). This higher pitch level calls attention to the new melody, and its songlike character makes it memorable to the listener, a goal toward which every marketing department surely hopes its band will strive. The chorus melody of "Idioteque" begins a fifth higher than the verse (as does the higher verse three of "Optimistic"). The higher tessitura lends an air of hysteria, which is followed by a descent that implies the subject's deflation at being allowed everything he wants, whenever he wants it. The addition of harmony vocals further marks the chorus, adding counterpoint to contrast with the fractured "two colors in my head" of the album's first half. After mumbling "laugh until my head comes off," the second voice then sings clearly in the chorus, in which the two voices work together to make what seems like an important declaration ("here I'm allowed everything all of the time"). These lyrics contrast with the imagery of the verses, making a blanket, sloganistic statement rather than offering a clarification of the hysterical lyrics in the verses earlier. It is not clear whether the subject is speaking from the "bunker," simply commenting on capitalism itself, or both hiding and commenting at the same time. The safety of the bunker is a metaphor for the false sense of security of modern society. In a capitalist society, almost everything is available for a price, within the constraints of the supply, but this is not necessarily a healthy state of being. Being allowed "everything" available inside a bunker is not the same as having unlimited pleasures within the world at large, but at least the bunker is a place that is easily controlled.

Prompted by revulsion at such doublethink, "Idioteque" ultimately rejects the indulgent present, as the subject "laughs until his head comes off" and "swallows till he bursts," again dissociating the subject's self from the body as he had in "Kid A" with the "heads on sticks" and "ventriloquists." The second verse of the song abandons the chords to emphasize the voice and the beat, and the hysterical stuttering cuts off the last "take the money" before the final chorus (2:35). The drums keep going, lending the vocals a primal urgency. Coming right after the chorus, this verse underscores the importance of the message ("we're not scaremongering, this is really happening") by making the vocals clearer. The song ends with babble over a strong dance beat; the music has been completely stripped away.[17] The constant negation of the earlier songs has grown into overindulgence, an excess of verbiage as babbling. Not only is the subject no longer denying his existence (he *is* here, and this *is* happening), he is simultaneously reveling in and decrying the effects of hedonism. His negation itself is hedonistic, or selfish, just as suicide is a refusal to own up to the responsibility of living within society, that is, of trying to change the world for the better. However, this existential suicide, a fall into cynicism, is no better than actual physical suicide; the negation of the subject demands the negation of that negation: not a return to the subjectivity that once was, but a return to the subject as one "cured" of cynicism. This cure is short-lived, however, as the subject soon pleads for release once more.

"MORNING BELL"

The penultimate song on *Kid A*, "Morning Bell," marks a further humanizing of the subject, with an opening up of the melody and a rise in tessitura. The song begins with a snare-drum riff that sounds over the last noisy gasp of the previous song, then a muted keyboard accompaniment comes in at 0:08. The drums remain far louder in the mix than the keyboard, adding to the anxiety created by the high vocal melody. The voice plaintively asks "release me," although it is not clear to whom the plea is addressed.[18] The harmonic accompaniment in "Morning Bell" fluctuates between A minor and A major. On the words "release me" (0:42), the voice alternates between A and F-sharp over accompanying G- (with an added A) and D-major chords before finally resolving down to E on "please" at the end of verse two (1:11). The accompaniment begins the A-major/-minor alternation under this "please," recreating the anxiety. In the third verse (1:32), which begins "where'd you park the car," a guitar enters the texture, repeatedly articulating an A as the voice emphasizes E and finally resolves to D over a G chord. As the voice resolves, a second guitar enters (2:06), strumming an A as the first guitar moves to a sustained E above it. For a moment it seems as though Radiohead has returned to its earlier, guitar-driven sound. This resolution offers a temporary respite in the form of what could be called a modal half-cadence on the IV chord of D major (itself the IV, or subdominant, of A). Functionally, however, it makes more sense to think of the harmonic motion simply as having moved down a whole step from the anxiety created by the prolonged A-major/-minor chords as the voice sings "round and round and round and round and round and round and round and round and" on E, moving to the D for the final "round" over the G-major chord (2:06). This G chord contains the non-chord member A, a remnant of the A-major/-minor chords as well as an anticipation of the move to D major that comes in the next measure. The moment when the voice and harmony decisively move to a resolution together marks a second of unity that creates a profound sense of relief in the listener. The singer immediately repeats the words "and round" on D, reiterating the union.

For what could be deemed the fourth verse, "cut the kids in half" (2:14), the song modulates, the muted keyboard now oscillating between E-minor and G-sharp-minor chords under a vocal that continues to emphasize the notes E and G. Rather than being the fifth of the underlying harmony (E above A major/minor), here the voice's E is the tonic. The D-sharp that emphasizes the word "half" at the end of each phrase would in conventional harmony mark a tonicization, functioning as the leading-tone to E, but it is harmonized here not by the B major that we would expect, but by G-sharp minor, a chord that normally functions to tonicize a secondary key area (such as A, the subdominant of E). The chords E minor and G-sharp minor have only one tone in common, B (the fifth of E and the third of G-sharp). Radiohead often uses third-related keys, but here the expected third of G is raised to G-sharp, creating a jarring sound instead, which emphasizes the drastic command given in the lyrics. The accompaniment returns to the key of A for the ending, still alternating ambivalently between A minor and A major. The song devolves into babble, with the voice singing "dum dum dum" (2:48) while floating between C and A, then "ohh" through a scalar descent C–B–A (3:05, emphasizing the tonic of A for the first time), ending with a mumbled but rhythmic "dum dum dum" and the tinny sound of a keyboard. The horror of sacrificing the children by cutting them in half has caused the subject to revert to a pre-verbal state—in effect reducing him to a child who will then be cut in half. The lyrics of verse four recall the biblical story of Solomon and the squabbling women who each claimed the same child as her own. Given the other imagery ("you can keep the furniture," "clothes are on the lawn with the furniture"), the song seems likely to be about divorce, but in a broader sense it could represent the wakeup call for someone who places too much importance on his worldly life and his possessions, including his progeny. The image of the "morning bell" is strange for this point on the album, if one were to try to construct a conventional narrative for the songs. If one considers that the subject has been spiritually dead for much of the album, however, then perhaps a last-minute alarm will jar him into action for the final song.

"MOTION PICTURE SOUNDTRACK"

The album's last song, "Motion Picture Soundtrack," evokes the song "Exit Music (for a Film)" from *OK Computer* (written for Baz Luhrmann's 1996 film *William Shakespeare's Romeo + Juliet*, though the song does not appear on the CD soundtrack).[19] Martin Clarke has described the final scenes of the Luhrmann film: "Juliet holds a Colt 45 to her head, which particularly disturbed Thom [Yorke]."[20] The same theme of suicidal lovers is repeated in "Motion Picture Soundtrack," but the subject here states that "it's not like the movies," implying that a happy ending is not necessarily going to follow. Of course the ending of *Romeo + Juliet* is not a happy one either; the unhappiness of the reality of the human condition sometimes spills over into film. "Motion Picture Soundtrack" actually makes a conscious attempt to end "like the movies," suddenly tying up any loose ends and smoothing over the drama that has ensued over the past duration of time with the subject's melodramatic rise into falsetto over a swirling chorus and synthesized harp.

The structure of "Exit Music" is fairly straightforward: verse one, verse two, bridge one, verse three, bridge two, and verse four. Verses one and two appear in succession and are based in B minor/major. In Schenkerian terms, the vocal part could be read as a 5-line, with the vocal line beginning on F-sharp (0:23, scale degree five) and descending to B (scale degree one). Although the song should not be given a strict Schenkerian reading, given how little it has in common with music of the high classical period, this vocal descent provides a soothing motion for the listener, particularly by ending on the tonic of B. The voice in the first bridge (1:26) creates anxiety by beginning on a C-natural (a non-diatonic pitch within the home key of B minor); its descent to the F-sharp (a tritone away from C) leads it only to the fifth of the B-minor chord rather than the tonic, as in the verses. The second bridge (2:50) presents an overall descending vocal sequence that first ascends to an F-sharp that also begins the final verse. Example 4.7 shows the beginning and ending pitches of each verse. The words "we

4.7. "Exit Music (for a Film)," neighbor-note motive

hope that you choke" in verse four (3:36) are stated three times over the harmonic motion F-sharp major to B minor, a conventional dominant/tonic relationship. The F-sharp–G–F-sharp neighbor-note motive from the beginning of "Exit Music" returns at the climax for the words "now we are one" (3:21), sung an octave above the prior melody, and then immediately begins to descend again. This marks a contrast to "Motion Picture Soundtrack," which ends on the F-sharp–E–G of "in the next life." Whereas the song meant to appear on an actual "motion picture soundtrack," "Exit Music," ends quietly, slipping away unobtrusively but with a logical resolution, the song "Motion Picture Soundtrack" itself ends with great dramatic flourish, despite having declared that "it's not like the movies."

Unlike the clear-cut harmonies of "Exit Music," the introduction of "Motion Picture Soundtrack" presents an ambiguity between C major and G major, recalling the ambiguity between F and C earlier on *Kid A*, in "Everything in Its Right Place." The song begins with slow organ-style chords and an introductory melody that continues throughout the song, under the vocals. After this "holy" sounding introduction, at 0:40 the singer describes decadent images of "red wine and sleeping pills" and "cheap sex and sad films." Each verse ends with a C chord that is then followed by a chorus in G major. The chorus states that "I think you're crazy, maybe" (1:15), the subject talking either to a love interest or to himself. The chorus ends on D major, the V chord in G, with the voice on A, then pauses before the next verse at 1:34. This pause sounds like a half-cadence in G, and the G-major chord reenters for the beginning of verse two. A harp's flowing chords add to the accompaniment as the second verse states that "it's not like the movies," recalling the imagery of the album's earlier songs with the words "letters always get burned" and "they fed us on little white lies." High voices at 2:15 add "oohs" above the subject's declaration in the second chorus; unlike the shimmering harp tones, which exist out of time with the rest of the music, the voices sing a regular rhythm with the chords and support the singer. The song ends on G, but the resolution seems forced because of the underlying chords (C-sharp minor to C major with an added ninth, and a G that appears only after the rest of the music has faded out). Example 4.8 shows the motion of the voice

"I will see you..."   "in the next life..."

4.8. "Motion Picture Soundtrack," resolution

and the underlying bass line. The line between the voice's G and the lower G in the bass shows that the two notes both provide closure, even though they occur at different points in the music. The subject seems to be on his way to achieving the release pleaded for in "Morning Bell." With the song's closing words, "I will see you in the next life" (2:36), marking the second, "real" (or bodily) death on the album, the singer's voice climbs to a high falsetto pitch (recalling the falsetto at the end of "How to Disappear Completely") that is subsumed into a heavenly chorus of other voices and harp strings. After over a minute's pause (3:14 to 4:18), the sound returns, first with a blip that sounds like a switch has been flipped, then a long tone on a D, and finally the harp music with a full choir singing an A; the harp moves to a G after the voices cease singing, then the harp and the tone gradually fade out, leading to about two more minutes of silence before the track ends. The music's return without the voice of the subject is yet another indication that the world not only continues to exist apart from him but is indifferent to his existence. The long moments of silence on this track remind the listener that this is a recorded object; the listener may even have forgotten in that first minute between the subject's death and the return of the harp music that the album was still playing, but the return of the music both shocks her into remembering and shows her that the subject exists somewhere apart from the recording, perhaps in that silence. The harp, choir, and organ of "Motion Picture Soundtrack" are false signifiers of church and religion, of which the subject has none. In the modern condition, the only god he can worship is that of capitalism, and the images on the album such as the Darwinian "big fish eating the little ones" belie any religious stance. The subject's false alignment with these heavenly signifiers does not produce any comfort in the listener that he has been redeemed; rather than an ascent to heaven, his move has been toward the silence of the empty last track. Any true redemption must come after the album's conclusion.

(HE) LOOKS LIKE THE REAL THING: THE SUBJECT AS *HOMME FATAL*

Although the two halves of *Kid A* can be parsed separately, the construction of the album-as-CD dictates that it be experienced as a whole. Even though listeners can hit "pause" at any point on the CD, a "second side" continues after the hollow midpoint of "Treefingers." The songs of *Kid A* are open-ended enough that they can have any kind of narrative attached, from the birth of the "first human clone," as Yorke has suggested,[21] to a new adventure with the aliens of *OK Computer*— *Kid Alien*, perhaps. Given the opaque lyrics and atypical interactions between the musical elements, however, any such reading seems overly forced. Conducting an analysis of reoccurring motives and lyrics allows for an interpretation that ties the album together as a whole greater than its two disparate halves.

One way of approaching such an interpretation of the vanishing subject of *Kid A* is to view this subject as a sort of *homme fatal*; Slavoj Žižek defines *femme fatale* within the context of the *film noir* or detective novel (such as *The Maltese Falcon*) as a "'pure,' nonpathological subject fully assuming *her own* fate [italics in original]" but donning "a series of inconsistent masks without a coherent ethical attitude."[22] Although the subject of *Kid A* is not as fully formed as the classic *femme fatale* and does not undergo the same series of actions (such as seducing a male protagonist in order to destroy him), he still has similar urges. Given the presumed male identity of the subject on *Kid A* because of the male singer who activates him, a more appropriate term might be *homme fatal*. Just as Radiohead's "ethical attitude" is somewhat contradictory—it is not always clear what the band stands for and against—the stance of *Kid A*'s subject is also inconsistent. Although the subject encourages solidarity against such entities as big business and government, his reasons for doing so are not clear. The subject complains about feeling "lost at sea" and being "fed on little white lies," but he is unwilling to take any steps toward helping others himself ("not my problem," "don't bother me"). The classic *femme fatale* reaches her "final hysterical breakdown" when she "*assumes* her nonexistence . . . [and] constitutes herself as 'subject': what is waiting for her *beyond* hystericization is the death drive at its purest."[23] The analogous moment for the *homme fatal* of *Kid A* is in "How to Disappear Completely," when he sings "I'm not here, this isn't happening" and then ascends into a falsetto wordlessness—ascension through feminization. The subject's hysteria leads to emasculation, which in turn leads to feminization. This progression might in turn lead back to a reconsideration of the "necessity" of gendering the subject, the impulse to "ground" subjective difference in nature, specifically the "natural" condition of anatomy. This line of thought questions the insistence that has been there all along on aligning sex and gender in defining the identity of the subject.

The subject finds his identity, according to Žižek, when he "freely assume[s] what is imposed on us, the real of the death drive," by "experiencing oneself as an object."[24] The subject of *Kid A* assumes this death drive first by literally disappearing in "Treefingers," and then by presenting a series of relentlessly negative scenarios (despite the slogans of "Optimistic") until departing for good in "Motion Picture Soundtrack" with the words "I will see you in the next life." The "second death," claims Žižek, goes "beyond mere physical destruction, i.e., entailing the effacement of the very symbolic texture of generation and corruption."[25] That is, when the subject dies for the second time, he seems at first to take the entire background environment with him, as normally happens at the end of a concept album when the music dies along with the subject. The second death, by contrast, is more a social problem of inscribing the subject into social memory than a problem for the subject himself, who is, after all, dead. The return of the harp and choir after the last notes of the final song have faded out is a sign that the world (even if it is a world beyond) has continued to exist apart from the subject, and that the world does not depend on the existence of the subject.

Kid A contains a reoccurring 3–2–1 line, that is, a motion that falls stepwise from an initial pitch down a major third (e.g., in the C-major scale, E–D–C, or scale degrees 3–2–1). In Schenkerian terms, this line would represent the *Urlinie*, or a fundamental melodic line that elongates the tonic triad and is accompanied by a 1–5–1 (or I–V–I) motion in the bass. For this discussion, however, the 3–2–1 motive is simply a melodic idea that reoccurs several times rather than a fundamental part of the harmonic structure. It is harmonized by different chords over the course of the album, none of which fit the Schenkerian demands of the I–V–I structure. Rather than trying to hear a melodic motive that forces an album of pop music into the mold of the high classical form, this motive can instead help guide the ear in a way that the lyrics and lack of narrative perhaps do not. This line, which can be deemed the *homme fatal* motive, comes from the crisis point of "How to Disappear Completely" and resurfaces throughout the second half of Kid A, as shown by example 4.9. The slurs over the notes in the treble clef indicate iterations of the *homme fatal* motive; additional slurs indicate where the vocal melody travels before or after singing the motive. As the example shows, the motive is harmonized in different ways, none of which function as the I–V–I of traditional harmony. The point of the example is not to try to assign a functional chord progression to the harmonic accompaniment but simply to note the differences in the use of the motive throughout the songs. This motivic link is far more subtle than the ones used in such "classic" concept albums as Pink Floyd's *The Wall* or *Dark Side of the Moon*. Allan F. Moore and Anwar Ibrahim note the use of "four linking passages" as a unifying factor in Kid A;

4.9. *Kid A, homme fatal* motive

the authors do not detail them, but evidently they are including the coda to "Motion Picture Soundtrack." The other links occur between "Kid A" and "The National Anthem," "Optimistic" and "In Limbo," and "Idioteque" and "Morning Bell," or tracks two and three, six and seven, and eight and nine.[26] Although these links do literally join the tracks together, they do not provide any narrative cohesion.

The *homme fatal* motive begins in "How to Disappear Completely" as A–F-sharp at the guitar's entrance in the intro (0:15), is expanded into A–G-sharp–F-sharp in the falsetto vocalese (4:37), and is later compressed back into just A–F-sharp by the other instruments at the end of the piece. After the melodic blankness of "Treefingers," with its slowly shifting harmonies, the motive returns at the beginning of "Optimistic" with the change of G-sharp to G, the addition of a B above the A, and the change of F-sharp to F-natural before the G. Whereas the motive in "How to Disappear Completely" had been sung on a plaintive "aah," the one in "Optimistic" is sung first on a more soothing "ooh." The chorus of "Optimistic" returns to the A for its initial pitch and then moves from G to F-sharp to form a 4–3 suspension over a D in the bass. The last half of the line transposes the motive to F-natural–E–D (a literal transposition of the motive in "Disappear") for the lyrics "the best you can is good enough" (1:14). The motive remains at that pitch level for the coda, "dinosaurs roaming the earth" (3:52), but interjects an E-flat, shown in parentheses in the example. Immediately after the 3–2–1 line with the E-flat, the voice begins to sing "aah" with its original 3–2–1 pitches (3:57, F–E–D). The voice then embellishes around these three notes until the outro (4:21), when the 3–2–1 line is sung at the original pitch level (A–G–F-sharp, with the added B and F-natural) and with the earlier vocalese ("ooh"). The *homme fatal* motive reappears at several transposition levels in "In Limbo." The vocal line moves G–F-sharp–E for the beginning of the verse ("I'm on your side," 0:35), and then E-flat–D–C for the midpoint ("trapdoors that open," 0:46). The chorus statement, "you're living in a fantasy world" (1:02), uses B-flat–A–G, emphasized again in "this beautiful world" in the coda. The melody of "Idioteque" is static, more of a singsong chant, but segments of the verse can be excerpted as the motive, such as "I laugh until my head comes off" at the pitch level E-flat–D–C (1:08). Rather than remaining on the 1, as in the earlier songs, however, the voice continually returns to the 2 and 3.

More than any other song on *Kid A*, "Morning Bell" is supersaturated with the *homme fatal* motive. The motive appears in the verse as G–F-sharp–E (0:34) and C–B–A (0:39), and at the original "How to Disappear Completely" level of A–F-sharp (1:02), with an interjected E. Significantly, this original motive appears at a poignant point in the song, the cry "release me," evoking the ending "aahs" of "How to Disappear Completely" as the voice is finally disappearing into the noise. Rather than ending on the F-sharp over a D-major chord (the third over the root), which would give the song a major (or "happy") sound, the voice moves to an E on the word "please" over an A-minor chord (the fifth above the root). The E is sung more softly than the A or F-sharp, and it seems like an afterthought, an attempt at a forced resolution that did not come the first time the motive was sung, in "How to Disappear Completely." The second verse proceeds in a similar fashion, and after a brief pause the voice again pleads "release me," but this time it does not move to E. The third verse grows more aggressive in its tone, confronting the listener and culminating in a hammered-out "round and round . . ." on an insistent E over an A-minor chord. The last "round" moves to D over a G-major chord that then moves to a D-major chord, but the resolution is brief. The third verse, "cut the kids in half" (2:14), moves from E to G in the same minor-third relationship from the original motive, but in the opposite direction (1–3 instead of 3–1). The line "cut the kids in half" perverts the 3–2–1 motion by introducing a D-sharp, which in the version of "Morning Bell" on *Amnesiac* ultimately resolves to a sustained E. Here, the motive resolves only briefly to an E before moving to the original D-major/A-major/A-minor alternation. The subject's extreme solution—the division in half—has briefly disrupted the fabric of the music, but the song then moves on to a less tentative resolution without the voice, as though to show that this lyrical eruption hasn't affected the music, which exists in a world apart from the subject and has progressed in spite of him.

Although the world is indifferent to us, we are indifferent to it only at the expense of ourselves. The challenge for the subject of *Kid A* is to live in the modern world; his attempted indifference to it ("not my problem") ultimately destroys him. The *homme fatal* motive is literally one of "grounding," of moving down to the tonic; existentially, it is a return to the world through death, the revenge of the world through mortality, and ultimately our grounding through death in the grave: dust to dust. Death, the fall to the tonic, is the only way for the subject to be grounded, which is also the point of impossibility for the subject. The last song of the album, "Motion Picture Soundtrack," brings back the *homme fatal* motive only at the very end, on the words "in the next life," which move F-sharp–E–G (2:41, 2–1–3). The motive has been transformed in a way that allows an escape into the upper boundaries of the voice; rather than moving to the "ground" of the tonic (1), the voice attempts to transcend its fate by ascending to 3. This pitch does fit into the underlying chord (C), but as the fifth rather than the tonic. When the music comes back in without the voice, it sounds a G chord, thus transforming the subject's G into the tonic and forcing him to be grounded. This forced resolution makes us question whether the subject really has escaped; since the world exists apart from him, and is thus superior to him, it can also attempt to reclaim him. Any redemption available to the subject must thus come from beyond the album. The absence of the *homme fatal* motive on *Amnesiac* lends credence to the idea that the experiences on *Kid A* are self-contained and that *Amnesiac* truly does represent the "next life" available to the subject, in which he will find a new way rather than continuing to retrace the 3–2–1 motive or being constrained by it.

Yet another way of viewing the narrative of *Kid A* is to continue treating "Treefingers" (track five) as the hollow midpoint, or "space between," but to link the songs on either side of it (see table 4.4). Not only can "How to Disappear Completely" (track four) and "Optimistic" (track six) be paired as bookends around this empty space, but the other songs can also be matched up around this midpoint. Like *The Wall*, the song sequence can thus be mapped onto a circle. Unlike *The Wall*, however, which proceeds in a never-ending loop, *Kid A* seems to fold in on itself and create relationships between the songs on either half. If "Treefingers" is the empty space between two sides, then "Motion Picture Soundtrack" (track ten) stands alone after the album has been completed, like the closing credits in a film. The subject first takes his leave in "How to Disappear Completely"; he does this more explicitly and arguably more cheerfully on "Motion Picture Soundtrack." Rather than denying that he is present ("I'm not here, this isn't happening"), he muses over his presence but ultimately says that he is leaving ("I will see you in the next life"). Instead of vanishing into vocalese, he exits melodramatically in full voice with clear lyrics. Whereas the last song on *The Wall* ("Outside the Wall") cycles around to the first song ("In the Flesh?") again in an endless loop, starting with the completion of a sentence that is begun at the end of the album ("Isn't this where . . . we came in?"), the last song on *Kid A* looks ahead to the next album instead ("I will see you in the next life"). It is hard to view *Kid A* as allowing for a renewal to take place within a continuous loop by playing the CD over and over, unless the first song is taken as a rebirth. If "yesterday I woke up sucking on a lemon" is a state of mind the subject wants to leave behind, referring to the previous playing of the album, then a loop becomes an entrapment because the subject is reborn into this negativity that persists over the course of the album. Regardless of

TABLE 4.4. Song Foldings in *Kid A*

5 "Treefingers"	
4 "How to Disappear Completely"	6 "Optimistic"
3 "The National Anthem"	7 "In Limbo"
2 "Kid A"	8 "Idioteque"
1 "Everything in Its Right Place"	9 "Morning Bell"
10 "Motion Picture Soundtrack"	

how "optimistic" the subject may seem in insisting that "everything" is "in its right place" in this new day or new life, he is still trapped in the human condition. "Motion Picture Soundtrack" can thus be read as either a springboard to the next album or, more philosophically, as a statement on the subject's perpetual cycle of death and rebirth within the same cycle of negativity. He escapes into falsetto, then the music returns and drags him back for track one as the CD is played yet again.

A look at *Kid A*'s lyrics shows some further similarities between the song pairs created by folding the song sequence in half. "Everything in Its Right Place" (track one) and "Morning Bell" (track nine) both deal with division, the former with an internal split ("two colors in my head") and the latter with an external split, or divorce ("cut the kids in half"). Whereas "Everything" insists on a surface calm dictated by the veracity of its title, "Morning Bell" devolves into hysteria and wordless mumbling. If we look at how the song pair might influence each other, the "morning bell" could be read as triggering the protagonist's awakening to a new day that is no better than the last ("yesterday I woke up sucking on a lemon"). The benign question of "Everything in Its Right Place" ("what was that you tried to say") is transformed into the accusatory "where'd you park the car" of "Morning Bell." The escape in "Morning Bell," the plea to "release me," is a recognition of the fact that "everything" is indeed not "in its right place." The babbling second voice of "Everything in Its Right Place" trying to strive for clarity becomes the mumbled "dum dum dum" at the end of "Morning Bell." The subject in the earlier song is still trying to make sense of his surroundings; later, the subject has accepted that things are not going well and wants to get out at any cost. Whereas the earlier song had attempted to force everything into place without admitting that it was not in place already, the later song is an admission of the wrong fit and an attempt at escape.

The similarities between "Kid A" (track two) and "Idioteque" (track eight) are more subtle. The subject can be seen as a "holy fool," or "idiot," who issues the Pied Piper–like call "c'mon kids" in "Kid A" and is later hysterically stuttering in "Idioteque." The subject complains lethargically in the former song of "rats and children" following him out of town; in the latter, he commands shakily that the "women and children" should go into the bunker first. In "Kid A" he seems to want to cast off his authority, whereas in "Idioteque" any authority he holds is undermined by his shaky delivery. The voice of "Kid A" is manipulated electronically, with the second voice coming in for harmony on the second line, "we've got heads on sticks." In "Idioteque," the two voices present a cogent harmony, but the second voice enters only after the words "laugh until my head comes off," suggesting an internal split in the subject. Whereas in "Kid A" the subject lazily suggests "c'mon kids," in "Idioteque" he urges himself or the audience to "take the money and run" after ushering the women and children into the bunker. The earlier song speaks of "ventriloquists" and "heads on sticks," suggesting an insurmountable divide but also an interplay between the two sides; in the later song, the subject wants to "hear both sides" about the "ice age coming," but this truer, non-manipulated voice is hysterical in its request for information (about issues like the effects of global warming) that may come too late.

"The National Anthem" (track three) can be paired with "In Limbo" (track seven). After the passive "we're all in this together, alone" stance of "The National Anthem," the subject at first takes a more active role in "In Limbo" ("I'm on your side") but then immediately relinquishes his leadership ("don't bother me"), admonishing the listener not to follow. Any initial sense of security in "In Limbo" is quickly seen as false, when the subject in the chorus abandons the pretext of being on the listener's side with the words "don't bother me" and "you're living in a fantasy world." The subject declaims an epitaph for the world, while shaking his head with the post-chorus comment "this beautiful world." The closing statement of "In Limbo" is a howled "I can't read," grinding down to an "aagh" that descends into machinery noises, whereas "The National Anthem" ends with a horn riff falling into chaos, a distorted orchestral recording, and the sound of a tape winding down.

Taken within the context of the folded song pairings, "Motion Picture Soundtrack" thus functions as an epitaph to the whole album. The schmaltzy synthesized harp and chorus emphasize the theatrical ending and the notion that "the world is but a stage." The *homme fatal* finally assumes his fate in the end by accepting his existence as an object of capital. The chorus begins with the words "I think you're crazy, maybe," dramatizing what one might have expected to be an ultimate proclamation of love after the verses about "red wine and sleeping pills . . . cheap sex and sad films." The "maybe" lends an air of doubt; the subject is not willing to cut ties with the person he addresses (possibly his schizophrenic self) by making a definitive statement about his or her mental stability. Then, too, if the subject is actually talking to himself, then making a final pronouncement and acknowledging his own schizophrenia could be the final straw that allows the world to consume him completely. As long as he does not admit his frailties, he has a chance at overcoming them and forging a productive existence within society. The forced resolution of the singer's falsetto and the music that reenters after his final pitch leave the listener wanting more, a salvation that comes only with forgetting the trauma of *Kid A*, on *Amnesiac*.

AMNESIAC
AS ANTIDOTE

Just as juxtaposing the two halves of *Kid A* can shed light on the album as a whole, *Kid A* attains further meaning when compared with Radio-head's 2001 follow-up, *Amnesiac*, recorded during the same sessions but containing songs that on the surface seem somewhat less experimental. Recognizing—or perhaps anticipating—the baffled reaction to *Kid A* by both fans and critics, the band claimed it would be returning, if not to the old sound, then certainly to more conventional song forms and marketing techniques. In a nod to the record industry, Thom Yorke stated that the band wanted to give *Amnesiac* "a fair chance within the giant scary cogs of the bullshit machine."[1] Yorke also claimed, somewhat facetiously, before *Amnesiac*'s release that "with the next one we are definitely having singles, videos, glossy magazine celebrity photoshoots, children's television appearances, film premiere appearances, dance routines, and many interesting interviews about my tortured existence."[2] His words are a caustic overreaction to the somewhat negative reception of *Kid A*, and they played on audience and critical expectations. Although the tracks for *Amnesiac* were not selected from the band's body of studio work until after *Kid A* had been released, Radiohead has resisted saying that *Amnesiac* comprises simply the dross left over after *Kid A* was compiled.[3] Allan F. Moore and Anwar Ibrahim state that *Amnesiac* is "more a consolidation of Radiohead's new experimental direction than another stylistic leap. As opposed to the sense of a coherent whole created by both *OK Computer* and *Kid*

A, the album is more akin to *The Bends* through being more a collection of separate songs."[4] The release of several singles from *Amnesiac* could further the perception of it as a "collection of separate songs," as it was possible for the singles to be heard apart from the album. James Doheny has argued that the difference between *Kid A* and *Amnesiac* is the "difference between coolly surveying 'new' influences and reconciling them with your existing music."[5] This impression is dictated as much by the release order of the albums as by their content, since by the time of *Amnesiac's* release listeners would have grown somewhat accustomed to, if not completely accepting of, the experimental sound of *Kid A*. If Radiohead's previous work is treated as the thesis, and *Kid A* the antithesis, then *Amnesiac* can be seen as the synthesis of the two. This perception is, however, as much a byproduct of the listener's comfort level with the material as any effort on the part of the band.

Yorke has said that *Amnesiac's* title refers to the Gnostic belief that "when we are born we are forced to forget where we have come from in order to deal with the trauma of arriving in this life."[6] If we believe that both albums have the same subject, which tends to be the assumption given the conflation of the singer (or at least his voice) with the lyrical-I-as-subject and in the absence of clearly drawn characters on either, then *Amnesiac* can be understood as an attempt to forget the trauma of *Kid A*, in keeping with the subject's promise on "Motion Picture Soundtrack" to "see you in the next life." Gnosticism is a school of theology/philosophy that flourished in the early centuries of Christianity and whose central doctrine is that salvation comes through an intuitive knowledge of the mysteries of the universe, ultimately overcoming the "grossness of matter" and returning to the universal spirit.[7] Mapping Radiohead's work onto Gnosticism could lead us to see the albums as an attempt on the part of the subject and the band itself to triumph over the commodification of modern society (expressed as "noise" on *Kid A*) to return to a "pure" musical state. The title *Amnesiac* also works as a fulfillment of Radiohead's promise that the album would be a return to its old sound, a forgetting of the experience of *Kid A* for both band and listener. However, since the band had recorded the tracks for *Amnesiac* at the same time as those for *Kid A*, this is a false construction. It is doubtful that the band somehow recorded all of *Kid A's* tracks first, and then recorded all of *Amnesiac's* in an attempt to erase the first batch of results. In that case, *Kid A*'s release would have been wholly unnecessary. The naming of *Amnesiac* seems a calculated attempt at repositioning the band in the audience's minds by dismissing *Kid A* as an aberration in Radiohead's output and by acknowledging the need of the subject, the band, and the audience to move on after the trauma of *Kid A*.

Although *Amnesiac* does succeed to some extent in blurring the memory of the traumas of *Kid A*, it cannot completely obliterate them. *Amnesiac*'s warmer and less distorted sound functions merely as a mask for a subject who, although definitely *present* from the beginning this time, is spiritually dead. The lyrics of the album form a dark, violent series of images that reveal the subject's true nihilistic status. The "amnesia" the subject experiences could be thought of as a kind of "directed forgetting," a term that refers to both the process of instructing someone to forget something, and a mechanism that survivors of trauma can use to make themselves forget a particular memory.[8] Successful directed forgetting seems to be a case of consciously initiating unconscious processes that determine what will later enter consciousness. Directed forgetting in a test setting involves the presentation of information (generally words in a list) followed by instructions to forget them. Whether such "directed forgetting" is applicable to autobiographical memories as well as simple lists of words is up for debate. Experimental results have shown that people are capable of forgetting events when instructed to, and if the event is a traumatic one from real life, they may be more motivated to forget it and will do so over a longer period.[9] Anne DePrince and Jennifer Freyd conducted an experiment in which "high dissociators" were found to recall fewer trauma-related words ("incest," "rape") than "low dissociators" and concluded that "This pattern is consistent with betrayal trauma theory's prediction that individuals who experience events high in betrayal will use dissociation to keep threatening information from awareness."[10] Perhaps the subject of *Kid A* finds it easier to erase his traumatic memories on *Amnesiac* because of his schizophrenic dissociation. A more sinister meaning for the phrase is the process of "directed forgetting" used to control the thoughts of the populace, as in George Orwell's *1984*. Orwell's "doublethink" involves not only forgetting but also forgetting the very act of having forgotten. Directed forgetting is different from thought suppression, however, in that in the latter, subjects are told not to think of a specific event or object, which initiates an automatic search for the suppressed object.[11] Given the short time period between the release of *Kid A* and *Amnesiac*, perhaps neither audience nor subject (if indeed still the same one) could forget *Kid A*'s traumas soon enough.

The relationship between *Kid A* and *Amnesiac* is nevertheless ambiguous. Colin Greenwood has stressed the continuity and cohesiveness of the albums: "I'm not sure they are two records. . . . [*Amnesiac*] is a combination of . . . more conventional, perhaps, but also more dissonant stuff. But it continues on from *Kid A*. It was all done in the same recording period. It is all a whole."[12] Like most critics, Yorke has argued that the cohesion between the two albums is a product of contrast: "*Amnesiac* is about seeing really awful things that you try to forget and can't quite. Whereas *Kid A* is deliberately trying to keep everything at a safe distance."[13] The irony in this statement is that the subject on *Kid A* was not actually able to keep the trauma of modern life at bay and requires *Amnesiac* in order to start over, to try again. Yorke also recognizes a continuity between the albums: "If you look at the artwork for *Kid A* . . . that's like looking at the fire from afar. *Amnesiac* is the sound of what it feels like to be standing IN the fire."[14] Here, the "fire" can be read as a metaphor for the human condition in modern society. R. J. Smith likewise wrote in the *Village Voice* that "If *Kid A*'s songs seem rooted in a pitched battle over the future, *Amnesiac*'s feel recorded the moment after."[15] In *Kid A*, the subject's effort to keep society's ills at bay is so traumatic that existential negation—suicide— seems the only rational solution. The subject of *Amnesiac*, by contrast, reacts to the same horrors with a deadpan nihilism as he learns to live with the inanity of the world.

For the most part, critical reception to *Amnesiac* has deemed it more accessible than *Kid A*, in part because of its reduced use of synthesized sounds, fewer filtered instruments, and more readily discernible lyrics. Ed O'Brien has quoted art designer Stanley Donwood, who has worked with Radiohead from *The Bends* to the present, as saying that "*Kid A* is like you pick up the phone, you call somebody, and there's an answering machine on the other end. With *Amnesiac*, you get through to that person. And you're engaged in the conversation."

This analogy views the subject of *Kid A* as being detached from and thus alienating the audience; fans had bought *Kid A* perhaps expecting to relate to it in the same ways they had to previous Radiohead albums, and were instead put off by it. *Amnesiac* was specifically marketed as a return to the band's old ways of connecting with its listeners, and critics picked up on this contrast between the two albums. David Fricke has stated that "the effect [of *Amnesiac*] is like *Kid A* turned inside out. . . . On *Kid A*, Yorke often sounded like a ghost trapped inside an ice sculpture. On *Amnesiac*, he sings in front of the music with confrontational intimacy. . . ."[16] Whereas the vocals on *Kid A* were for the most part heavily filtered and distorted, *Amnesiac*'s were moved to the forefront and stripped of effects. At times even the singer's breath is audible; he literally animates the subject. *Amnesiac* was described by *Q* magazine as "similarly shy, textural and embroidered by electronica, but where it differs vitally from *Kid A* is in being 1) better balanced, 2) more emotionally intelligible and 3) even more grimly beautiful."[17] This implies that in the production of *Amnesiac*, the band managed to integrate those elements that had interrupted the texture of *Kid A* into something that the listener could better relate to; however, it could also be true that listeners were simply more accustomed by then to the strange electronic sounds the band was employing and were themselves integrating these sounds into an accessible musical experience. The band claimed to be using *Amnesiac* as an antidote to the bafflement of *Kid A* and the critics followed suit, recognizing *Kid A* as a problem-as-artistic-statement that needed to be resolved by the band's next release.

The vocals and lyrics on *Amnesiac* are easier to decipher than those of *Kid A*, at least on an audible level,[18] because they are less filtered or distorted. The album packaging does not include lyrics, however, despite the limited-edition release taking the form of a book. The inside cover of this book has a sleeve for a library lending slip, which is labeled "Ref: F Heit451." The sleeve is labeled "Nosuch Library" and lists "Radiohead" and "Amnesiac" along with "ACC No. F heit 451." This labeling links *Amnesiac* to the Ray Bradbury classic *Fahrenheit 451* and the idea that in the future, dangerous books will be burned. The sleeve contains date stamps from 1996 through 2007, and the lending slip has the date 06 Feb 2012. The date range slots the album into a time period ranging from the recent past into the near future, emphasizing that any traumas or dangers on the album exist essentially in the present. The CD fits into the sleeve pasted into the inside cover. The track list for the album and the writing and production credits are given inside the back cover. The compact disc is credited to Radiohead, and the book to "Stanley Donwood and Tchocky [Yorke's alias]."[19] The book contains some artwork similar to that of *Kid A*, with overlaid computer graphics and hand-drawn art, but *Amnesiac*'s artwork also includes many sketches of people and the reoccurring image of a weeping Minotaur.[20] The Minotaur (a man/bull monster) of Greek mythology lived at the center of a labyrinth, and Radiohead acknowledges the similarly labyrinthine structure of their music by stating on the lending sleeve that "Labyrinthine structures are entered at the reader's own risk." The effect of leafing through the book is that of looking at someone's private sketchbook scribblings. Some of the pages have typewritten lyrical fragments from songs on *Amnesiac*, recalling the handbill art of *Kid A*. Whereas other albums sometimes contain lyrics in a "handwriting" font to give the appearance of having been written out longhand by the songwriter, lending a sense of authenticity, *Amnesiac*'s packaging functions more as a scrapbook constructed to do no more than hint at the album's meaning. The book contains what seem to be photos from an archive left behind, to which the archivist must assign importance and meaning. If the "reader" enters, at his own risk, then he is responsible for finding meaning in the labyrinth as well as avoiding any horrors. However, the artist gives him no useful clues to help guide his way. The album is in some sense an ironic rant against commodification because the band derives its income from selling its music as a commodity, managing its critique in such a way that its protest is not simply a means of further commodification. So too is the album-as-book an empty vessel without meanings to its words beyond those the reader identifies or assigns. Perhaps in Radiohead's post-apocalyptic world, commodification has caused words to lose all meaning; the commodity with no value beyond its status as a commodity is an empty signifier.[21] Amnesia here is figured as a loss, a forgetting, a decontextualization, an emptying, and ultimately a condition of survival in a world emptied out by the universal form of the commodity. For Radiohead to succeed on a level beyond the commodity, reaching the status of "artist," it must at least pretend to forget its condition as a product of the recording industry and create art that furthers that forgetting—ultimately an impossible act.

As mentioned, the instruments of *Amnesiac* are less distorted than those of *Kid A* and support the musical structure rather than overtly working to split it apart. Some have commented that the "warmer" sound of *Amnesiac*'s songs (echoed in the artwork, which for the most part has the appearance of being hand-drawn rather than computer-generated) offers a respite from the harshness of *Kid A*, in which even the so-called "natural" sounds are synthesized, filtered, and used to disrupt the musical texture and alienate the subject. Stephen Dalton has noted that *Amnesiac* "appears to build a bridge between its sister album's *avant*-noise post-rock soundscapes and more traditionally recognizable pop forms, from acoustic ballads to big band jazz."[22] Some of the elements that had disrupted the musical texture of *Kid A* are altered into a more conventional and thus redeeming state on *Amnesiac*; the "Charles Mingus horns" that were given only a repeated minor-seventh riff on "The National Anthem" of *Kid A*, for example, return as an ensemble of intertwining solo lines to support the vocalist on *Amnesiac*'s "Life in a Glasshouse." Alex Abramovich writes that "On *Amnesiac*—the more accessible, and more rewarding, of the two records—electronic experimentation alternates with straightforward melody, often within the confines of a single song."[23] It is debatable whether an accessible album is automatically a rewarding one; a listener may feel a greater sense of accomplishment, for instance, when she can understand and appreciate a progressive-jazz album than a collection of bubblegum-pop singles. What Abramovich describes as electronic sounds alternating with straightforward (accessible) melodies can be variously interpreted as the musical elements finally taking control of and suppressing the noise; as the noise still managing to interrupt the more conventional pop-rock structures; or as the elements of music and noise having negotiated a common ground in which they are both allowed to exist. Whereas on *Kid A* the noise had constantly interrupted the musical texture, on *Amnesiac* the noise is to some extent controlled, or at least managed, by the voice and the return of the non-filtered guitars. Greg Hainge disputes the notion of *Amnesiac* being "more listener-friendly or, rather, more old-Radiohead-fan-friendly"; he quotes

Ian Watson as saying that "the sequencing of the songs and often bleak lyrical tone makes *Amnesiac* a very troubling album indeed. Where *Kid A* eased you in with the comforting warmth of 'Everything in Its Right Place' and rewarded you after that draining emotional journey with the serene beauty and reassurance of 'Motion Picture Soundtrack,' *Amnesiac* is a far more desolate experience."[24] Watson here is reading beyond the surface comfort of *Amnesiac*'s more conventional song structures and instrumentation, recognizing that the subject is just as disturbed, and possibly more so, as he is now repressing the agonies of *Kid A* to pretend that everything is "in its right place." The temptation, again, is to read *Amnesiac* as an antidote, to perceive its sounds in opposition to those of *Kid A*, as trying to redeem the lost subject. However, a peek beneath the album's surface shows that the subject is still trying desperately to find meaning in modern society.

Just as the less distorted vocals do not make *Amnesiac*'s lyrics any less opaque than *Kid A*'s, the album's apparently more straightforward musical elements do not mean that a clear narrative is present. Despite the band's statements about *Amnesiac*'s accessibility and the release of several singles from it, because it is so similar to *Kid A* it can be treated as another concept album, albeit another resistant one. Its resistance is more subtle because of its singles, but the band continued its experimentation with this album and generally thought of it and *Kid A* as cut from the same cloth. Table 5.1 shows some musical elements of *Amnesiac* divided into the same categories as those of *Kid A*. The elements are better integrated than on *Kid A*, although a reading of *Amnesiac* as integrative implies that it was recorded subsequent to and as a reaction to *Kid A*, and as mentioned above, since all the content of the two albums was recorded together this isn't strictly the case. Rather, any perceived integration of the sounds is due largely to the listener's newfound comfort with Radiohead's innovations, after the confusion of *Kid A*.

Mapping the songs of *Kid A* and *Amnesiac* onto one another suggests that initially *Amnesiac* appears as a salvation of sorts for the subject condemned in *Kid A*—or for the listener baffled by the album. This impression turns out to be false: although at a surface level the music draws the listener in and offers comfort that the subject can find a place of reconciliation, in fact the subject remains alienated;

TABLE 5.1. Binary Oppositions in *Amnesiac*

Song	Sense	Nonsense	"Acoustic"	Electronic	Music	Noise
"Packt Like Sardines in a Crushd Tin Box"	voice ("I'm a reasonable man")	muttering voices, sound effects	"gamelan," voice (breathy, sibilant)	drum beats; "gamelan," keyboards	repetitive melody (chorus)	distorted voice, sound effects
"Pyramid Song"	voice	meter (out of time), dreamy "oohs," sound effects	voice, piano, strings, "live" drums, builds	sound of "wind," sirens, fluttering strings/keyboard effects	piano, strings (supporting)	fluttering string sounds under piano
"Pulk/Pull Revolving Doors"	all words, no melody	rhythm drops in and out, hard to understand lyrics		samples; broken-up text; drum loops	bells	all beat, no melody, effects (sirens), distorted
"You and Whose Army?"	vocals (begins with breath)		voice close to mike, guitar, "live" drums, piano, string bass	radio mike	guitar, voice, harmony vocals	
"I Might Be Wrong"	catchy chorus ("let's go down the waterfall")	reverb on vocals, falsetto, "covered" voice	guitar/bass riff, "live" drums	synthesized sounds	harmony vocals, postlude (string melody), local "aahs" and riff returns	relentless riff
"Knives Out"	catchy chorus, speaks directly to listener ("I want you to know")		non-distorted vocals		guitar, bass, drums, guitar solo	

"Morning Bell/Amnesiac"	same lyrics as Kid A (familiar)		"bells"		stripped of all but chords, counter-melody[1]	synthesized chords
"Dollars & Cents"[2]	strings in unison with voice (heart of album)	hard to understand words	strings	relentless bass riff	strings counter-melody	
"Hunting Bears"	no lyrics/vocals (nothing to say)	guitars, sound of fingers on strings			all pitch, no beat	fingers on frets
"Like Spinning Plates"	"backwards" vocals rearranged into new phonemes	source = backwards song		effects, playing song backwards	voice	sound effects, strobing effect
"Life in a Glasshouse"	clear vocals	meandering voice, as jazz instrument	jazz ensemble	sound effects, begins with burst of "god music" from end of Kid A, erases previous song	interweaving instrumental lines	sound effects, erupting solo lines

Notes:

1. The counter-melody comes in especially at the statement "cut the kids in half" and ends with the Beatlesque recorders at approximately the same tempo as the next song. This melody is cut off by the riff of "Dollars & Cents," so it functions as a counting-off to the next song.

2. The statement "won't you quiet down" is an attempt at quashing the erupting noise (equivalent to "How to Disappear Completely"). The command "quiet down" returns over the clear statement "we are the dollars and cents," when all instruments except the guitar and cymbal drop out.

this reconciliation is only an apparent one. As table 5.2 shows, many of the same musical elements that had caused such anxiety on *Kid A* return throughout *Amnesiac*: drum loops, sampled text, jazz riffs, and so forth. "Pyramid Song," for example, contains musical elements similar to those in "How to Disappear Completely" but presents them more conventionally—or rather, less subtly. Martin Clarke notes that Yorke's "ethereal vocals are clearer than on *Kid A*, buoyed up, rather than drowned, by gentle drums and instrumentation."[25] Likewise, the strings and other instruments on *Amnesiac* work in tandem with Yorke's vocals rather than against them. The overall musical impression is that of a scenario where the subject is fully present, surrounded by peaceful images of "a moon full of stars and astral cars" rather than the violent "strobe lights and blown speakers, fireworks and hurricanes" of "How to Disappear Completely." The "warmer," more natural sound of *Amnesiac* has also been perceived as more commercially accessible than that of *Kid A*, an idea supported by the promotion of two singles from *Amnesiac* ("Pyramid Song" and "Knives Out"). However, the subject that is present on *Amnesiac*, although produced through less technologically distorted means, seems insincere and overblown—more willing to accept the commodification of the world, if grudgingly—than the vanishing subject of *Kid A*, who struggles for survival in a musical texture fractured by the clash of music and noise. Offering the furthest thing from authentic expression, the "commercial" subject who occupies *Amnesiac* is constructed and sustained through his investment in an artificiality that only appears authentic. The "authentic" subject promised by commodity culture in this sense becomes a chimera: he appears only at the point of existential negation, the point where he disappears completely.

The initial listener reaction to *Amnesiac* is already different from that of *Kid A*. Because the earlier album had no singles, though its tracks had been "leaked" ahead of time, the first sound the listener heard would have been track one, "Everything in Its Right Place." With *Amnesiac*, by contrast, it was at least possible for listeners to have heard a single, "Pyramid Song," before the album's release. Thus, the eventual track two set the stage for the album's reception. Without the album to contextualize its meaning, the song first appears as a pure musical commodity, the definition of a single. Its tone is quite unlike

TABLE 5.2. Song Mappings between *Amnesiac* and *Kid A*

Amnesiac	Kid A	Common elements
"Packt Like Sardines in a Crushd Tin Box"	"Everything in Its Right Place"	broken-up texture
"Pyramid Song"	"How to Disappear Completely"	slow tempo, dreamy quality
"Pulk/Pull Revolving Doors"	"Kid A" "Idioteque"	sampled and broken-up text sampled drum loop
"You and Whose Army?"	"Motion Picture Soundtrack"	lyrical imagery, instrumentation
"I Might Be Wrong"	"The National Anthem" "In Limbo"	repeating bass riff lyrics
"Knives Out"	"Optimistic"	catchy sound, "single"
"Morning Bell/Amnesiac"	"Morning Bell"	same lyrics
"Dollars & Cents"	"In Limbo"	lyrics
"Hunting Bears"	"Treefingers"	lack of vocals/lyrics
"Like Spinning Plates"	"Everything in Its Right Place" "Kid A"	sampled text played backwards sampled and broken-up text
"Life in a Glasshouse"	"The National Anthem"	jazz horns

that of *Kid A*, but also dissimilar to Radiohead's earlier singles, such as "Paranoid Android" and "Karma Police," each of which had immediately grabbed the listener with a hook. "Pyramid Song," by contrast, begins with muted piano chords playing a syncopated rhythm. The voice enters on a falsetto "ooh" (0:18), recalling the beginning of "Optimistic." Heard on its own, as a reaction to *Kid A*, the song gives the impression that the subject will be spared this time—if the forthcoming album will even contemplate subjective existence. Within the context of the album, however, the song takes on a distinctively darker hue, and we recognize an affinity with the theme of *Kid A*. The subject's one moment of peace comes from beyond the grave ("we all went to heaven in a little row boat," 1:30): before the album even arrives, we know that the subject is already dead. Lyrical imagery from *Kid A* returns throughout *Amnesiac*: most strikingly, the subject who had

TABLE 5.3. Image Trail of *Amnesiac* Lyrics

Track 1	"Packt Like Sardines"	"your life flashed before your eyes"
Track 2	"Pyramid Song"	"we all went to heaven in a little row boat"
Track 3	"Pulk/Pull Revolving Doors"	"there are trapdoors that you can't come back from"
Track 4	"You and Whose Army?"	"we ride tonight, ghost horses"
Track 5	"I Might Be Wrong"	"I used to think there was no future at all"
Track 6	"Knives Out"	"he's not coming back"; "cook him up, squash his head, throw him in the pot"; "he's frozen and bloated"
Track 7	"Morning Bell/ Amnesiac"	"release me"; "cut the kids in half"
Track 8	"Dollars & Cents"	"we're gonna crack your little souls"
Track 9	"Hunting Bears"	instrumental (missing subject)
Track 10	"Like Spinning Plates"	"you feed me to the lions"; "my body's floating down a muddy river"
Track 11	"Life in a Glasshouse"	"packed like frozen food and battery hens"

been floating "down the Liffey" in "How to Disappear Completely" is now jumping "in the river" and swimming with "black-eyed angels" in "Pyramid Song." In "Like Spinning Plates," however, his dead body is "floating down a muddy river." The "trapdoors that open" in "In Limbo" become "trapdoors that you can't come back from" in "Pulk/ Pull Revolving Doors." Rather than offering the subject escape, then, *Amnesiac* offers him only further imprisonment. The surface positivity of "Optimistic" returns in "Dollars & Cents" (a link to the false, buyable happiness offered by commodity culture) with the lyrics "there are better things to talk about, be constructive" and in "I Might Be Wrong" with the words "think about the good times, never look back" and "have ourselves a good time, it's nothing at all." These commands exemplify the very definition of amnesia, the forgetting of past trauma (i.e., of *Kid A*). The song's lyrics can also be read as implying that it is impossible to actually have a "good time," because a state of happiness doesn't exist; that is, "it's nothing at all."[26] The lyrics of *Amnesiac* provide an "image trail"[27] of death and violence, as shown in table 5.3.

Rather than being possessed by a suicidal drive to existential negation, as on *Kid A*, the subject here is in essence already dead. Such is Radiohead's depiction of "life" in modern society; any happiness and comfort in the album, as in the human condition, exist only at the surface level.

"PACKT LIKE SARDINES IN A CRUSHD TIN BOX"

Amnesiac contains many of the compositional techniques used in other Radiohead albums, including the pivot tone and the accumulative groove. The album begins with "Packt Like Sardines in a Crushd Tin Box," discussed by Mark Spicer as having an accumulative beginning.[28] Spicer does not delineate the instrumental entrances, but they can be mapped out as in table 5.4. Track one of the album functions as an erasing of the single "Pyramid Song," creating a new first impression for the listener. This impression is very different from the one created by "Pyramid Song"; in contrast to the former song's soothing piano chords, "Packt Like Sardines" begins with a rhythmic "gamelan" sample (technically a "'field recording' of the gently modulated Hare Krishna 'water drum,'"[29] but in any case a new "morning bell" to wake the listener from her slumber) and is followed by the entrance of a drum kit and then a keyboard. The voice finally enters at 0:51 with the nihilistic statement "after years of waiting, nothing came." This time of waiting could refer to the six-month period between the release of *Kid A* and *Amnesiac*, which may have seemed like an eternity to fans who deplored the band's new sound, or to the longer (four-year) wait between the band's last album in its guitar-driven style, *OK Computer*, and the release of *Amnesiac*, which had promised a return to that sound. Doheny notes that George Harrison of the Beatles, who famously converted to Krishnaism, was interested in Eastern instruments and the quest for enlightenment; here, Radiohead ironically juxtaposes the sounds of the former with lyrics that mock the latter.[30] The lyrics may have more to do with the concept of nirvana as a state of nothingness, the abnegation of the self, which is the fulfillment of the years of waiting (meditation), in which case the "nothing" that arrives should be warmly received. The challenge is being receptive to the nothingness when it arrives. Here, the emptiness of the album-as-commodity has displaced, even instrumentalized, that place of nothingness for which

TABLE 5.4. The Accumulative Groove in "Packt Like Sardines in a Crushd Tin Box"

(X = entrance; O = exit)

CD timings	Intro 0:00	0:15	0:36	Verse 1 0:52	1:18	Chorus 1:23	Verse 2 1:38	1:55	Chorus 2:09
"Gamelan"	X			O	X		O		
Keyboards/ bass/ guitar		X							
Drums			X						
Voice				X					
Second voice								X	
Sound effects									

CD timings	Bridge 2:32	2:47	2:55	3:01	Verse 3 3:03	Chorus 3:18	Outro 3:49
"Gamelan"		X				O	
Keyboards/ bass/guitar	O	X					
Drums	O			X			
Voice	O				X		O
Second voice	O				X	O	
Sound effects	X						O

the subject longs. The disillusionment that comes with unmasking the illusion that a successful spiritual quest will escape the emptiness of the commodity could thus be read as a comment on Radiohead's dissatisfaction with the conventional pop-music world typified by the Beatles—who of course passed out of the mainstream in their own time but have since come to represent the "classic" pop band.

This allusion could also be read as a recanting after what Tim Footman sees as "acknowledgment of the previous holders of that ['greatest band in the world ever'] title," the Beatles. The "overblown, neo-classical arrangement" of "Motion Picture Soundtrack" recalls "Good Night," the final song on the Beatles' "White Album"; there is a long pause after the song, as at the end of *Abbey Road*; and *Kid A* "closes with a burst of abstract noise," like *Sgt. Pepper.*[31] The juxtaposition of "Motion Picture Soundtrack" as the last song on *Kid A* next to "Packt Like Sardines" as the first song on *Amnesiac* furthers the interpretation that Radiohead is reacting against the Beatlesque elements of its previous album. "Packt Like Sardines" mocks the quest for enlightenment and the hopefulness of the "next life" that are evoked in "Motion Picture Soundtrack." It casts the lyrics in the second person (1:07, "as your life flashed before your eyes . . . you realize you're looking in . . . the wrong place"), drawing listeners in and making them feel as though the subject is passing judgment on them. The lyrics also create the confusion characteristic of the second person, whether it is meant to be a plural and general "you" that includes the speaker, a dialogue between a lyrical "you" and "me," or a direct address to the listener. The structure of "Packt Like Sardines" is conventional (intro, verse one, chorus, verse two, chorus, bridge, verse three, chorus, outro), though verse three cuts up the lyric and intersperses it with drums and "gamelan." Each chorus (beginning at 1:22, "I'm a reasonable man, get off my case") grows four bars longer (from eight bars to twelve and then sixteen). Conversely, each verse grows briefer: the first verse (0:51) is a full sixteen bars, as is the second (1:37), but the second four bars of the second verse are instrumental. A bridge section of keyboard noises interrupts the verse/chorus sequence at 2:34, followed by the reappearance of the "gamelan" at 2:47. The third verse (3:02) is only eight bars long, and its second four bars too are instrumental (keyboard sounds that return at the end of the song). The effect is that the subject is growing more insistent with his claim of being a "reasonable man," as those lyrics are repeated over and over. The syncopated reiteration of "get off my case" underscores the subject's insistence. As example 5.1 shows, the vocal melody emphasizes D major/minor (mixing the F-natural and F-sharp) and is tightly confined to a mere fifth (D to A), furthering the notion of social confinement and claustrophobic musical space articulated on *Kid A*, particularly in "The National Anthem." The song's chorus is even more confined, to a minor third (D to F-natural). In both the verse and the chorus, the voice ends on the tonic of D, grounding the vocals. With the chorus, the subject asks the listener to leave him alone: "I'm a reasonable man, get off my case." The small melodic range and the repetition first of "get off" and later of "get off my case" lend the chorus a singsong or chantlike melody. As the voice repeats "get off my case," it remains for the most part on the D, though it occasionally reaches up to the F-natural for the word "get," making it sound as though the command is growing more insistent. The voice sings a syncopated rhythm, recalling that of the "gamelan" introduction. A second voice comes in at the middle of verse two (1:53, the second "after years of waiting" statement of that verse) and sings in unison with the first voice until the final chorus ("I'm a reasonable man").

The title of the song echoes the claustrophobic melody; even the words of the title are confined, with letters missing or substituted ("packt," "crushd"). The word "reasonable" in the chorus is also contracted to something more like "reas'na'ble," sung with only three syllables. The verse states that any meaning must be found elsewhere, as meditating for "years of waiting" has led only to the realization that the subject's confinement has forced him to look in the wrong place. (On an allegorical level, this could be read as an admonishment to Radiohead's fans not to look for meaning in the band's music.) The "wrong place" of Amnesiac is a contrast to the insistence on everything being in its "right place" on Kid A; instead, the subject of Amnesiac is willing to admit from the outset that things are wrong. This realization has come as the result of a near-death experience, in which "your life flashed before your eyes." As the first song after Kid A, "Packt Like Sardines" serves as a reaction to the death(s) of "How to Disappear Completely" and "Motion Picture Soundtrack." With the subject's continued insistence that he is a "reasonable man," he seems to be advocating a return to logic, to Enlightenment reason, and thus to the confinements that this form of reason places on action and thought. However, in being confined and contracted in the lyrics, language no longer represents a logical syntax, and thoughts and actions may be short-circuited. The first verse elides with the chorus, forming the lyric "you realize . . . I'm a reasonable man," implying that any epiphany has to do with the subject rather than with the listener (that is, with the listener's perception of the subject). The words "you realize" at 1:15 hang suspended on a G (over the D emphasized in the minimal harmonic accompaniment), resolving melodically into the D of the chorus that then reinforces the original tonic of D minor.

"After years of wai - ting no - thing came"

"I'm a reas'nable man get off my case, get off my case, get off my case"

5.1. "Packt Like Sardines in a Crushd Tin Box," verse and chorus

Verse three of "Packt Like Sardines" ends with an electronic manipulation of the voice on the word "case" (2:32) that emphasizes the
C-sharp leading-tone to the tonic of D. After the bridge, the voice sings
"after years of waiting" once again, then moves into the final chorus
(3:17) while a second, distorted voice is heard in the background. The
song ends with just the keyboard/drum machine, a reversion to technology's dominance. If *Amnesiac*'s subject is the same as *Kid A*'s, his
statement on his "reasonable" state of being seems strange, given that
he had attempted suicide over the course of the earlier album, not
the most reasonable of actions under normal circumstances. In his
repeated insistence on the reasonableness of an unreasonable action,
the subject articulates the idea that the most reasonable, or rational,
response to modern society is an attempt at escaping it, which thus
sets up the nihilistic style of *Amnesiac*. Mark B. N. Hansen states
that "Packt Like Sardines" establishes the tone for the album just as
"Everything in Its Right Place" did for *Kid A*: "[The song] begins to
explain the rationale of its demarcation from *Kid A* despite its having
been compiled from the same recording sessions. . . . 'Packt' gives us
a feeling for the dominant movement of the album, a movement that,
through the preservation of a certain autonomy of both voice and
instrumentation, will begin a perhaps more complex process of reterritorialization [voice and instruments becoming grounded rather than
unmoored as on *Kid A*] . . . toward a post-rock mode." Hansen further
states that this process is completed on the live *I Might Be Wrong* recordings,[32] made in circumstances under which it is not possible to play
as many effects, producing a more "authentic" musical performance.
Kid A had, by contrast, deterritorialized the voice and the guitar by
filtering both until they were nearly unrecognizable. The territory
normally occupied by Radiohead's prominent lead vocals and three

guitars had been redistributed on *Kid A* by heavily filtering the voice and mostly exchanging guitars for keyboards; when guitars do appear on the album, they are filtered to sound like keyboards. This bold move not only reimagined Radiohead's own sound, but also threatened the standard of voice/guitar interplay and co-dominance in pop-rock music (think of the Rolling Stones' Mick Jagger/Keith Richard or Aerosmith's Steven Tyler/Joe Perry), which probably contributed to the album's ambivalent reception. On *Amnesiac*, the guitars return unfiltered, and the vocals are much clearer. Since "Packt Like Sardines" introduces these more conventional elements right away, the album immediately reclaims the musical space as belonging to both voice and guitar. The sounds that appear later on the album (the sharp intake of breath in "You and Whose Army?" and the hands sliding along the guitar strings on "Hunting Bears") function as not only a reterritorializing of the musical space, but an almost physical one.

"PYRAMID SONG"

The heavy, syncopated feel of "Packt Like Sardines" contrasts with the slow, dreamy rhythms of the next song, the single "Pyramid Song," in which the syncopated piano creates a sense of timelessness, especially with the voice's counter-rhythms over it (see example 5.2). The "oohs" in the intro and chorus can be linked back to the *homme fatal* motive or 3–2–1 line of "aahs" in "How to Disappear Completely" and through-

5.2. "Pyramid Song," rhythm of verse

out *Kid A*. This time, however, the voice enters on scale degree two (F-sharp) and extends down two more notes to D and C-sharp. The song's structure presents an intro, two verses, a chorus, two more verses (the same as before), and a final chorus repeated twice. The intro and chorus "oohs" are a fifth higher than the vocals in the verse, lending an unearthly feel to the chorus in particular that furthers the song's dreamy quality. The song feels more conventional in the sense that the verses are full lyrical statements and the sounds are not filtered like in the songs of *Kid A*, even though the rhythms make it seem unmoored. Each verse offers a return to reality, as it were, from the otherworldly chorus. The vocal line emphasizes C-sharp but descends to F-sharp at the end of each line. The C-sharp largely fits into the underlying accompaniment of planing chords that move stepwise from F-sharp major to G major 7 (G–B–D–F-sharp, only a passing harmony) to A and then back down to G major 7 and F-sharp major, moving back to G major 7 under the F-sharp in the voice; thus the voice's F-sharp, which had sounded stable in isolation, becomes an unresolved seventh over the harmony. Although the higher C-sharp sounds harmonious, since it is both the fifth over F-sharp and the third over A, the voice continually descends to the tonic of F-sharp at the end of each line. The harmony itself finally resolves to F-sharp after the voice has died out in the coda with the repetition of the words "there was nothing to fear, nothing to doubt" (3:45). The accompanying instruments here, rather than battling the subject, instead confirm his comforting state-ment by moving to the voice's home key of F-sharp.

Another way of exploring the sounds of "Pyramid Song" is to look again at the interplay of music and noise. Rather than dividing the instruments into the binary oppositions of electronic and acoustic, however, it is perhaps more productive to look at whether the other instruments support the subject/voice by playing a harmonious melody or chords, or work against him by creating a disturbance in the texture. The song begins with gliding piano chords, but in the background is a faint suggestion of ambient noise. This noise grows louder when the voice comes in with its "oohs" at 0:18; here, the noise sounds like strings playing a tremolo and a distorted tape being played backwards. When the voice sings its first verse (0:36, "jumped into the river"), the noise fades, leaving only the piano as accompaniment, but the noise returns when the voice pauses after the line "all my past and future" (1:22). When the voice sings "nothing to fear, nothing to doubt," at the end of the line (1:39), noise in the form of sirens enters the texture. At the first chorus (1:50, "ooh"), the strings enter on the same pitch as the voice and play along with its melody. A few beats into the melody (1:59), a drum kit (snare and cymbals) enters to play the syncopated rhythm along with the piano.

When verse three begins (2:25), the howling sounds from the faint ambience heard earlier accompany the voice for the first line. As the second line begins (2:33, "black-eyed angels"), a second voice comes in to provide harmony. The supportive strings enter for the third line (2:43), "moon full of stars," and play a counter-melody. The howling sounds are heard when the strings and voice fade out; these sounds are low in the mix and are consequently less threatening. The voice is alone with piano and drums for "nothing to fear, nothing to doubt" (3:27), but after the third repetition (with vocal harmony) the supportive strings enter and take over the song at 3:51, sounding a melody along with the piano's rhythm. The howling reenters after a few seconds (4:08) and gradually grows louder until it takes over the texture after the strings, piano, and drums have faded out. In contrast to "How to Disappear Completely," the subject's leave-taking here seems to be of his own volition. He has described peaceful scenes of a world beyond his own (with the moon, astral cars, and heaven), a contrast to the modern world in which there is plenty to fear and plenty to doubt. Here, the strings work with the voice, enhancing the texture under and around him rather than trying to swallow him up as in "How to Disappear Completely." The other instruments take over the texture only when he abandons it, and the noise claims the song only in the absence of the voice and strings. If we look for a narrative in the song, we can pose the theory that the subject is confident enough to ward off the possibility of encroaching noise, but given the nihilistic statement in the album's first track, a better guess might be that he is simply resigned to his condition and is no longer interested in fighting for his musical space. The split in the subject's voice between melody and harmony sounds calm rather than fractured, which could indicate either that he has made peace with his schizophrenia or that he is no longer in the midst of a dissociative episode. The noise that ends the song reminds the listener that all is still not well in the world of *Kid A/Amnesiac*.

The ending of "Pyramid Song" is only a surface calm, as the memory of past trauma can only be temporarily erased; the subject can only momentarily forget his human condition. The music of "Pyramid Song" continues after the voice leaves, with a postlude of synthesized strings over the same syncopated piano chords, finally ending on F-sharp. "Pyramid Song" soothes the manic energy of "Packt Like Sardines" but fails to progress harmonically, though it does build and finally "resolve." Doheny states that "Pyramid Song" began its life as a song called "Nothing to Fear" and was then called "Egyptian Song," taking as its subject matter the flight of Moses and the Israelites from Egypt by way of Charles Mingus's song "Freedom."[33] This imagery can be linked to Footman's discussion of the purported slaughter of the "first of the children" in *Kid A*'s "Idioteque."[34] By changing the song's title over time, Radiohead buries its meaning, similar to the way that Yorke's vocals and the various musical sounds are buried in layers of filtered electronica on *Kid A*, and similar also to the very method that Radiohead uses to market itself, burying its political leanings and anti-corporate messages in riddles for its audience to solve. Just as Radiohead cannot ultimately both evade and function successfully within the commodity culture it decries, so the subject's escape in "Pyramid Song" is only a temporary one. As a human being living in modern society, he must eventually return to face the trauma he is trying to forget.

"PULK/PULL REVOLVING DOORS"

Track three, "Pulk/Pull Revolving Doors," erases the security of "Pyramid Song" and returns to the full-blown paranoia of *Kid A*. Whereas "Pyramid Song" contains mostly "natural" sounds (itself a false impression, as sounds must be subjected to electronic recording in order to appear on an album), "Pulk/Pull" is all filtered electronica and drum loops. Its computerized voice is built up from sampling Yorke's voice and playing it back in snippets, similar to the technique on "Everything in Its Right Place" but in contrast with *OK Computer*'s "Fitter

Happier," which had used the computer's "actual" voice to read lyrics written by Yorke. Here, the human subject has apparently been merged with machine. Hansen notes that the "technical mediation" present on "Pulk/Pull" "does not so much blur the voice and sound as bring them together into a productive relationship while continuing to preserve their separation."[35] This "productive" relationship (like being an "empowered and informed member of society") comes at the cost of maintaining one's individual identity, a goal traded in favor of working for societal good. If machines are the way of the future, then the subject's identity must be entombed in them via the computer. Hansen states that "Pulk/Pull" allows the voice to produce "vocalic effects that mimic the content of the utterances" and thus gives it "its most characteristic, most articulated function: speaking complete sentences."[36] Filtered by the machine, the vocal melody loses its expressiveness and is confined mostly to a major second. The lyrics list various types of doors, liminal spaces of transition, points of escape—barn doors, revolving doors, sliding doors, and so forth—and end with the statement "there are trapdoors that you can't come back from" (2:18). At the word "trapdoors," the voice is further distorted by feedback, but the rest of the line is stated clearly. This line jumps out at the listener as a mark of the real; the escape described in "Pyramid Song" is only a temporary one after all, and a slide through a trapdoor means no coming back (a downward slide that leads to the statement in "Knives Out," track six, that "I'm not coming back"). The sounds of sirens, heard earlier in "Pyramid Song," come in just after the line about trapdoors, marking the bulk of "Pulk/Pull" as only an interlude between danger signals. The voice is flattened and mechanized, so that the subject's cry is dehumanized and taken as a statement of fact rather than an urgent plea or a warning of danger. The last words spoken by the subject are those about trapdoors; evidently he has been absorbed into the "machinery" of technological sounds, and the earlier reterritorialization of clear vocals and unfiltered guitar is threatened by this absorption. Though the musical sounds on *Amnesiac* are less altered than on *Kid* A, the album's subject is no less threatened by technology. In merging with the subject, the machinery does not just threaten his humanity; it actually defeats it and forces the continuance of a zombie-like existence animated by technology.

"YOU AND WHOSE ARMY?"

The next song, "You and Whose Army?," track four, immediately brings a human bodily experience back into the album, beginning with a sharp intake of breath followed by a short pause before the voice begins singing. The subject has reclaimed control from the electronic elements of the previous song, although his voice is obviously coming through a microphone; this breath could represent a gasp of horror at the trapdoors of "Pulk/Pull" or at the merging of the subject with the machine, or it could simply represent the subject/singer getting ready to perform the next song, simulating a live performance. The microphone and echo effects used recall the vocalists of the World War II era, but the harmonic structure shares little with the ballads of that time (e.g., "We'll Meet Again," "I'll Be Seeing You," etc.), which emphasized a particular key even when using chromatic pitches to show off the singer's skill. The structure of the song is verse one, verse two, bridge, and chorus, again departing from the WWII ballads, which often included a repeated chorus for audience members to sing along. The verses of "You and Whose Army?" present a series of chords related by fourth and fifth: D-sharp minor, G-sharp, C-sharp minor, F-sharp, B minor, E, A, and finally C-sharp minor again. The circle-of-fifths progression lends the song a feeling of many temporary tonicizations; that is, D-sharp to G-sharp is a V–I (pseudo-dominant/tonic; normally the dominant would be major) relationship, as are G-sharp to C-sharp, C-sharp to F-sharp, F-sharp to B, B to E, and E to A. Typically a circle-of-fifths progression is used to lead into and reinforce a given tonic, but although the progression here sounds stable, it has no one tonic upon which to rest. Likewise, the voice meanders through the melody rather than emphasizing a particular note.

Doheny calls "You and Whose Army?" "probably Radiohead's most politically pointed song to date." Yorke admits that the song is about Tony Blair's election and his subsequent perceived betrayal of his electorate,[37] which might have expected radical social change from the Labour Party (rechristened "New Labour" during Blair's tenure) even if it wasn't explicitly promised during the campaign. The lyrics address "you and your cronies" (1:34) but mention the "Holy Roman Empire" (0:45) rather than the British Empire (Blair formally converted to Catholicism after leaving office). Despite the hearty first breath, the voice starts out sounding weak and highly filtered, like the radio-static sound of the song "Kid A." Doheny notes that the WWII-style vocals "underline the third-wave conflict between Big Money and the anti-globalization/No Logo movement."[38] The "third wave" of corporate branding involves multinational corporations launching local brands to try to connect with the consumer at a personal level; consumers in the know would presumably feel conflicted between supporting a "local" brand that was owned by a large corporation and seeking out a brand that had more relevance to the community. Given the superior marketing resources available to the larger corporations, it becomes difficult for small, truly local brands to attract enough attention to survive. It is possible that Yorke uses WWII-style vocals here in order to recall the radical social programs instituted by the British Labour Party at the end of WWII (national health service, welfare state). The style also evokes the rise of global brands at the end of WWII, point-ing toward the politics that has come to accept the emptiness of the commodity form as "natural" and consumer capitalism as the way of the world. Such a way of thinking creates a cognitive dissonance when Radiohead's message is considered against its actions; the band simultaneously decries the capitalist culture and thrives within it. In purchasing a Radiohead product, the consumer is supporting both a global entity (Radiohead) rather than a local one (a bar band with a homemade CD) and a multinational corporation (its record company). Radiohead manages to successfully participate in the third-wave style of branding by building internet communities among its audience and creating a positive "whispering campaign"; its No Logo tour in support of *Amnesiac* was facilitated through this technique, as was the distribu-tion of the "leaked" *Kid A* throughout an underground community of listeners. The anonymity of the internet allows for both a feeling of localized access to the band and its material and the false perception that the band has a personal relationship with its own "army" of listen-ers. The band furthers this perception by posting cryptic messages and occasional blog entries such as reports of the band being in the studio on its website through the RSS feed Dead Air Space.[39] Fans "in the know" can follow the band's comings and goings and even download the occasional song.

Footman notes that the syncopated "come on, come on" intro of "You and Whose Army?" recalls *OK Computer*'s "Karma Police."[40] In the bridge (1:20), the voice questions the person he has been addressing, asking "you and whose army?" The melody sounds questioning as well, outlining an E-major chord (falling B to G-sharp to E) over chords that move C-sharp minor to A-sharp minor before re-tonicizing D-sharp minor to G-sharp major after the vocals cease. At the second half of the bridge (1:47), a drum kit comes in just before the words "you forget so easily"; the voice ends on a G-sharp that provides a dominant relationship to lead into the C-sharp major of the chorus. A rollicking barroom-blues piano comes in for the chorus (1:54), lending a humanizing influence to the previously soulless-sounding tune. Doheny notes that at the climax of the song, the chorus, the "mood . . . [swings] completely from irony to evocation to rallying call,"[41] offering hope and an escape for those betrayed: "we ride tonight, ghost horses." The subject includes the listener for the first time, singing the more inclusive "we ride tonight" (2:01) instead of the accusatory "you." Along with this inclusiveness comes a warmer chord progression emphasizing C-sharp and G-sharp (with no third, making it neither major nor minor). The vocals alternate between the pitches C-sharp and E, with the fifths G-sharp and B above in harmony. The E in the voice is supported by an E-major chord (related by third to the C-sharp) in the piano, which moves to an F-sharp to create a seventh dissonance (F-sharp to E) before moving back to the C-sharp. Even though F-sharp is the subdominant rather than the dominant of C-sharp, which would tonicize the main key in traditional harmony, this progression is still more stable than the earlier circle of fifths because it emphasizes a single tonic. The chorus ends with the repeated words "ghost horses" (2:49) on the falling pitches C, B, A, G-sharp, with a second voice in harmony a sixth above (after the initial fifth of G-sharp above the C-sharp, the voice stays on G-sharp and then moves to F-sharp and finally E). This "ghost" voice is a return to the falsetto "oohs" in "Pyramid Song" as well as the wordless sections of "How to Disappear Completely" and "Optimistic." The voice and accompanying instruments (just a subdued piano by the end) conclude the song together for the first time thus far on the album. Again, although the listener may be comforted by this peaceful ending, it does not mean that the subject is vibrant and has attained some kind of happiness. Rather, the subject, who has died over and over again, first consumed by the noise of the violent musical texture of "How to Disappear Completely," then choosing suicide in "Motion Picture Soundtrack," here is attempting to escape on a "ghost horse," being already dead from the beginning of the album. The false cheer of the rallying cry, "we ride tonight," leads only to another futile attempt at escape: a "ghost horse" that is intangible and ethereal and cannot bear the subject's weight. There is no escape within the modern human condition, just as there is no escape for Radiohead itself trapped inside the capitalist machine.

"I MIGHT BE WRONG"

The falsely hopeful attitude expressed in "You and Whose Army?" is undermined by the next song, "I Might Be Wrong," track five, in which even the title is an admission of insecurity. The structure of "I Might Be Wrong" is intro (synthesizer/guitar/drums), verse one ("I might be wrong"), pre-chorus[42] ("open up"), chorus ("let's go down"), verse two ("what would I do"; second half is truncated), pre-chorus, chorus, bridge ("keep it moving"), instrumental break, and outro/coda ("aah"). The song begins somewhat tentatively, with a few synthesizer notes outlining a D^7 chord (no third) that are followed by a rhythmic guitar riff (0:15; see example 5.3) and a drum kit four measures later

5.3. "I Might Be Wrong," guitar riff

(0:24). Rather than gradually accumulating, the groove instead coalesces immediately after the free-time intro. The emphasis on rhythm links this song to "Packt Like Sardines," and the first verse refers back to the empty search for enlightenment in the earlier song ("after years of waiting, nothing came"). Here, the subject states at 0:33 that "I might be wrong, I could have sworn I saw a light coming on." The subject thinks he has caught a glimpse of the light of enlightenment, a utopian flame that he senses but can't quite catch hold of, unsure of whether it is real or an illusion.[43] This light could also represent a reanimation of the subject's defeated spirit, but that light has been extinguished for good, and the subject admits as much. The next line (0:56) recalls the nihilism of *Kid A* but suggests that the subject has moved on: "I used to think there is no future left at all." The next "I used to think" is then cut off at 1:12, lending ambiguity to the lyrics: has the subject ceased to think at all? This part of the verse can, alternatively, be read as separate statements: "I used to think" and "there is no future left at all." The pre-chorus begins at 1:16 with the words "open up, begin again" in falsetto, showing that the subject, rather than beginning anew, has been denaturalized and in fact emasculated. Though the subject seems to be reminding himself to leave his previous nihilism behind, the higher voice sounds slightly hysterical, as though the subject has regressed to a childlike state. The chorus presents conflicting ideas: the imagery of "let's go down the waterfall" (1:32), which Footman links to the "fake idylls of 'Nice Dream' and 'In Limbo,'"[44] suggests risk-taking behavior, but also a return to the natural sublime, with a current of inevitability as the subject races headlong over the edge of the cliff. The next line, "think about the good times, never look back" (1:40), recalls the hedonism of "Idioteque" ("here I'm allowed everything all of the time").

In the second verse (1:57), the singer addresses the unnamed "you," on whom he seems to rely, asking "What would I do . . . if I did not have you?" The subject could be speaking to Radiohead's listening audience, a sarcastic question since although within the capitalist culture an album would have no reason to exist without someone to buy it, the band has consistently articulated a message of resistance against that very culture. Instead of an appreciation of the listener's purchase, the statement becomes a defiant suggestion that perhaps the band could be doing something more productive with their time than simply producing albums to be consumed. Since the verse ends after these words, the subject does not provide an answer to his rhetorical question. In the second pre-chorus, "open up and let me in," the singer continues to address the unnamed person, and the chorus furthers the notion of an interaction between the subject and another, suggesting again the trip down the waterfall, where they can "have ourselves a good time, it's nothing at all." These last words are repeated twice more ("nothing at all"), emphasizing the nihilistic viewpoint of the singer and providing a link to the earlier statement that "there is no future left at all."

The song's harmony is based in D minor, and the voice continually returns to A, the fifth of the chord, throughout the verse, revealing the idea of the frozen scale degree five: the indecision of the lyrics is reflected in the voice's inability to descend from this scale degree. The voice ends on a D over the guitar riff (3:35), which is played for several measures of an instrumental break and then abruptly stops (3:47). After about four beats of silence, the guitar comes back to start a coda on a real melody (3:53); the drum machine joins it to provide a backing rhythm (4:02), and the voice eventually comes in on a falsetto "aah" (4:12). The vocal melody recalls the *homme fatal* motive from *Kid A*: A–F, A–F–G–B-flat–A on "aah" (see example 5.4). Here the

5.4. "I Might Be Wrong," voice in outro

subject sounds out of place, as though he is trying to find room in a musical texture that has moved on without him. In the songs of *Kid A*, the voice's A falls to F-sharp or G (the latter in "Motion Picture Soundtrack"), whereas here the voice instead circles the A with neighboring tones and then ends on the A, the fifth of the underlying D chord. The subject has moved up an octave, from one A to another, but functionally he has not moved on at all (despite the words "keep it moving" heard in the bridge). The guitar riff begins again just after the falsetto voice ends (4:30) and then carries the song until the end, when the guitar and drums stop at the same time.

Footman states that "I Might Be Wrong" "fulfills a similar function to 'How to Disappear Completely,' a relatively conventional song that startles because it sounds so out of place in the midst of all this experimental noisemongering."[45] "How to Disappear Completely" emerged uneasily out of the noise of the album's three previous songs, none of which had presented coherent lyrics, let alone a conventional verse/ chorus structure. Because of the straightforward song presentation, the subject on *Amnesiac* seems more clearly articulated, more fully present, if even less hopeful than that of *Kid A*. Rather than devouring the subject, in "I Might Be Wrong" the other instruments are indifferent to him, continuing on even when the vocals end and, to be yet more contrary, stopping the song after the subject suggests that they "keep it moving." The continued existence of the subject propels the album forward; there is no space between sides as on *Kid A*. The subject's zombie state, however, leads to a second-side single ("Knives Out") that is a simulacrum of death and decay. Although the subject has been fully present in one sense, in that his vocals are relatively undistorted and he has sung or spoken on all of the tracks thus far, he is spiritually dead and just as ambivalent to the world around him as the soundscape is to him. His exhortation to "keep it moving" (3:17), as half-heartedly issued as the "c'mon kids" of "Kid A" and sounding as though he is gritting his teeth as he sings it, could be an address to himself; rather than attempting to leave the album as he had on *Kid A* with "Treefingers," here he has decided to remain within the commodity of the album until the second side has been reached. The final falsetto recalls that of "How to Disappear Completely," suggesting that the subject is about to make his escape again, yet the vocalese is false because his statement has indicated that he is not going to abandon the texture this time. The subject has realized that he is bound to the commodity and that his success at survival within modern society is tied to the success of the album—ultimately measured in sales, but here gauged by whether it can retain its subject until the end of the final track.

AMNESIAC
AND BEYOND

Rather than next presenting a "hollow space" between imaginary sides, as *Kid A* does, *Amnesiac* instead proceeds immediately to its next single, track six, "Knives Out." In contrast to *Kid A*, here the second-side "single" is real, in the sense that it was actually released on its own to the public to promote the album. However, unlike "Optimistic," with its sloganistic, surface-positive lyrics, "Knives Out" makes no pretense at positivity. Thus it inverts the construction on *Kid A* to present a "false" version of a "true" single.

"KNIVES OUT"

The song begins with a catchy guitar riff over the stepwise, descending harmonic progression C minor–B-flat major–A-flat major–G minor–F major–E minor. The full band is present from the initial notes, presenting a single that could easily be heard on the radio. The ensemble seems to be "putting on a good face" so people will buy the album based on that first impression; a close listen to the lyrics, however, soon reveals the horrors behind the mask. The first line (0:19) draws the listener in with the words "I want you to know," followed by the statement that "he's not coming back," a reference to the subject who has been present throughout both *Kid A* and *Amnesiac*. The second line (0:38) brings the listener even closer, asking her to "look into my eyes." The singer then states that "*I'm* not coming back" (italics added), aligning himself with the subject and his insistence on *Kid A* that "I'm not here, this isn't happening." Rather than schizophrenia, here the singer recognizes that he and the subject are one, that their fates are the same.

The chorus (0:57) presents a different harmonic progression, with a series of chords that transform from minor to major in order to create the dominant for a temporary tonic: A minor becomes A major, which tonicizes D minor; D minor moves to D major, which tonicizes G major. The chorus ends on E minor, also the ending chord of the verses, which leads back into the C minor of the verse (as a third-related chord rather than a dominant). Over these chords, the voice sings a melody with the chromatic pitches C-sharp and E-natural, notes that fit into the underlying chords but create a rupture in the diatonic line. The lyrics give instructions for surviving in the modern world, beginning with the command "knives out." Rather than defending herself against a perpetrator, however, the listener is instructed to "catch the mouse . . . shove it in your mouth." Verse two (1:22) notes that everyone is at the mercy of society: "if you'd been a dog, they would have drowned you at birth." The verse goes on to again ask the unnamed "you" to "look into my eyes" to discover the sincerity behind the words, because "it's the only way you'll know I'm telling the truth." Of course, this does not allow for the possibility that the subject could be lying. The band has created a real single with a falsely soothing return to the old guitar-driven sound; is the invitation to learn the truth a legitimate one, or are they simply trying to fool the listener? The lyrics restore the Enlightenment privileging of sight: only the eyes can see the truth. The irony is that the subject is beyond sight, technologically—in being represented through the recording—and existentially—in being no longer present. "Truth," which depends on the presence of the subject, forces "you" (the listener) to fend for "yourself" in a violent society in which we all look out only for ourselves. Here the premise of existence is self-preservation: "knives out, catch the mouse, don't look down, shove it in your mouth." You should eat without looking at what is being eaten, lest the horror be too great. Not looking down also ensures that someone else cannot surprise and kill you for the mouse. The lesson here is that because we are so intent on protecting ourselves and what is ours, we do not notice the destruction we must necessarily inflict on nature in order to survive—or, that humankind will always put the needs of its own small group over those of the larger civilization. Destroying the environment or eating the last of an endangered species does not matter so long as one's own stomach can be full.

The second chorus (2:00) furthers the violence, commanding the listener to "cook him up, squash his head, put him in the pot," an exploitation of the other constructed by culture's managing of nature. Whereas in the first chorus the listener was expected to eat the mouse raw, catching it and then immediately shoving it into her mouth, here she is at least allowed to cook it. Generally a pot is used to cook more than one thing at a time, so there is a possibility that the mouse is being added to a pot full of other mice; the excess of modern civilization is being celebrated as the listener accumulates more than enough food and begins to hoard it. An instrumental interlude (2:24) the length of a full verse comes in between the second chorus and the third verse. Rather than presenting a guitar solo, as a conventional single might, the accompaniment remains the same as that throughout the rest of the song—the stable musical space within which the subject is operating (again, the music exists apart from the subject). The third verse (3:03) is the most startling, repeating again the words "I want you to know he's not coming back," as if there were any doubt by now. A second voice comes in a third below for the words "not coming back," echoing the message with a declaration from the schizophrenic split in the subject. This time, the subject states that "he's bloated and frozen, still there's no point in letting it go to waste" (3:22). The subject himself is now to be cannibalized, creating a literal dog-eat-dog (or man-eat-man) society. The mouse/object has been displaced by the human/subject. Though undesirable and unappetizing under normal circumstances, as a "bloated and frozen" "it"—no longer a lyrical "I" or even a "he"—the subject can still be consumed.[1] There is an efficiency in exploiting nature, in that the damage we do to nature is a reflection of the damage we do to ourselves. As we strip the earth of its treasures, we are figuratively cannibalizing our own bodies. The last repetition of the chorus (3:42) makes clear how the subject's body will be used: "catch the mouse, squash his head, put him in the pot." Thus, it becomes clear that the "knives out" are to be used for butchering and serving up dinner. A link can be made here back to the fairy-tale Pied Piper of "Kid A," and the rats who were to follow the subject out of town. The subject has become like one of the "three blind mice" of another sinister children's fable, with an Enlightenment-style blindness corresponding to the inability to "see" the truth. The song ends right after the third chorus, as though the subject has nothing more to say on the matter; as in the aborted verse three of "Optimistic," with its "nervous, messed-up marionette," the horror of the imagery is too great to continue. Once the subject has literally been consumed, of course, there is no point in continuing the song. By releasing such a trauma-inducing song as a single, Radiohead may erase the traumas of the previous album, but it surely creates new ones.

"MORNING BELL/AMNESIAC"

After seeming to reconcile the schizophrenic split in "Knives Out," the subject returns to the theme of division and the longing for release in the next song, track seven, "Morning Bell/Amnesiac." *Amnesiac* itself cannibalizes not only the theme of the vanishing subject lost in modern technological society, but also the song "Morning Bell," the penultimate song on *Kid A*. The *Amnesiac* version exorcises the song's driving rhythm and changes its key to an alternation between A minor and C-sharp minor, from the A-major/-minor alternation on *Kid A*. The slowed-down rhythm emphasizes the vocals, which already sound hysterical when separated from the rhythmic harmony of the *Kid A* version. The alternating chords recall the tolling of a bell. James Doheny notes that on *Kid A* the harmonic rhythm takes five beats, while on *Amnesiac* it takes only two. Though recording technology has made it possible to create multiple versions of the same song, most often in the form of alternate mixes, the *Amnesiac* version of "Morning Bell" is given greater weight by virtue of its being the "title" track: "Morning Bell/Amnesiac."[2] Mark B. N. Hansen states that *Kid A*'s "Morning Bell" had been a "tour de force in vocalic doubling and complex fusion of fragmented voice with machinic instrumentals," thus forcing the voice to be subordinate to the instruments. In contrast, "'Morning Bell/Amnesiac' invests in the harmonic interchangeability of voice and instrumental sound . . . as if the band has simply lost its fear of vocalic imperialism."[3] This statement is true of *Amnesiac* in general, however, as the vocals remain audible and undistorted for much of the album.

In contrast to the version on *Kid A*, here the voice begins the song with no instrumental or rhythmic introduction. After his declaration that he's "not coming back" in the previous song, the subject makes his presence known immediately. The subject's continued presence makes the listener question his earlier statements, particularly his assertion that he is telling the truth; on the other hand, the subject may have called attention to the possibility of his own lying: it is impossible for the listener to see the eyes of the subject, given the recording medium; therefore, it is impossible to see that he has been lying. The keyboard accompaniment sounds like chiming bells, and a bass synthesizer enters the texture halfway through verse one with a low counter-melody that wends chromatically against the voice. The vocal line prolongs its resolution to E on the line "cut the kids in half" (1:38) stressing the neighbor tones around it (D-sharp and F-sharp) and sustaining the E for longer than it had on *Kid A*. The voice's plaintive repetitions of "release me" in the coda (2:08) occur on an A–F-sharp that recalls the *homme fatal* motive. Although the A does not fit into the G chord beneath it, the F-sharp does fit into the D chord. The overall effect is one of softly supporting the subject in his goal to be released, although that release may come only with death. Perhaps the subject's declaration in "Knives Out" that he was not coming back has been harder to achieve than he had initially thought, and he needs the help of the musical accompaniment to attempt to escape the form of the commodity.

Whereas the *Kid A* version of "Morning Bell" had a driving intensity, the *Amnesiac* version has desperation instead, with its lack of rhythm and its foregrounded vocals. The line "cut the kids in half" is particularly clear, and its resolution to E is poignant in that the voice-as-subject is making the choice to be released, rather than being subjected to the effects of the harsh musical environment as on *Kid A*. Doheny reads this line in the *Kid A* version as being the "heart-wrenching climax" of the song, but the line on *Amnesiac* as simply a "comically horrific denouncement of what we've suspected from the song's start."[4] That is, the subject is seen as a raging madman bent on revenge for the split with his spouse; after throwing the "clothes out on the lawn with the furniture," the final indignity is to divide up the children too. The resolution to E after "cut the kids in half" is ambiguous, meant to signify either a real solution or a mere surface fix to a deeper dilemma. The near-immediate return to the A-minor/C-sharp-minor alternation indicates that such a solution was only temporary, in any case. Placed here, after the statement that "he's/I'm not coming back" of "Knives Out," the plea in "Morning Bell" to "release me" takes on a new meaning: the subject seeks a release from the dog-eat-dog society of capitalism, in which he is at least figuratively being cannibalized. The "morning bell" can also evoke a monastic call to prayer. So the phrase "light another candle" signifies an appeal to a higher power after the bell for matins, or morning prayer, has rung. This light is also an image of enlightenment, which still has not been achieved. Whereas on *Kid A* the bell had led immediately to the escape of "Motion Picture Soundtrack," here there is no true release for the subject, as the subject himself becomes commodified in the next song.

"DOLLARS & CENTS"

"Dollars & Cents," track eight, is *Amnesiac's* most overt statement on capitalism; Radiohead makes a literal reference to the band as commerce in the chorus: "we are the dollars and cents, and the pounds and pence, and the mark and yen" (3:44). The fact that the dollar is listed first suggests that the U.S. is at the center of this universalizing global capitalism; "cents" is perhaps a pun on the "sense" of Enlightenment reason. This statement is followed by the words "we're gonna crack your little souls," a startling image for a normally nonvolatile system of commerce. Doheny describes this section of the song as the proponents of the No Logo movement rising up against globalists[5] ("we" being the No Logo proponents and "you" being the globalists). Tim Footman refers to "Dollars & Cents" as Radiohead's "first explicitly political song, taking on the identity of global antichrists like the WTO [World Trade Organization] and the IMF [International Monetary Fund]."[6] In this sense the band is speaking of the "common people" as a commodity for global capitalists. The song is somewhat freely composed; its lack of reoccurring verse or chorus presents a resistance to the commodity form of music embodied in the closed form of the pop song. Given that the song is about global capitalism, its critique may be anarchist, but it also becomes rather amorphous, the musical image of the disorganized masses. A seductive bass riff continues throughout the song under alternating B-major/-minor chords played on a strummed guitar and a heavy synthesizer that enters with the voice in verse one. Table 6.1 shows the interaction of the voice, instruments, and noise eruptions. The synthesizer enters with the voice's pitches and/or rhythms except where noted, when it brings a counter-melody in the fifth verse. The function of the second voice changes over the course of the song. At first it exists only as feedback behind the lead vocal, but it becomes a shouted counter-melody behind the first "quiet down" statement (verse three, 1:52), then harmony in thirds, and finally joins the synthesizer with a counter-melody for the words "quiet down" in the final verse.

The song can be parsed as six discrete verses, as shown in example 6.1. Because the chordal harmony is so static, it is more useful to examine the vocal line in order to make sense of the music. The general direction of the vocal line is shown by a slur. The pitch at the end of each slur represents the last note in a given lyrical statement. For the most part the voice ends on a chord member of the underlying B-major/-minor harmony (B, D-sharp, or F-sharp), but when it emphasizes a different pitch (such as the E in verse one or the G-natural in verse three), it creates a rupture in the texture. When the subject begins singing (0:12), he first states that "there are better things to talk about," hoping perhaps to distract from the horrors of having the knives out and then cutting the kids in half over the course of the previous two songs. He then suggests that the listener "be constructive," recalling the exhortation in "Optimistic" to "try the best you can." The melody of verse one emphasizes B and E; the latter pitch would function as a subdominant to the B chords but does not fit into the underlying harmony. Instead, the verse is left feeling unfinished as the voice ends on E. The second verse (1:09) ascends stepwise from the root of B to the sixth above but instead emphasizes the F-sharp that functions as the dominant. The lyrics listed in the published score for this verse, "even when it's only warnings, even when you're talking wargames," recall the phrase "we're not scaremongering, this is really happening" from *Kid A*'s "Idioteque." A comprehensive listing of Radiohead's lyrics on the website Radiohead At Ease[7] (this site's URL could also be parsed as Radiohead, A Tease, though "at ease" is a phrase from "Fitter Happier") transcribes this line as "even when he turn [*sic*] the water blue," referring perhaps to the frozen and bloated subject in the previous

TABLE 6.1. Noise Eruptions in "Dollars & Cents"

(X = entrance; O = exit)

CD timings	Intro 0:00	Verse 1 0:13	0:26	0:40	0:44	0:48	Verse 2 1:09	1:17	1:23	1:36
Guitar/bass	X									
Drums	X									
Voice		X								
"Noise"/synthesizer		X	O	X	O	X	O		X	
"Noise"/sound effects										X
Second voice								X (feedback)		

CD timings	Verse 3 1:53	2:24	Verse 4 2:35	Verse 5 3:02	3:30	Verse 6 3:44	4:12
Guitar/bass	(X)						
Drums	(X)						
Voice	(X)		X				
"Noise"/synthesizer	(X)			X (counter-melody)	O	X (voice in unison)	O
"Noise"/sound effects	(X)	O					
Second voice	X (shouting)	O	X (harmony)			X (second melody with synthesizer: "quiet down")	O

6.1. "Dollars & Cents," verses

song, and on the *I Might Be Wrong* live CD it sounds as though Yorke is singing "even when *you* turn the water blue" (italics added), recasting the listener as the subject. Regardless of the actual lyrics, as no official version has been issued by the band (the "official" Radiohead site does not give lyrics), the vocal line creates a disruption in this verse. The voice holds out a C-sharp (1:22), a major second against the root of the underlying B-major chord; this discordance is emphasized by a loud chord cluster played by the synthesizer. Each half of verse two ends on a note within the underlying B chord: B and D, respectively.

In verse three (1:52), the voice seems to be talking to the noise disrupting the texture with the phrase "why don't you quiet down," which is repeated four times, with the guitar, bass, and drum accompaniment growing louder each time. After initially confirming the B-major chord by outlining the triad, ending on D-sharp, the voice then emphasizes a G-natural. Behind the statements of "quiet down," a second voice is singing an unintelligible rant that ends with what seems to be the half-shouted word "free." The lyrics on Radiohead At Ease give a statement about democracy and being on the streets, seemingly speaking of a protest held by the common people. If these are indeed the lyrics to the background vocals, then the command to "quiet down" could be read as a command from the government leaders for the crowds to stop their protest. All the instruments except the bass (on the same riff) and the drums drop out for the interlude before verse four (2:27). The next verse (2:34), which the score transcribes as "you don't live in a business world," employs vocal harmonies in thirds to sweeten the texture. The subject chastises the listener for not being able to understand his situation, an ironic statement since although the subject may live in a "business world," a world of commerce and commodity, he does not fit into it easily and has himself become only a commodity within it. Addressing the listener as "babe" at the end of the verse seems insincere and out of character for the band, despite the change to a major-third harmony, normally a marker of sincerity, in that the major mode connotes positivity. Perhaps the only expression of humanity left in the music is the commodification of the infantile love object, expressed throughout pop music in songs such as "Baby You Can Drive My Car," "Be My Baby," "I Got You Babe," etc. The vocals in this verse more than any other confirm the underlying harmonies, at first singing in thirds on D-natural and F-sharp (from B minor) but then ending the verse on B and D-sharp (from B major). Ending a phrase on the major triad is a typical device even in Western art music (the Picardy third, in which the third of the tonic is raised a half-step to make the final chord major, dates from at least the time of Bach, if not earlier) and makes the piece seem to have a happy ending. The harmony here moves immediately back to B minor, erasing the harmonious B-major sound from the listener's ears, or at least creating further ambiguity.

The lyrics of verse four (3:02) are largely unintelligible, but the guitar/tablature/vocal score to the album[8] gives them as "it's all over, baby's crying . . . all over the planet's dead" (the crying baby representing hunger, and the baby itself representing humanity's self-propagation). The one line of the verse that is easy to make out is "I can see out of here . . . let me out of here." Despite the ambiguity of the other lyrics, the subject's cry for release is comprehensible, and a second voice comes in on the second "out of here," emphasizing the split in the subject's psyche as he tries to make sense of modern life. This verse emphasizes B minor, with the voice largely focused on D-natural. Against the vocal line is a soaring synthesizer line that ends on an F-sharp, the fifth of B minor. In *Amnesiac* the synthesizer almost becomes another protagonist, as it is given its own prominent counter-melody in several songs. The voice makes one last statement, "all over the world" (3:30), outlining B major again, and studio effects make the words echo after their initial statement. The guitar chords move immediately back to B minor for the final verse. Whereas the melody of the first five verses had been focused around B, the root of the underlying harmonies, the final verse (3:44), "we are the dollars and cents," hammers out a rhythm on F-sharp. The riff of the vocals occasionally lines up with that of the guitar (see example 6.2). The song's melody constricts as the message tightens to a slogan that, rather than a puffed-up, false message as on "Optimistic," acknowledges the reality of the world, that our true value to society is our economic worth. Over this new vocal riff, presented almost as a chant, is the soaring "quiet down" melody. The subject's "true" message about being reduced to a commodity is being silenced by the counter-melody above, which is joined by a synthesizer in unison. The melody that the listener might want to sing along to ("quiet down") is an imposition by the "false" world of pop music onto the

* = lines up with riff

6.2. "Dollars & Cents," guitar riff and rhythm of voice

"real" message that pop music is just a commodity, the literal "dollars and cents." Mapping this message onto the human condition means that humankind itself is only a commodity to be exchanged for dollars and cents by those in power. The subject makes one final statement (4:12) over just the guitar line—"we are the dollars and cents"—forcing his message to outlast the melody. The guitar line and a few stray cymbal noises end the song quietly, as though the music is petering out after the realization that there is no meaning to it beyond its status as a commodity.

"HUNTING BEARS"

"Hunting Bears," track nine, recalls the "all music, no lyrics" form of "Treefingers," though it occurs after the "capitalist triptych" of "Knives Out," "Morning Bell/Amnesiac," and "Dollars & Cents" rather than at the midpoint of the album as "Treefingers" had. Doheny calls "Hunting Bears" a "timbral tone poem,"[9] words that could also be used to describe "Treefingers." After the lack of "real" (i.e., nonfiltered) guitars in *Kid A*, "Hunting Bears" presents sounds that are so clearly made by guitars that the sound of the player's fingers moving along the strings is audible. The body is reclaimed here as it was in the opening breath of "You and Whose Army?" Like the singer's breath, however, the sounds are only signs—that is, representations—of human presence, or authenticity; despite these sounds of live performance, the album remains a recording. Ironically, the subject is absent from this song, though the title "Hunting Bears" implies some kind of action. The action implied is ambiguous: the bears are as likely to be hunt*ing* as being hunt*ed*. Images of grimacing cartoon bears had appeared in the limited-edition release of *Kid A*; Hainge discusses these images along with the Minotaur of *Amnesiac*'s packaging as problematizing the idea of nostalgia: the menacing bears evoke a childhood of "trauma that we do not wish to go back to,"[10] and they likewise evoke the trauma of *Kid A*. The menacing bears could be seen as hunting the subject. Since the subject is absent from this song, perhaps the bears have already caught and eaten him, "squashed his head, thrown him in the pot." This action can be mapped onto the band members' feelings at this point in their career, as being hunted by the critics, the media, or even their audience, in danger of being smothered with adulation.[11]

This instrumental piece is in D minor, with the guitar providing a low D drone under its higher melody. The noise of the fingers sliding along the strings makes it sound as though the player is searching for the correct notes. The free meter lends a contemplative air to the piece. The whole piece is repeated, and about halfway through the repetition, quiet synthesizer chords enter the texture, providing a slight accompaniment to the guitar gesturing. The piece could be heard as being in rounded binary (a repeated A and B followed by a truncated A; the whole piece is then repeated); the first ("A") section contains a reoccurring riff suggesting D minor that moves D–G–A–D, D–G–A–C–D–C–A (see example 6.3), and this motive returns at the very end

6.3. "Hunting Bears," guitar in "A" section

of the B section (0:56 and 1:53) to make the piece sound complete. The B section (0:32 and 1:29) emphasizes E and A, indicating a move to the dominant of A. Any real tonality is simply implied, however, as there are no true cadences or harmonic progressions. It is somewhat ironic that a song with the most overt marker of the "rock" sound, the electric guitar, abandons the traditional pop form of verse/chorus in favor of a more classical structure. It is as though the guitar that had been jettisoned from *Kid A* (by virtue of being filtered to death) has reappeared here in its true, undistorted form, claiming the musical space from the voice. The guitar-only song could also serve as distraction from the statement of the real form of the commodity at the end of the last song. If the voice is going to make statements of truth, then another instrument must claim the sonic space from it to distract the listener.

"LIKE SPINNING PLATES"

Next to the rhythmless "Hunting Bears," the heavily rhythmic, spliced-up intro to "Like Spinning Plates," track ten, is that much more striking, and recalls the "gamelan" sound of "Packt Like Sardines." Although the rhythm is incessant for the first half of the song, it too feels out of time, even though the published score notates it in $\frac{4}{4}$. The song is slight in its vocal presentation, presenting only a single verse and a chorus between a long intro and a short outro. "Like Spinning Plates" begins with sounds that evoke a movie reel being spun backwards, so that it only gradually coalesces into an image that makes sense. An eighth-note pattern of alternating octaves begins at 0:20 to establish the rhythm, then a few chiming tones enter at 0:49 before a longer synthesizer note (recalling the coda of "Motion Picture Soundtrack") provides a flourish of sound above the texture at 1:32, just before the vocals come in at 1:46. The harmony of "Like Spinning Plates" was constructed by playing a song called "I Will" (which was first heard in *Meeting People Is Easy* and would appear on the later album *Hail to the Thief*, backwards); Thom Yorke then wrote new lyrics based on the phonics of the backwards (cannibalized) melody.[12] The lyrics speak to politics and the harsh truth behind them: "while you make pretty speeches, I'm being cut to shreds." In the next line (2:07), the subject is being "fed to the lions." The person making the "pretty speeches" could be a government leader, with the "lions" representing the cogs of the capitalist wheel. The lyrics have a double meaning, however, as the "pretty speeches" could also refer to the words of the subject himself, and the "lions" to the record industry that rips the soul from the artist, or the audience that consumes the commodity by buying it. The melody is in G-sharp but has a Middle Eastern feel to it due to wending through chromatic pitches. Each line of the verse ends on G-sharp, lending the melody a temporary stability. The rhythm of the alternating octaves continues throughout the verse, adding to the choppiness of the vocal. A synthesizer chord enters the texture between lines of the verse but retreats when the voice reenters. The verse has no chords under its chromatic melody until the last word or syllable of each line, when the synthesizer comes in; this lack of harmony adds to the starkness of the song.

The vocals of the verse are muted and distorted, using a covered tone, as though they are still backwards, but the subject's voice grows clear at the chorus (2:28): "this just feels like spinning plates." Again the "real" is poking through, just as the statement "we are the dollars and cents" had emerged from the distraction of the command to "quiet down." The image of spinning plates evokes a variety-show juggling act, a pointless and anxiety-producing activity, much as the act of listening to the album produces an anxiety in the listener and any act of interpretation seems both necessary *and* impossible. The melody leaps to a high G-sharp for the word "plates," an example of text-painting as the voice mimics the altitude of the spinning plates. The phrase "spinning plates" has an unnatural break in the syllables, leaping a fourth (D-sharp to G-sharp) for the second syllable of "spinning." This puts an unnatural emphasis on the second syllable as well. Behind the voice, the synthesizer gradually swells and then diminishes; here, it sounds in unison with the subject rather than entering only after he has ceased singing. The subject next makes the statement "I'm living in cloud cuckoo land" (2:42), a reference to a fantasy world, but later sings "my body's floating down a muddy river" (3:09), a sign of the real, as the subject had been described as already dead in "Knives Out." This marks also the end of the subject's journey from "floating down the Liffey" in "How to Disappear Completely" to "jumping in the river" in "Pyramid Song." The body floating down the muddy river in the verse is a stark contrast to the chorus image of plates spinning in the air, bringing the subject immediately to ground. The vocal line for "cuckoo land" ends on D-sharp, the fifth of G-sharp major, sounding like a resolution, but the final ending of the song, on "river," from C-sharp to B-sharp, the third over the G-sharp-major chord, sounds incomplete and as though the subject has given up. The chorus's underlying chords move from A major to C-sharp minor (recalling the use of those chords in "Morning Bell/Amnesiac") and then back to G-sharp major—an atypical harmonic progression in Western art music that sounds stable here due to its repetition. A second voice enters for the second half of the chorus (2:49, on the first "land"), singing in unison with the subject—a return to the split in his personality evident in this second voice heard throughout the album. The subject sings the words "spinning plates" by himself, but the second voice returns for the line about the body floating down the river. The synthesizer continues to sound the progression from A major to C-sharp minor to G-sharp major as the alternating octaves grow louder in the texture, having been in the background all along. The song gradually fades out, floating away with the body of the subject.

"LIFE IN A GLASSHOUSE"

After beginning with a burst of synthesized tones similar to the music extraneous to the subject that had ended *Kid A*, "Life in a Glasshouse" brings back the horns (led by trumpeter Humphrey Lyttleton) from *Kid A*'s "The National Anthem," but this time the horns are in concert with the voice and present a unified accompaniment from their initial entrance. The voice in the verse seems more like another ensemble instrument than a lead, with its chromaticism winding around that of the other instruments. The bluesy sound of the instruments accompanying the singer gives the air of a jazz funeral, providing a counterpoint or sympathetic accompaniment to the singer's words. A bluesy piano riff with horns playing along begins the song in earnest at 0:20, and the subject enters at 0:29 with the words "once again, I'm in trouble with my only friend." The piano riff is notated in the score as being on the beat, with the vocals shifted slightly before or after the beat, but the actual experience of listening to the song produces the opposite effect. The voice is heard as being tied to the "real" beat, and the instruments as syncopated.[13] The lyrics suggest that someone (the subject's "only friend") is trying to help him overcome a mistake, presumably that of throwing a stone at his own glass house, since "she [the friend] is papering the windowpanes." The second verse (1:07) returns to the imagery of "Knives Out" with the words "packed like frozen food and battery hens," admonishing the listener to "think of all the starving millions" that could be fed with this unappetizing food. The subject admonishes "your royal highnesses" in the next line: "don't talk politics and don't throw stones." He is asking for compassion rather than politicizing the world's problems and casting blame for them. The subject and listener are equally frozen and packed like battery hens (or like "sardines in a crushd tin box"). Battery hens are raised in cages so small that they cannot spread their wings; their only purpose in life is to lay eggs, just as the band's only purpose is to produce albums to be consumed by the listening audience. The underlying melody of "Glasshouse" is rooted in A minor, but the added sevenths and the meandering melody that emphasizes the B destabilize the harmony. The voice's B-flat is added to the C-minor chord in the accompaniment, another seventh relationship that is common in jazz music. Although the voice ends on an A, nominally the tonic of the progression, the accompaniment plays an F-sharp-diminished chord, so that the A becomes the third rather than the root. The sudden move to a diminished chord at the end of the verse, a rare ending for a cadence in typical harmony, emphasizes the subject's sarcasm on the words "your royal highnesses" (1:39).

The words that begin the chorus, "well of course I'd like to sit around and chat," at 1:46, lend a false positivity to the subject's tone, along with the sudden move back to A minor after the F-sharp-diminished chord (a minor-third relationship that has A and C-natural in common). The underlying harmony includes the dominant of A (E moving to E^7), then moves to F before returning to A minor (another major-third relationship). Between statements by the voice, the jazz ensemble erupts into soloistic lines. Despite having articulated a plea for release throughout the album(s), here the subject expresses regret at needing to leave. He sings the same melody three times, with the same harmonies, and the other instruments drop out for the final line of the chorus (2:14): "there's someone listening in." Here, a cognitive dissonance is created; of course someone is listening—the person who bought the album and for whom it was originally produced. Yet the subject seems not to want anyone to listen, trying to cast off his status as a commodity. The rhythm of the accompaniment is more regular, as the horns play block chords under the chorus. At the line "there's someone listening in," the horns play a more discordant, arpeggiated rhythm. In contrast to the twice-voluntary leave-taking of *Kid A*, the subject here seems reluctant (at least on the surface) to bid farewell; his inability to stay is excused by the fact that "there's someone listening in." The vocal line's rhythm is fluid and contrasts with the squarer horn line. The vocal rhythm at the chorus is much more rhythmically rigid and moves A–B–C (the inverse of the *homme fatal* motive) instead of meandering through a B-flat as it had in the verse. The voice ends on a C above an A-minor chord, and the descending clarinet arpeggio immediately afterward creates a feeling of sudden instability.

The clarinet line and the syncopated piano/drum riff from before begin verse three (2:25), in which the subject observes that "once again we are hungry for a lynching"; someone is looking for a scapegoat, and the "hunger" evoked by this violence echoes the cannibalism of the earlier songs. The subject admonishes those looking for the lynching that they "should turn the other cheek, living in a glass house." The subject conflates "we" and "you" in making a statement about society's appetite for finding a scapegoat and casting stones while remaining open for scrutiny ourselves. In the final chorus/coda, the subject again expresses regret at not being able to stay because "there's someone listening in." The voice breaks out of its confined minor-third melody, moving to the F and E above the C (functioning as the fourth and third scale degrees above the note that the voice last articulated as tonic) at 3:31 for the repeated words "only, only, only, only, only, only" before again stating at 4:11 that "there's someone listening in." For these final words, the instruments cease to play, lending the same irony that came on "The National Anthem" when they all dropped out for the word "everyone" as though they were listening to the subject. The horns end the album with a blatted held A-minor chord, no "god music" this time as on *Kid A*. The ending of the vocal line uses the neighbor tones to C (B and D), which would seem to be tonicizing C but occur over an A-minor harmony. Footman notes that "the theme ('don't talk politics and don't throw stones') goes back to the central figure in [*OK Computer*'s] 'No Surprises,' a man who's given up the political fight and retreated into bourgeois conformity."[14] This is a surface reading, however; the subject is acutely aware that he cannot say too much (when he articulated the "real" earlier, the guitar took over the entire next song); the truth could only be spoken if someone were not "listening in," which is of course impossible given the status of the album as a recorded trace of his words. Rather than giving up, the subject is instead being cautious; after his mention of "frozen food and battery hens," he immediately censors himself: "don't talk politics." The final burst of jazz tones after the subject's last words lends an ominous air to the album's ending. Although the improvised jazz had once been heard as noise (on "The National Anthem"), here it has become the new ground within which the subject can move. Because the noise has the last "word," it also outlives the subject. Unlike on *Kid A*, the subject here is not coming back (as he told us in "Knives Out") and is in fact encased in a glass house. The subject is not concerned with people watching, but with them listening, which is both appropriate, encased as he is within the album, and ironic, for the glass house is airtight and the subject hermetically sealed.

"Life in a Glasshouse" can also be linked to the statement "I'm a reasonable man, get off my case" of "Packt Like Sardines." Doheny describes the message of "Life in a Glasshouse" as the "strange way that fame can both provide a privileged platform from which to speak, and at the same time be used to undermine the credibility of whatever might be said from it." The band is clearly aware of the contradiction between "railing against the greed of multi-national corporations" and "simultaneously collaborating with them in the creation of million-dollar fortunes for all concerned."[15] The band members have continually retreated from their own political statements: as Yorke has said, "I should shut the fuck up because it's pop music and it's not anything more than that."[16] The members of Radiohead themselves are the ones living in a glass house, and any criticism they make of the commodity culture can be lobbed back at them as hypocritical. The "someone listening in" at the end of each chorus is both literally the listener of the album (*Amnesiac* itself being the glass house) and figuratively the hegemonic scrutiny applied to those who would point out the world's problems: we too live in capitalism's glass house, and thus we cannot speak the truth without casting stones. To the extent that truth can appear, it appears only face-to-face, through the eyes ("look into my eyes, it's the only way you'll know I'm telling the truth") rather than in the words expressed. The last refuge of humanity occurs face-to-face,

I MIGHT BE WRONG · 163

when one can find what little truth of humanity remains by looking into the eyes of the other. Behind this idea, however, lies the ideal of authenticity, the suspicion of representation and of writing, and a belief in the power of presence (the mouth taking in breath, the fingers sliding down a guitar string). Yet, even in reading the truth from the eyes of the other, one is still "reading," that is, deferring the presence of the truth. In the same way, the listener "listening in" has become a form of Big Brother, an unwitting agent of capital by virtue of the very act of buying and consuming the album. This is perhaps the final irony: that we can only "see" the other and recognize the "truth" of that other's words insofar as the other is willing to let a Big Brother figure see, determine, and appropriate that truth. We are apparently left with the open "truth" of Big Brother, making what community we can out of it, or with the closed delusions of the self, an escape from the world that leads to the prison of self-delusion. Yorke's statement that "it's pop music and it's not anything more than that" breaks the spell of the commodity, the myth that the commodity is more than what it is, that we should look to public figures (whether entertainment celebrities or politicians) for our beliefs. Only our mythologizing discourse, a discourse promoted by the music industry, prevents us from recognizing the commodity character of the music we buy. Of course, Yorke should not be taken literally as saying that music ought therefore to simply give itself over to its commodity status; it must continue to resist the commodity form—not as a marker of authenticity that simply serves as the terms under which the mythologization takes place, but as a means of unveiling the very process of mythologization, the ways in which the commodity appears as the illusion of something more than a commodity. In the end, music as a commodity must become self-critical, must confess its commodity character without surrendering its utopian content: that the world could be otherwise.

Although *Amnesiac* succeeds as a resistant concept album, in the sense that the listener must puzzle out any sort of meaning without overt clues dropped by a named protagonist undergoing the trials and tribulations of a narrative, it is not, after all, an antidote for the bleakness of *Kid* A. Rather, it is an unsympathetic eulogy for a subject who is dead before the album even begins, a zombie who is animated only through the voice and by the fact of the listener's album purchase. Although *Amnesiac* does succeed to some extent in blurring the memory of the traumas of *Kid A*, foregrounding the voice and the guitar rather than burying them, it cannot completely obliterate the trauma of the modern condition. The message of the unredeemable subject remains clear throughout both albums, articulating a resistance against commodification while simultaneously stating that resistance is futile, that we are all ultimately both the cannibals and the cannibalized, we both consume and are consumed, and this is simply a fact of the modern human condition. The warmer and less distorted sound of *Amnesiac*'s "singles" functions merely as a mask for the nihilistic subject, whose humanity is unable to be redeemed in the face of commercialism. In the end the subject is, like the album and Radiohead itself, only a commodity, something to be exchanged for "dollars and cents" in the marketplace of modern society, a trauma that neither the band nor the listener can escape.

TRAPDOORS THAT YOU CAN'T COME BACK FROM: *AMNESIAC* AS A WHOLE

Although some authors have treated *Amnesiac* as a collection of disparate songs rather than an organized sequence with an underlying structure, Radiohead has stated that *Kid A* and *Amnesiac* are at least related, if not one huge album. Though it is not clear whether the two should be read in sequence, the latter should at least be considered as a companion piece that enriches the meaning found in the former. By virtue of its release after *Kid A*, *Amnesiac* thus becomes by default the consequent to the antecedent of *Kid A*, the solution to the problem presented by the lack of a subject. Footman states that *Amnesiac* "seems less of a sequel or companion piece . . . more of an indecently hasty remake. Which doesn't make it a waste, just something of a disappointment—although, if *Amnesiac* had been released first, opinions might well have been reversed." Doheny notes that if Radiohead had released *Kid A* as a double album, as they had considered, they would have prevented this misinterpretation[17] (although the order of the two discs would have had a similar effect). But although the songs of *Amnesiac* can be linked to and perhaps shed light on those of *Kid A*, there is no linear narrative to "solve" the problem posed on *Kid A*, that of the subject's would-be suicide or self-negation.

Looking from afar at the structures of the albums may aid our interpretation. Whereas *Kid A* starts tentatively, with a repeated keyboard melody, *Amnesiac* starts boldly with a loud, rhythmic gamelan figure. It takes just as long for the voice to enter, however, and we hear that the band has put one over on us again; rather than returning immediately to the conventional guitar-based, melody-driven sound of the earlier albums, Radiohead has presented another experimental anomaly in the rock music soundscape. Doheny discusses the song sequence of *Amnesiac* and how it relates to those of Radiohead's previous albums, making the case that *Amnesiac*'s sequence is not so different after all.[18] Greg Hainge, however, goes so far as to link the despair and anguish of *Amnesiac* to Jean-Paul Sartre's *Nausea*, in which the protagonist "undergoes a kind of breakdown following his realization of the terrible contingency of the universe." Eventually Sartre's subject realizes that his nausea can be cured only by a jazz melody that "seems . . . to have an internal coherence and justification, for every note in its melody needs to be in its place for the melody to work" (in other words, "everything in its right place"). Rather than presenting a solution, despite the jazz feel of the final "Life in a Glasshouse," Radiohead's music instead "serves merely to express this sense of being lost, to give voice to the space of trauma that modern man can feel when faced with a global economy in which the individual can have little effect."[19]

Although *Amnesiac* did present a salvation in the form of a warmer, non-filtered sound and songs that work as companion pieces, if not antidotes, to those of *Kid A*, the subject present on both albums is similarly damned in his position in modern society. The band toured in support of *Amnesiac* but included songs from *Kid A* in its set list as well. For many listeners, it took the tour to make sense of both albums by presenting selections from them together in performance. Apart from a few TV appearances and tour performances presenting earlier versions of some of the songs that would be released on *Kid A*, that album did not exist as a live performance until *Amnesiac* was released. Perhaps without the saving sound of the songs from *Amnesiac*, performing songs from *Kid A* would have further confused the audience and led them into a different kind of alienation, a distancing from the band rather than a shared "us against the world" mentality. Fans normally attend a concert with the expectation of hearing how the band treats album material live, hoping for a performance that matches the recording as closely as possible, but in this case they might have been looking to have the songs interpreted after not being able to make sense of them from the albums. Jonny Greenwood has stated that "the more concerts we do, the more dissatisfied we get with trying to reproduce the live sound on the record. In a way it can't be done and that's a relief, really. When you just accept that, recording becomes a different thing."[20] Amazingly, given the technology involved in the albums' production, Radiohead managed to realize the material live without resorting to hiring additional tour personnel. The band's performance of "The National Anthem" and "Idioteque" on *Saturday Night Live* in 2000 came across as an experimental music/art collective, with Jonny Greenwood furiously twiddling the knobs of his electronic equipment. Seeing the struggle between man and technology onstage brought the conflict expressed on *Kid A* and *Amnesiac* to life. The question remains whether the band's mastery of the electronic instruments lets them triumph over the dehumanizing influence of modern life, or whether their concert tour itself bound them more firmly to capitalism, as they were being paid to perform for the masses—who bought concert tickets, concession food, tour programs, and of course T-shirts.

Despite the supporting tour for *Amnesiac*, the album failed to sell in the numbers that *Kid A* had (though *Amnesiac* did reach number 1 on the U.K. charts and number 2 on the U.S. charts). Perhaps listeners were wary of being fooled again, despite Radiohead's promise of a return to the guitar-driven sound. It was no secret that the albums had been recorded during the same studio sessions, and the timing of *Amnesiac* only six months after *Kid A* might also have discouraged listeners from buying both if they did not like the first album. The tour, however, sold out across the U.S. Listeners were obviously eager to hear the band play live again after the long wait between the *OK Computer* tour (1997–98) and this one (2001). The band, too, seemed to have renewed energy, ready to give the crowds what they wanted instead of holing up petulantly and refusing to bow to commercial demands. Presumably the band had earned enough from the massive success of its second and third albums that there was no immediate financial need to tour. Too, the band members might have realized that it was to their benefit to keep their presence active in the minds of fans rather than retreating to the insular world of the studio. Joseph Tate notes that in the song "Dollars & Cents" from *Amnesiac*, the "we" of the statement "we are the dollars and cents" is "metaphorically Radiohead, a product we buy with pounds and pence."[21]

The tour rooted the band in a reality that the studio experience could not, which further breaks down the categories of the real and the unreal and brings full circle Jonny Greenwood's statement about all studio recording ultimately being equally unreal as a reproduction of acoustic/live sound. The touring experience humanized the band for its fans in a way that the studio album could not, and brought band and fans together in a group sense of alienation against the rest of society rather than isolating them from one another as well as from society. The band was quite willing to make money from selling tour merchandise, also sold through its subcompany W.A.S.T.E.[22] Now fans could declare their alienation on a T-shirt or hooded sweatshirt. Radiohead once declared that they would never again perform "Creep," after touring with it incessantly when it was a hit single. Now, however, they seemed to recognize the benefits of supporting their albums and singles on the road.

I MIGHT BE WRONG: LIVE RECORDINGS

After "reanimating" the subject of *Kid A* and *Amnesiac* with the live tour, Radiohead subsequently released a recording of several songs from the summer 2001 tour, entitled *I Might Be Wrong: Live Recordings*. The cover artwork of the album continues the imagery of the *Amnesiac* special-edition book, with typewritten fragments of words interspersed with hand-drawn and computer-generated artwork. A single weeping Minotaur, hand-drawn, covers his eyes and gnashes his teeth on the CD cover. When the cover is unfolded, a series of Minotaurs is replicated in the middle, as though they are mass-produced. The image of a multilevel bridge is behind the Minotaurs. The weeping man on the cover of *Amnesiac* has gained horns, teeth, and a tail and has been transformed into the Minotaur; the subject now has weapons at his disposal, but he still weeps at the human condition and at what he has become. The title of the live album, *I Might Be Wrong*, echoes that song from *Amnesiac*, and if put into the past tense, the phrase casts doubt on the preceding releases ("I *might have been* wrong," i.e., the band should not have released those two albums). The very fact that Radiohead took material that critics, fans, and even the band itself seemed at first to decry, and managed to perform the songs live at all, let alone on a sold-out tour, *and* issue a recording of them, indicates that *Kid A* and *Amnesiac* were actually smart marketing decisions. The strategy behind the live CD can be read in many ways. The decision to release a live album of songs that few deemed accessible on the first or even subsequent listens could be read as a cynical one, as the band dictating what their fans will buy because they realize that the insider culture created by their marketing strategy will demand that the album reach chart status by virtue of fans collecting it. Or, the band could have been trying to prove that its "experimental" albums were worth their salt by virtue of translating well into live performance. There is also an authenticity that comes from being able to replicate studio albums live, an authenticity that the Beatles never reached with *Sgt. Pepper*. Radiohead does not perform entire sets acoustically as did several of the 1990s acts seeking similar authenticity, but their live album is a triumph in a similar vein to the "Unplugged" acts that were once showcased on MTV.

The track sequence of *I Might Be Wrong*, as shown in table 6.2, mixes up songs from *Kid A* and *Amnesiac* and includes a newly recorded song, "True Love Waits," at the end of the album. Interspersing the tracks from both albums recontextualizes them and "proves" that a narrative can be created from any sequence of tracks. None of the singles from either album (real or imagined) appear here. The live recording begins with "The National Anthem," perhaps reminding the audience right off the bat that they are all together, alone, both at the Radiohead concert and in modern society. Being at a concert with other people, from just a few to the several thousand that typically attend a Radiohead show, creates a shared experience. Experiencing "The National Anthem" as part of that audience, even virtually by listening to the recording, furthers the illusion of the "insider" status that Radiohead's marketing has created as well as reminding people that

TABLE 6.2. Track Listing for *I Might Be Wrong: Live Recordings* (2001)

Track 1	"The National Anthem"	*Kid A*
Track 2	"I Might Be Wrong"	*Amnesiac*
Track 3	"Morning Bell"	Hybrid
Track 4	"Like Spinning Plates"	*Amnesiac*
Track 5	"Idioteque"	*Kid A*
Track 6	"Everything in Its Right Place"	*Kid A*
Track 7	"Dollars & Cents"	*Amnesiac*
Track 8	"True Love Waits"	New

they are trapped within capitalist culture. The song begins with radio noise in a foreign language, then the bass riff (distorted as though it is overloading the amp) comes in at 0:08. Synthesized horn noises and the ondes martenot come in at 0:19 before the voice at 0:46, which sings a series of rhythmic grunts before beginning the lyrics at 1:28. Unlike the original, which kept the interruptions to a minimum until the end, here the noise disrupts the lyrics before they even begin. Yorke's voice sounds strangled and hysterical as he sings the lyrics about "holding on." After each verse, he lapses into vocalese; it is not clear from the recording how much of this is being produced live and how much is pre-recorded. The cries on the high A–G-sharp near the end (3:18) sound even more pained, and a guitar solo enters the texture at 3:30 among the bass riff, drums, and ondes martenot. The voice babbles until the end, over the increasingly busy texture. The song ends with electronic sounds and the ondes martenot, then a high guitar screech at 4:40 that fades into ambient audience noise. A shaken tambourine provides a link to the next track, "I Might Be Wrong."

The placement of the "title track" as the second track on the album echoes the tentativeness of the title. Performing the song live before thousands of people (and as a live recording, potentially before millions) shows courage, however; the subject *might* have been wrong, but he is going forward with his message anyway. A burst of cheering erupts as the audience recognizes the opening bass riff. The lead vocals are muted, but the audience obviously recognizes the song. The main change from *Amnesiac*'s version to the live track is the addition of audience noise, begging the question of whether the crowd is agreeing that the singer might be wrong or is applauding him so he understands he has made the right decision. The addition of the spectators lends an extra dimension and makes the listener wonder whether they are cheering his decision or his indecision. The song ends abruptly with what sounds like the word "stop," and the crowd cheers wildly again; the noise leads into the next track as though the songs were actually played in sequence live, doubtful since the album was recorded at multiple locations on the band's world tour.

The third track, "Morning Bell," can be heard as a hybrid of the two versions heard on *Kid A* and *Amnesiac*. Doheny states that the live version on *I Might Be Wrong* uses "*Kid A*'s $\frac{5}{8}$ blues lament reading" but is a "far more swung version."[23] That is, the live version is performed at the quicker tempo of the *Kid A* version but sounds "warmer" by virtue of being a live recording. A loud guitar comes in for the verse beginning "where'd you park the car" (1:31) and sounds angry until the resolution to "round" (2:04), at which point the guitars' swirling descent sounds even more emphatic than on the album. The audience's cheers can be heard again during the move to "cut the kids in half" (2:12), when most of the non-vocal instruments drop out of the texture. This again begs the question of what the audience is cheering—is it simply that the home listener can hear the audience better at this point in the album because the band has grown quiet, or are they cheering the subject's proposed solution? Rather than the "dum dum dum" babble at the end of the song, we hear instead a chant that ends with the repeated words "walkin', walkin', walkin'" (2:46) along with a second voice that comes in with "dididid" above it. The "angry" guitar gradually takes over the texture, wailing and then screeching over the electric piano. Hansen states that on the live recording, "something like the effect of balance achieved via the acoustic mode of 'Morning Bell/Amnesiac' is wrought through second-order simulation."[24] That is, the band uses guitars to realize *Kid A*'s electronic sounds. It seems fitting that the one song that appears on both albums is heard after a song from each. The live version of "Morning Bell" functions as a symbol of the process of integrating both albums into some semblance of meaning for the listener. Just as the listener had to try to make sense of either album for herself, so too did the band have to learn to realize the recordings live in a way that was true enough to the studio work to be satisfying but was also reinterpreted in a way that was true to the band's artistic ideals. One can surmise that an acoustic version of, say, "Treefingers" on piano might not produce the same effect in the listener as hearing the original in the right context might.

Cheering again provides the bridge between tracks, as a gentle piano melody begins track four, "Like Spinning Plates." This song may have required the most modification from recording to live performance, given that Yorke's original vocals were spliced together from a backwards melody; the instrumentation has also been completely changed. Synthesized strings enter the texture after over a minute of solo piano (at about 1:00) but fade in and out throughout the rest of the song. The voice finally enters at 1:27, and this time the lyrics are clearly understood. The song gradually builds to the second repetition of "this just feels like spinning plates" (2:34), and the strings come back in for the line "my body's floating down a muddy river" (2:50). The live version of the song can be heard as more of a poignant lament than the recorded one, which was wholly electronic, whereas the live one is wholly "organic" (apart from the synthesized strings). The original version also featured a long introduction, with the voice entering at about 1:45. As the ending to the virtual side one of the live album (that is, if the album is divided in half by the number of songs, though the vinyl version of the album actually ends with "Idioteque" for side one), the song provokes anxiety and can be read as the subject's comment on wanting to escape from reality as he did in the two studio albums. He is staying present in modern life, but "it feels like spinning plates"; that is, his existence is tentative and unstable like the plates balanced high on a pole. The challenge is to keep his balance as well as his sanity in the modern human condition.

The second half of the CD begins with "Idioteque," here the simulacrum of a side-two single. The song is fully realized with a heavy techno beat and evokes the dance clubs where it would make for good entertainment. After the initial beat, the audience again erupts in a cheer. In a virtual sense, they are welcoming the album's second single (this placement works even on the vinyl recording, if George Martin's advice to "go out with a bang" at the end of side one is followed). A loud, syncopated keyboard part is added to the texture above the beats used on the original recording. Again the vocals are clearer here than on the original, and the singer's breath is audible, snatched between words as he strives to articulate the apocalyptic message. The texture is reduced at the verse that begins with "ice age coming" (1:40), and the singer's angry tone is echoed in the crowd, who is singing along. It could be argued that the fans are simply latching on to the familiar words, rather than actually understanding the desperately important message. The crowd's voices are not audible for the chorus (2:21), "here I'm allowed everything all of the time," but this is probably simply because the music is too loud for them to be heard. After the final chorus, the texture breaks down at 2:54 into howling electronic sounds over the incessant techno beat and another eruption of audience noise. The singer comes back in for "the first of the children" (3:31), which he stutters until the end of the song.

Track six is "Everything in Its Right Place," which had opened *Kid A*. At the end of the previous track, between the songs, we hear the first words spoken from band member to audience, or rather muttered, which end with "okay, okay." Here, the song seems to start winding down the album by presenting the message that, despite the subject's earlier anxiety, he has now found his rightful place in society. The pace of the song also slows down from the frenetic tempo of "Idioteque." The song begins with the sung (and presumably improvised) words "here comes the flood" over undulating guitar/keyboard tones; after Yorke intones "one, two, three," the original piano melody from "Everything" begins at 0:49. The crowd immediately starts clapping along in recognition, erasing the memory of the lonely experience of *Kid A*'s opener. The singer's voice echoes after each initial statement of "everything" (1:08), but the delay seems to come from recording the live vocal as it happens rather than from prerecording. This delayed echoing of the voice reoccurs throughout the song, repeating the words that were sung just before it. The mix of the keyboard higher in the texture makes it sound as though it is supporting the voice. At the second series of "everything" repetitions (2:08), other sounds begin to disrupt the texture, sounding like old orchestra tapes being played backwards or howling voices or bursts of radio static. The noise becomes more active with the words "tried to say" (2:53) and a babbling voice continues below the held tone of the final "say" (3:21), then is spliced up and played back over itself to the point where we wonder whether the band has manipulated the recording in the studio. Layers of spliced vocals weave in and out as though the subject is lost in a labyrinth of mirrors, seeing himself reflected and distorted until he does not know which "he" is the original anymore. After an extended sonic collage of distorted vocals, electronic sounds take over the texture and distort the vocals even further, mimicking the sound of the singer on helium. Eventually the sounds fade to just the distorted electronic piano and static, followed by crowd noise (relief that the song is over?). This version of "Everything" clocks in at 7:42, nearly double the 4:11 of the original.

After reassuring the listener that everything is in its right place, the next track, the final offering from one of the studio albums, is "Dollars & Cents." Perhaps that "right place" is, after all, the place of the commodity. With this final song from the resistant album pair, Radiohead underscores its own status as something to be bought and sold in a capitalist society: "*we* are the dollars and cents" (italics added). The song begins with cheering at the familiar theme (despite the fact that none of these songs were released as singles). A loud keyboard tone enters the texture along with the words "there are better things" (0:12) and maintains its presence until the end of that verse. The vocal presentation is fairly straightforward, articulating each verse in turn as in the original. The shift between major and minor in the accompanying riff is more audible here than on the studio album, underscoring the ambiguity of the message. During the plea/command to "quiet down" (1:49), the drums grow louder, seeming to resist as they play a free rhythm, but then at the final command "quiet down" (2:17) the texture drops back drastically, as though the instruments are finally listening to the singer. The crowd noise is audible here in their absence. A quiet second voice enters for the fourth verse (2:32), but the words are nearly incomprehensible. As the fifth verse begins (2:59), a loud keyboard counter-melody enters just before the voice, providing a nice contrast. The final verse (3:40) provides the same contrast between the "quiet down" voice and the one stating that "we are the dollars and cents," the latter erupting with a shout on "crack" in the line "crack your little skulls" (transformed from the "little souls" of the original). The song ends with an extended guitar riff on the major/minor alternation along with tambourine (4:07) and ends with a crash that sounds as though the music has hit a wall, followed by cheering.

Just as *Kid A* had presented a "final final" song in the music heard after "Motion Picture Soundtrack," *I Might Be Wrong* presents an "encore" of "True Love Waits," a straightforward voice-and-acoustic-guitar piece that presents a marked contrast to the songs of *Kid A* and *Amnesiac* and even to much of the band's earlier material. The song only occasionally lets the crowd noise (whistling) break through, sounding almost like a studio recording otherwise. Yorke ends "True Love Waits" by saying "Thank you, everybody. G'night," a further recreation of the concert experience for the CD listener. Thus the song functions as a simulacrum of an interaction between singer and audience. Instead of evoking robots, aliens, or cannibalism, the song describes a lover with "tiny hands" and a "crazy kitten smile" (1:59). Despite the subject's statement that "I'm not living, I'm just killing time" (1:35), he pleads "just don't leave" in the chorus (1:09, 2:20, and 3:54), perhaps a feigned request for the audience to stay after the encore. This statement is ironic given the subject's own leave-taking over the course of two full albums and his crass statement that "I think you're crazy, maybe," in the chorus of "Motion Picture Soundtrack." Too, he seems not to care anymore that someone might be "listening in," as on "Life in a Glasshouse." On *I Might Be Wrong*, of course someone is listening in, because the songs were recorded live. Perhaps it has taken the live audience for the subject to feel comfortable expressing the "human" feelings of love and regret.

According to the Radiohead fan site Green Plastic, the band had been performing "True Love Waits" since even before *OK Computer*'s release, but its inclusion on *I Might Be Wrong* marks its first availability for sale.[25] The website setlist.fm is a searchable resource to which concert attendees can upload set lists from events they have attended; it lists "True Love Waits" as being performed at twenty-one of 391 shows (though only once prior to 2001), always in an encore.[26] Green Plastic calls this song "one of the most requested live songs that Radiohead has in their catalog," despite the fact that it had never been recorded in a studio and was released only in 2001; clearly having knowledge of the song and being able to request it is the mark of an insider.[27] Ed

O'Brien noted in his online diary in 2000 that the song had been "kicking around for about four years now."[28] It is possible that this song is a character piece, that is, one written from the perspective of someone unrelated to the subject of the rest of the *Kid A*- and *Amnesiac*-based set (such as songs from classic concept albums like *Tommy*: "Acid Queen," "Fiddle About," etc.). Yorke has said that the image of "lollipops and crisps" (British for "potato chips") comes from a newspaper story in which a young child was locked in his house for a week and survived on junk food. In this case, the line "true love waits in haunted attics, and true love lives on lollipops and crisps" (3:09) becomes a sinister image: that of the abandoned and forgotten child slowly dying as he waits for his parent to return. This image could be extended to the subject's entrapment within the album, longing for release, or to the band's own status within the record industry. The comments about the song on the band's official website, quoted on Radiohead At Ease, state: "you, like everyone else [*sic*] need to feel important."[29] The quote could refer to the original abandoned child, as it comes immediately after a mention of the origin of the "lollipops and crisps" line, but it could also be a veiled message to the listener. Yes, everyone needs to feel important, but Radiohead's work continually reminds us that we are all mere cogs within the capitalist machine. Any voice coming from the subject, abandoned in the attic, is simply a child's plea (like the baby cry at the end of "Kid A"), left to be unheard or disregarded. Like the subject's longing for "true love," any hope of escape from modern culture is doomed to failure. His promise to "drown his beliefs" (0:26) and "dress like your niece and wash your swollen feet" (0:48) is a hollow one, as his beliefs can never be wholly abolished because true doublethink is not possible. Given the conflation of the subject with the adult male singer, we can assume that the subject has reached maturity, and that even if he dresses as a child he will still be an adult. Yorke addressed the "niece" line by saying that "the difference between young and old [is] when people start to dress sensible and act their age. this person is offering not to do that to keep the other. alles klarr?"[30] Yorke's "alles klarr" quip underscores the ambiguity present in much of Radiohead's work, that appeal to the insider that is so crucial to the band's marketing strategy. Of *course* the meaning is not clear, because Yorke refuses to make it so, and his statement is a cynical crack at those who try to puzzle out the meaning of his words even as it brings together those who think they *do* understand. The implication of Yorke's statement is that the subject's act of trying to change himself to keep a loved one (calling into question the notion of "true love") will ultimately fail; his words can also be read as a statement against trying to change the band's sound in order to please the listener.

After *Kid A* and *Amnesiac*, many fans probably longed for a return to the band's old sound, but despite the band's statements saying they were going to return to that sound and start conforming to listener and industry expectations yet again, that was not to be. Similarly, the subject's declaration that he will change for his loved one is also doomed to fail. The imagery of the niece's clothes and the lollipops and crisps recalls the reversion to childhood nonsense and babble that occurred on *Kid A*, particularly on "Everything in Its Right Place" and "Idioteque," and even at the end of "Morning Bell." Since the subject does not actually revert to babble here, he has triumphed over it and moved on to adulthood along with the band. This longing for the innocence of childhood, while realizing that beneath the surface innocence of the fairy tale lurks the heart of darkness, would permeate the next Radiohead album, *Hail to the Thief.*

RADIOHEAD AS COMMODITY

Radiohead has continued its articulation of resistance against the record industry since the release of *Kid A* and *Amnesiac*. For their sixth studio album, *Hail to the Thief* (2003), the band once again promised a return to the guitar-driven sound, at first glance an apparent dismissal of the two "resistant" albums as anomalous despite the success of the supporting tour and its live album. Thom Yorke has stated that the sound of *Hail to the Thief* is "*OK Computer 2*," though in terms of album packaging and lyrics *Hail to the Thief* was just as obscure as, and possibly more sinister than, the band's previous two releases. Despite its similar opacity, however, this album went to number 1 in the charts. Yorke went on to say that "What we will do from now on, should not be anything like we've done before. . . . Radiohead will be completely unrecognizable in two years. At least, I hope so. It's the only perspective of the future that I can live with."[1] Thus he acknowledged that, rather than being an aberration, a mere blip in Radiohead's output, *Kid A* and *Amnesiac* represented an early signal for the band's new direction. Ed O'Brien seems to agree with Yorke's assessment, saying that *Hail to the Thief* is "the end of an era."[2] Yorke's and O'Brien's comments could be taken as a reflection of their boredom with the band as it was, a reluctance to stay with the same musicians they had played with since their teens, or as a rebuke of the record industry and the capitalist culture within which Radiohead and every other musical act must function in order to survive. In the end, however, just as the subject must continue to plod on despite his dissatisfaction with his life, so too must the band members continue to find a way to maintain peace with the record industry if they are to continue their careers as musicians.

HAIL TO THE THIEF

Allan F. Moore and Anwar Ibrahim note that opinion is divided on "whether *Hail* is the 'real' successor to *OK Computer*, with the more extreme experimentation of the *Kid A/Amnesiac* sessions the work of a band fleeing the responsibility of writing a 'proper' follow-up, or that *Hail* is somehow the inevitable outcome of these albums, in the same way as Radiohead viewed *Kid A* as the only way forward from *OK Computer*."[3] Table 7.1 shows the song placement on Radiohead's first six studio albums; *Hail to the Thief* returns to the conventional formula of presenting a single as the first song and interspersing others throughout the tracks. The three singles of *Hail to the Thief* charted similarly to those from *Amnesiac*, just as both albums had gone to number 1; thus, any deviation in the band's sound was not reflected in the fans' purchases of their recorded material. Either fans were willing to follow the band's output, sheep-like, purchasing anything it produced, or they were supportive of the band's new direction. The possibility also remains that even non-fans were compelled to buy albums that they might have heard were different in some way from the mainstream. *Hail to the Thief* presents, at least on the surface, a further defragmenting of the narrative expected from a conventional album, concept or otherwise. The cover art and booklet that accompany the special edition of the album present a series of maps that serve not to clarify but rather to further obscure any meaning. Joseph Tate has described the album in terms of Gilles Deleuze and Félix Guattari's "rhyzomatics," a way of looking at something as a series of connections from any one point to any other rather than as a clear linear path or progression.[4] Davis Schneiderman also notes the use of this strategy on the band's website.[5] This way of reading *Hail to the Thief* neglects the music altogether in favor of the lyrics, although it does open up the text to multiple possibilities rather than pinning a single narrative on it. The labyrinth of the Minotaur, the point on *Amnesiac* from which "he's not coming back," has become instead an open system with no

TABLE 7.1. Song Placement on Radiohead Albums (singles are in bold)

Track	Pablo Honey (1993)	The Bends (1995)	OK Computer (1997)	Kid A (2000)	Amnesiac (2001)[1]	Hail to the Thief (2003)[2]
1	"You"	"Planet Telex"	**"Airbag"**	"Everything in Its Right Place"	"Packt Like Sardines in a Crushd Tin Box"	**"2 + 2 = 5"**
2	**"Creep"**	**"The Bends"**	**"Paranoid Android"**	"Kid A"	**"Pyramid Song"**	"Sit Down, Stand Up."
3	"How Do You?"	**"High and Dry"**	"Subterranean Homesick Alien"	"The National Anthem"	"Pull/Pull Revolving Doors"	"Sail to the Moon"
4	**"Stop Whispering"**	**"Fake Plastic Trees"**	"Exit Music (for a Film)"	"How to Disappear Completely"	"You and Whose Army?"	"Backdrifts"
5	"Thinking about You"	"Bones"	**"Let Down"**	"Treefingers"	"I Might Be Wrong"	**"Go to Sleep"**
6	**"Anyone Can Play Guitar"**	"Nice Dream"	**"Karma Police"**	"Optimistic"	**"Knives Out"**	"Where I End and You Begin"
7	**"Ripcord"**	**"Just"**	"Fitter Happier"	"In Limbo"	"Morning Bell/Amnesiac"	"We Suck Young Blood"
8	"Vegetable"	**"My Iron Lung"**	"Electioneering"	"Idioteque"	"Dollars & Cents"	"The Gloaming"
9	"Prove Yourself"	"Bullet Proof...I Wish I Was"	"Climbing Up the Walls"	"Morning Bell"	"Hunting Bears"	**"There There"**

TABLE 7.1. (continued)

Track	Pablo Honey (1993)	The Bends (1995)	OK Computer (1997)	Kid A (2000)	Amnesiac (2001)[1]	Hail to the Thief (2003)[2]
10	"I Can't"	"Black Star"	**"No Surprises"**	"Motion Picture Soundtrack"	"Like Spinning Plates"	"I Will"
11	"Lurgee"	"Sulk"	**"Lucky"**		"Life in a Glasshouse"	"A Punchup at a Wedding"
12	"Blow Out"	**"Street Spirit (Fade Out)"**	"The Tourist"			"Myxomatosis"
13	"Creep" (Radio Version)					"Scatterbrain"
14						"A Wolf at the Door"

Notes:

1. Chart placements for Amnesiac: "Pyramid Song" 5 U.K., "Knives Out" 13 U.K. Amnesiac reached number 1 on the U.K. charts and number 2 on the U.S. charts. http://en.wikipedia.org/wiki/Radiohead_discography (accessed 8 December 2009).

2. Chart placements for Hail to the Thief: "There There" 4 U.K., "Go to Sleep" 12 U.K., "2 + 2 = 5" 15 U.K. Hail to the Thief reached number 1 on the U.K. charts and number 3 on the U.S. charts. http://en.wikipedia.org/wiki/Radiohead_discography (accessed 8 December 2009).

clear endpoint. Rather than trying to escape, the subject is now trying to negotiate an endless series of possibilities. A limitless set of choices leading to no clear resolution may be a more apt representation of modern life but is just as bewildering as the labyrinth or the "spiral down" is entombing. And, a life with too many choices ("here I'm allowed everything all of the time") can be just as unfulfilling as one in which no choices are available.

With *Amnesiac*, the visual album trappings that had developed over Radiohead's releases attained the level of art-object: the limited-edition book of drawings complete with a fake library reference card inside the front cover. The band members created a false artifact that artist Stanley Donwood has said is "designed to be left for decades in a drawer, in an old cupboard, in a dusty attic, in an abandoned house, and found after I am dead."[6] The packaging for *Hail to the Thief* contains, along with the map of drawings with anti-capitalist slogans, what looks like a playbill with actual song lyrics, the first included since *OK Computer*. The design of the packaging recalls Jethro Tull's concept album *A Passion Play* (1973). Thus the band presents what seems on the surface to be a concept album, without the coherence in the music to support it, making it an empty signifier—whereas with *OK Computer* and *Kid A*/*Amnesiac* listeners were initially puzzled but were given a variety of musical and lyrical themes from which to divine the concept.

Many fans assumed that the title of *Hail to the Thief*[7] was a reference to the "stolen" U.S. presidential election in 2000, handed to George W. Bush by the U.S. Supreme Court, but Jonny Greenwood has stated that the album's subject matter reaches much further: "We'd never name a record after one political event. . . . The record's bigger than that."[8] By making such a statement, Greenwood retreats from stating any overt political opinions on behalf of the band and positions Radiohead as being somehow above or outside the political system. Such a remark perhaps overstates the importance of the band's music, but it does at least point toward their future direction. It also contrasts with Yorke's remark that "it's pop music and it's not anything more than that," positioning the production of pop music as even *more* important than any statement about capitalism or politics that the band might make (of course, for many people, systemic critiques of capitalism *are* the bigger topic, transcending any specific political event like an election). Martin Clarke calls *Hail to the Thief* "a coda to *OK Computer, Kid A* and *Amnesiac*, rooted in Thom's concerns about the dark political forces that move in the shadows."[9] Even if we take Jonny Greenwood at his word that *Hail to the Thief* does not refer to a single political event, it still contains numerous references to Orwellian dystopias: the very title of the first song, "2 + 2 = 5," warns the listener that she is entering the same type of world described on *Kid A* and *Amnesiac*. One image trail for *Hail to the Thief* shows its dystopian/political references. The first song uses the phrase "you have not been paying attention," recalling O'Brien's conversation with Winston Smith in 1984.[10] "Backdrifts" contains the line "all evidence has been buried, all tapes have been erased," which recalls Watergate and hints at both the future of 1984, in which history is continually revised, and the policies of the Bush era, in which e-mails between government officials can be easily erased or hidden through the claim of executive privilege. The song's subtitle, "Honeymoon Is Over," could refer to the end of the "honeymoon" period after an election, in which the elected leader is given the benefit of the doubt by the legislature and his proposals are treated favorably. "Go to Sleep" suggests another alternative to political action: "I'm gonna go to sleep, let this wash all over me." In the modern condition, compassion fatigue is a common response; that is, people grow so weary of continually caring about the environment, health-care reform, the poor, etc., that they simply start shutting it all out. Tate suggests a link to Slavoj Žižek's "estimation of the situation that what we do in the face of technological change is simply 'go to sleep' and let it wash all over us. The perfect response is to let the capitalist machinery go on without interruption."[11] The narrative of "A Punchup at a Wedding (No No No No No No No No)" can be described as simply the action in the title, but it can also be given a more political reading than just "corrupted societal functioning."[12] Yorke has stated that "Myxomatosis" has to do with mind control rather than being a literal statement about the rabbit-killing virus,[13] another Orwellian theme. Tate notes that the words "a flan in the face" in "A Wolf at the Door" are a possible reference to cabinet minister Clare Short being hit in the face with a pie in 2001.[14]

A second image trail shows the connections between *Hail to the Thief* and the band's earlier albums. The words "we're rotten fruit, we're damaged goods" in "Backdrifts" recall the imagery of "Optimistic" and "Knives Out." The words "over my dead body" in "Go to Sleep" indicate that the subject is threatening to stop some type of action, saying that it will happen only if he is dead and cannot prevent it. This marks a contrast to the earlier subject who longed for death or was reanimated after his demise. "Where I End and You Begin" has the line "the dinosaurs roam the earth," a link back to "Optimistic," as well as "there'll be no more lies," recalling the "little white lies" of "Kid A" and "Motion Picture Soundtrack" but a false promise given the album's other imagery. The words "I am up in the clouds," sung to the same melody (harmonized this time), followed by "I can watch but not take part," indicate that the subject is somehow apart from the action this time; he is no longer the one being eaten. With the words "I will eat you alive," the subject has moved from being the devoured to the devourer. The voice outlasts the instruments, making the threat sound even more menacing. Tate notes that the last line of "Where I End," "I will eat you alive," which recalls the cannibalism of *Amnesiac*, segues nicely into the first line of the next ("We Suck Young Blood"): "are you hungry?"[15] In "We Suck Young Blood," in contrast to the "bloated and frozen" body that was to be eaten in "Knives Out," here the subject seeks "young blood" and "sweet meats." The line "our veins are thin, our rivers poisoned" brings the idea of environmental activism into the song and suggests a parallel between the cannibalization of the subject and that of the earth. The greatest moment of harmonic cohesion comes with the line "we suck young blood," in which the voice ascends against a chromatic piano and background "oohs." The song ends with "aahs" in the voice with backing harmonies; again the voice has outlasted the other instruments.

From the very beginning, *Hail to the Thief* indicates that the subject, or at least the band, is present. Whereas *Kid A* had begun with a seductive electric-piano riff and *Amnesiac* had presented the sound of a synthesized "gamelan," *Hail to the Thief* instead furnishes the sound of instruments being plugged in and some background chitchat ("are we rolling?") that tells the listener that the band is back in the recording studio. The song even presents a bit of a false start, as the guitar sounds like it is unplugged and then plugged back in, whereupon it begins the opening riff to "2 + 2 = 5." Likewise, the singer enters in full voice, with backing harmony, singing a verse immediately after the opening riff, at 0:25. This subject even states the title of the song at 0:42, as though it is a chorus slogan similar to that of "Optimistic." This ends up being a false chorus, however, as the real chorus at 1:53 chides the listener with the words "you have not been paying attention." After the seductive falseness of the verse, the subject begins almost screaming in the bridge (2:26) as he sings "don't question my authority or put me in the dock." This song can be perceived as a cry from the real that is hastily silenced by the falseness of the commodity, as the next song returns to the techno beat and what sounds like a subdued glockenspiel for "Sit Down Stand Up." The subject has made his brief outburst and is now being told how to behave. Yorke's voice sounds flat here, a marked contrast to the emotion of the opening track, as though the subject is once again resigned to the modern condition and his inability to make a real change in his life or in society as a whole. The subtitle of track two, "Snakes & Ladders," evokes the imagery of the packaging, with its endless routes back and forth between different conditions. In the children's game Snakes and Ladders (called Chutes and Ladders in the U.S.), a random toss of the dice could send a player up a shortcut via a ladder or back down a snake/chute away from the goal. Similarly, a chance decision by a subject in modern society could lead to a windfall of riches or a pit of despair. Even in a society with too many choices, there is always the chance of being affected by something beyond your control, making these choices futile. "The Gloaming" (the subtitle to the whole album, according to the limited-edition booklet), track eight, begins with crackling sounds evocative of the first track; this song functions as the second-side single.

Yorke's voice is less filtered or abstract on *Hail to the Thief* than on either of the two preceding albums, possibly because his message is clearer, or because he wishes to convey it more strongly. Kevin J. H. Dettmar claims that the clarity of Yorke's voice on *Hail to the Thief* stems from the more overtly political character of the album (despite the band's denial) and notes that the "somewhat cleaner distinction between man and machine" hearkens all the way back to *The Bends*.[16] On *Hail to the Thief*, the voice is no longer simply part of the texture, but a subject in its own right. In a sense, Yorke has undergone his own disappearance/self-effacement and reemergence similar to that of the subject on "How to Disappear Completely" through "Treefingers" and "Optimistic." The instrumentation, melody, and dreamy quality of "Sail to the Moon" are similar to "Pyramid Song" and "How to Disappear Completely." The lyrics continue *Amnesiac*'s theme of escape with the words "build an ark and sail us to the moon." The instrumentation and imagery recall "Pyramid Song," with its "moon full of stars and astral cars"; perhaps the ark could be used to escape the "muddy river." The lyrics are more negative than those of the earlier song, however, stating "I spoke too soon . . . I was dropped from moonbeams and sailed on shooting stars." An ascending keyboard arpeggio accentuates the "shooting star" imagery, lending a positive aspect to the texture over the guitar and piano. A second voice in fifths harmony under the word "moon" in the line "sail us to the moon" (3:00) grounds the subject before the final line, a repetition of "sail us to . . ." that fades into electronic echoes as the piano plays ever higher pitches to the end. Despite the cohesion of the individual tracks, *Hail to the Thief* sounds much less coherent when taken next to *Kid A* and *Amnesiac*; the previous two albums had required more work on the part of the listener to make them hang together, with the lack of singles on *Kid A* contributing to the idea that there must be an overriding concept controlling things. Since *Hail to the Thief* immediately brought to mind, for many, taunts about the 2000 U.S. presidential election, a concept can seem more apparent from the outset. It is possible to read an underlying politicism into all the songs on the album, but that could also be said of Radiohead's other works, at least if one expands the definition of political writings to include statements on man's alienation in modern society. Even the band's first single, "Creep," could be read as making a statement on alienation, albeit at a very personal level.

Radiohead's *Kid A* and *Amnesiac* ultimately succeed in a way that *Hail to the Thief* does not, by being resistant in both their musical and lyrical presentation, mostly refusing to offer complete and coherent pop songs, and thwarting expectations about Radiohead's musical style. The band subverts the concept album tradition by presenting material that requires effort on the part of the listener to comprehend, yet offering little to no plot, characters, or dramatic action to clarify the concept. The band also challenges the progressive-rock tradition to which Radiohead has so often been compared by disavowing any claims of meaning in the albums. Despite embracing the technology required to produce these albums, the band also decries the effects of technology not only on the albums' vanishing subject, but ultimately on mankind; in the end, we are each dehumanized and made into a commodity, just as the band itself has been. It is of course ironic that a band making its living from the sale of goods in a capitalist society would be so vehemently anti-capitalist in its work, at least on the surface. By articulating the subject in *Kid A/Amnesiac* in relation to the culture of consumption, Radiohead maps itself onto that subject as well. The whole notion of the rock band is itself constructed within capitalism, and by operating within the system Radiohead at some level relinquishes its autonomy and thus its power over its own product, making the band subject to control by its fans, its record company, and the marketplace. In the end, the "concept" is larger than simply one, or even two, albums: Radiohead the band ultimately becomes Radiohead the brand, yet another empty signifier for the consumer to buy, despite the band's pretensions to the contrary.

THE ERASER AND IN RAINBOWS

After the *Hail to the Thief* tour, Radiohead took a year off and then spent two years in and out of the studio, writing new material and playing it live to rework the arrangements before releasing their seventh studio album, *In Rainbows*.[17] In the meantime, Yorke released a solo album, *The Eraser* (2006). One could speculate that the title continues the process undertaken by *Amnesiac* in erasing the memory of its predecessor, *Kid A*. If Yorke himself is the "eraser," then his album could be seen as superseding Radiohead's material. Likewise, the title could indicate that Yorke's previous output through the band should be erased. This is a false assumption, however; Yorke's solo work sounds much like Radiohead's, and the packaging of the album recalls that of the limited-edition releases of *Kid A* and its descendants. Black lines on a white background recall both the artwork of Edward Gorey and Edvard Munch's *The Scream*. The artwork for *The Eraser* was created by longtime Radiohead collaborator Stanley Donwood, who made a linotype called "London Views."[18] Donwood has stated that the "artwork and the music have a symbiotic relationship, tending towards the parasitical. The music being the host and the artwork being the leech. . . . Listening to a record take shape is a good way of attempting to adhere the pictures to the songs." Donwood has also stated that "often Radiohead make music that makes something close to my stomach squirm and twist, like an odd vertigo. It's the beauty of abandoned factories, of lines of pylons marching to the horizon. It makes pictures in my head, movement and landscape, solitude and sadness, like watching someone you love leaving the house and wondering if today is the day that they'll never come back."[19] When questioned about whether his work on album covers falls into the realm of fine art, Donwood said, "Absolutely not. It is commercial art, designed to shift units and add to the wealth of record-company shareholders. But then I suppose that fine art itself isn't really that morally respectable either. Paint pictures for an advert or an ad-man. You decide."[20] This statement foregrounds Donwood's part of Radiohead's product as a commodity.

The Eraser charted at number 2 in the U.S.[21] and was described in the LA Times as "an evocative portrait of life made slippery by urban sprawl, murky political alliances and global warming—and given hope through individual and communal resistance."[22] In other words, it continued the same themes as the previous three Radiohead albums. In an NME review of the album, the author notes that the members of Radiohead had retreated from Kid A's "icy brink" until the release of Yorke's solo album, which returns to the earlier album's "phantom presence of synthesizers, mechanical rhythms, and eerie, inhuman dislocation." The review notes that this dislocation results in a profound change for Yorke's voice: "Freed from Radiohead's titanium heaviness, here it soars unimpeded." The review predicted that The Eraser would split Radiohead fans as Kid A had: "Some will mourn its lack of viscera; its coldness; its reluctance to rock. But it's yet another revealing glimpse into Yorke's cryptic inner-world, and one that has the courage not to hide its political message in code."[23] Indeed, Yorke himself has linked the album's lyrics to world governments' lack of attention to global warming.[24] Rolling Stone played up the emotional content of the album, rather than its foregrounded political stance: "it's intensely beautiful, yet it explores the kind of emotional turmoil that makes the angst of OK Computer or The Bends sound like kid stuff."[25] Yorke notes that on The Eraser, "The music, no matter what way you look at it, is coming out of a box. . . . It has its own space. We consciously decided to not expand it beyond that. The vocals are exactly the same, right there in the speakers. The record was built to be listened to in an isolated space—on headphones, or stuck in traffic."[26] This way of envisioning the album casts it as a direct message to the listener, an appeal through the insider marketing strategy, and recalls "Everything in Its Right Place," in which the main voice speaks audibly while babble interferes on either side. *Rolling Stone* similarly notes the emphasis on the voice: "The structures are tighter than in Radiohead songs, centered on the vocals—fans hoping for ten-minute ambient dub doodles will be disappointed. Yorke's voice has never sounded so fragile; his melodies have never sounded so mournful. In a word, he sounds alone. And it wears him out."[27]

Yorke himself links his solo project to the song in which the subject of *Kid A* found *him*self completely alone: "My favorite tune from that time [the *Kid A/Amnesiac* period] is 'How to Disappear Completely,' because we didn't care how it could be seen as pretentious or anything. It just sounds glorious. What Jonny did to it is amazing."[28] Ironically, in creating a solo album, Yorke seemed to still want to "disappear completely." He has stated that he and producer Nigel Godrich disagreed on how prevalent to make the voice in the mix: "I kept begging Nigel to put more reverb on it. 'No, I'm not doing reverb on this record.' Please hide my voice. 'No.'"[29] *Rolling Stone* sees *The Eraser* instead as reclaiming not only the voice, but the subject's persona: "these aren't Radiohead songs, or demos for Radiohead songs. They're something different, something we haven't heard before. . . . Yorke is asking new questions, looking for clues to the same old mystery: how to appear, incompletely." Ultimately the album, though appreciated, was perceived as falling short of Radiohead's band output, in part because it discarded the idea of the accumulative groove: "*The Eraser* is full of moments when you wait for the band to kick in, and it doesn't happen. It reminds you how much Radiohead thrive on their sense of collective creation—even at their most downbeat, their camaraderie gives off a life-affirming energy."[30]

The rest of the band spent this hiatus thinking about ways to create a new business model for their next album. Yorke stated in an interview about *The Eraser* that he "would love for us to drop a chemical weapon within the music industry. But I don't see it as our responsibility, either."[31] In an interview given after the release of *The Eraser*, Yorke expressed his feelings about the corporate structure within which commercial artists are expected to function: "My big problem with corporate structure is this bizarre sense of loyalty you're supposed to feel—towards what is basically a virus. It grows or dies, like any virus. And you use it for your own selfish ends."[32] Yorke had told *Time* after the release of *Hail to the Thief* that "I like the people at our record company, but the time is at hand when you have to ask why anyone needs one. And, yes, it probably would give us some perverse pleasure to say 'F*** you' to this decaying business model [expletive masked in original]."[33]

The radical new direction that Radiohead had indicated it would pursue after *Hail to the Thief* finally came with the release of *In Rainbows*, which occurred in an unconventional fashion. Fans were invited to pre-register online for access to the album's download, and they could choose the amount they wished to pay, anything from $0 to $99.99. On the day before the album's release date of 10 October 2007, fans who had signed up on inrainbows.com received an e-mail about the download:

> THANK YOU FOR ORDERING IN RAINBOWS. THIS IS AN UPDATE.
>   YOUR UNIQUE ACTIVATION CODE(S) WILL BE SENT OUT TO-MORROW MORNING (UK TIME). THIS WILL TAKE YOU STRAIGHT TO THE DOWNLOAD AREA.
>   HERE IS SOME INFORMATION ABOUT THE DOWNLOAD:
> THE ALBUM WILL COME AS A 48.4MB ZIP FILE CONTAINING 10 × 160KBPS DRM FREE MP3S.[34]

DRM stands for "digital rights management"; "DRM-free" means that the tracks could be burned onto CDs by the listener or shared without restriction. Jonny Greenwood notes that the idea for this marketing gimmick came from a music-software package whose developers told the band to pay them what they thought it was worth. Yorke says that the policy was "a way of letting everybody judge for themselves" what the worth of the album would be. The new album was Radiohead's first since fulfilling its multi-album contract with EMI in 2003, and the first for which they owned the rights to their own music. Yorke says that releasing another major-label album would have been a "worst-case scenario. . . . Sign another deal, take a load of money, and then have the machinery waiting semi-patiently for you to deliver your product, which they can add to the list of products that make up the myth. . . ."[35] The *New York Times* reports figures from ComScore stating that 1.2 million people visited the *In Rainbows* website in October, and that a "significant percentage" of them downloaded the album. The band has consistently refused to release data on how much was earned from the download sales; manager Chris Hufford says, "People made their choice to actually pay money. It's people saying, 'We want to be part of this thing.' If it's good enough, people will put a penny in the pot."[36] The irony, of course, is that people were asked to put a price on the product without knowing how good it was, though of course the songs on the album might have been familiar to fans who had heard them live or on bootlegged downloads. The band had dropped hints that it might be releasing a new album soon, and *Rolling Stone* playfully attempted to decode the band's cryptic messages, posted using a cipher tagged "Worm Buffet Code" by fans at Radiohead At Ease.[37] Hufford and Radiohead's other manager, Bryce Edge, had wanted to release only the digital download and a box set containing "the album and a bonus CD, two vinyl albums, artwork and a fancy package for $80," but the band "overruled them, noting that many of its fans are neither downloaders nor elite collectors."[38] The official announcement of the album's release stated simply: "Hello everyone. Well, the new album is finished, and it's coming out in 10 days. We've called it *In Rainbows*. Love from us all."[39] The band released the track listing shortly after this announcement,[40] and *Rolling Stone* then presented a track-by-track commentary on what listeners might expect to hear from the download of both the regular CD and the bonus one included in the deluxe package, based on live bootlegs via YouTube.[41]

Colin Greenwood describes the excitement surrounding the release of *In Rainbows*:

> When they sent the album I was having breakfast and checking my e-mail. A file download thing appeared at half seven in the morning, which was quite exciting. Then I read reviews of it from people staying up in the small hours in America. Some had exams the next day but they were drinking loads of coffee and staying up anyway. It was really mad. We were trying to create an event. Why not?[42]

Time magazine described the download process this way:

> Drop *In Rainbows'* 15 songs into the online checkout basket and a ques-
> tion mark pops up where the price would normally be. Click it, and the
> prompt "It's Up To You" appears. Click again and it refreshes with the
> words "It's Really Up To You"—and really, it is. It's the first major album
> whose price is determined by what individual consumers want to pay for
> it. And it's perfectly acceptable to pay nothing at all.[43]

NME reported a year after the release of *In Rainbows* that the album had "generated more money before it was physically released . . .
than the total money generated by sales of the band's previous album.
. . ."[44] The article also reports that Warner/Chappell, the publishing
company that oversaw the album's release, along with Radiohead's
management, had monitored the daily average price paid for the download and were "prepared to cancel the download facility if the average
price became too low." The album ceased to be available for download
once the physical CD (not the deluxe box set, which was released at the
same time as the download and reportedly sold 100,000 copies) became
available for sale, on 1 January 2008. The album still went to number
1 in both the U.S. and the U.K. after its physical release, suggesting
that the download did not negatively impact its sales.[45] According to
research published by Big Champagne, a media tracking and technology company, and the MCPS-PRS Alliance (now called PRS for
Music), which manages royalties for British artists, around 2.3 million
people downloaded the album illegally through BitTorrent.[46] A writer
for musicradar.com further notes that "people paid more at the start
than later on, the early purchasers being committed Radiohead fans
who thought the music was worth more."[47] Richard Manners of War-
ner/Chappell had stated that the company "fully supports Radiohead
in their desire to find new ways to present their music to their fans and
to the wider world. These new ways are iconoclastic in nature; they
acknowledge the realities of a digital society and they challenge existing commercial assumptions. It is in this spirit that band and publisher
are working together."[48]

In contrast to previous studio experimentation, the band created
some initial ideas in the studio, then worked out the songs live (as fans
bootlegged them), then returned to the studio again. The *New York
Times* called *In Rainbows* "Radiohead's most gracefully melodic album

in a decade."[49] NME noted that "Six years on from its release, Kid A occupies a unique place in Radiohead's discography. Depending on who you ask, it's either the moment they learnt to fly without being weighed down by rock'n'roll's leaden corpse, or the day they cast off the guitars and drifted up their own collective arsehole."[50] Time speculated that future artists might follow Radiohead's model in turning their full-length albums into "loss leaders," since more income can potentially come from touring (and presumably the merchandise sold at concerts): "under the most lucrative record deals, the ones reserved for repeat, multi-platinum superstars, the artists can end up with less than 30% of overall sales revenue (which often is then split among several band members)."[51]

In 2009, Radiohead continued to fuel speculation about its future releases. Colin Greenwood announced in May that the band had returned to the studio.[52] A blog entry on Dead Air Space on 5 August announced that the band had released a track called "Harry Patch (In Memory Of)" in honor of the last surviving U.K. veteran of WWI, who had died at the age of 111 on July 25. The track was sold for £1 per download, and proceeds went to the British Legion.[53] On 9 June the band made available through W.A.S.T.E., its online store, the digital purchase of several albums, including both discs of In Rainbows, The Eraser, and Jonny Greenwood's There Will Be Blood soundtrack. The band added a new song, "These Are My Twisted Words," for free download on 17 August. The zip file for this track included a tiff image entitled "artwork" with overlaid images of trees, a text document that attributes the artwork to Donwood and the track to Radiohead with production by Godrich, an mp3 file, and a pdf called "twisted woods" ("twisted woods" being a play on words as well as an allusion to the twisting tree branches) with the message "this is an artwork file to accompany the audio file. we suggest you print these images out on tracing paper. use at least 80gsm tracing paper or your printer will eat it as we discovered. you could put them in an order that pleases you." The pdf contains fourteen pages of tree-branch images like those in the "artwork" file. Thus, the band now placed part of the creative input as well as the task of assigning value to the product in the hands of the fans. This act stands in contrast to the band's decision not to use Donwood's artwork for In Rainbows until the CD release. Donwood states:

"There was one [album cover] but because it was an mp3 we decided not to use it."[54] The band and/or the artist had obviously moved beyond that stance by the release of "These Are My Twisted Words," seeing the mp3 as a commodity just as the CD is. With this enhanced status comes the opportunity for artwork to be created for it. Along with the official download site through W.A.S.T.E., the band provided a link to a BitTorrent site where listeners could also download the new song for free for a limited time period.

And as to a new Radiohead album? Jonny Greenwood stated in an August 2009 interview with the *Australian* that "Traditionally we'd be looking for 10 or 11 songs and putting them together, but that doesn't feel as natural as it used to, so I don't know what we'll do. Maybe we'll find four songs that work together and we'll call that a release. I don't know. . . . No one knows how to release music anymore, including us. How to put it together, in what format, how long. We're in the dark as much as anyone I think."[55] After Greenwood's statement, speculation ran rampant on the Radiohead At Ease website, as fans discussed a possible new Radiohead EP to be entitled *Wall of Ice*.[56] An article posted on 17 August 2009 in *Contagious* magazine explained that fans took their "treasure hunt" to the extreme, based on a leaked track (posted on an At Ease message board on 17 August) and a cartoon from XKCD (a series of online comics on math, science, and computer themes). The cartoon shows a Donwood-esque stick figure standing on the edge of an iceberg with the words "Dear Sony, Microsoft, the MPAA, the RIAA, and Apple: Let's make a deal. You stop trying to tell me where, when, and how I play my movies and music, and I won't crush your homes under my inexorably advancing wall of ice."[57]

Contagious stated:

"Wall of Ice" is not only an exercise in crowd manipulation, it's a genuine acknowledgement of the way in which the music industry now works, and one in the eye to the archaic and crumbling systems from which Radiohead have struggled to liberate themselves. The band is fast becoming as synonymous with technological mischief as they are with music, and for that. [*sic*] we can only salute them.[58]

What, then, of our continually vanishing subject? The possibility that Radiohead would no longer release full-length albums loomed large in 2009, as downloads trickled from both official and fan websites onto fans' computers. Radiohead had managed to move on after releasing a set of albums that resisted conventional notions of subjectivity in the world of capitalism by presenting a series of songs in which the subject either died or was reanimated after death. *Kid A* and *Amnesiac* both "resist" the lure of the concept album, with its narrative and characters, and this resistance echoes the band's resistance toward the record industry—first by releasing no singles, then by touring in as eco-friendly a way as possible, then by allowing consumers to assign a value to the product they purchase, and finally by dispensing with the conventional album altogether and releasing only individual songs as digital downloads. By continually reinforcing the status of the album (and even of the cover artwork) as a commodity, the band creates an ironic distance between themselves and the industry that fostered their success. Giving the listener the feeling that she is being "let in on" knowledge of a new commodity adds to the mystique of the band even as it sells product after product to the same "insiders" who purport to be anti-capitalist. The band creates its own microcosm of capitalism with special downloads and deluxe-edition box sets; it builds its own buzz by dropping clues about future tour plans and tickets that require a special password to access. This insider culture is insular but appealing to outsiders who may be looking for a sense of community among similarly alienated humans living in the twenty-first century. The band posts enough "casual snapshots" of itself in its RSS feed to foster the illusion that the five members are just like their fans; their reputation rests on the audience believing the exterior illusion and continuing to support their work.

In what could be seen as a cynical move, EMI/Capitol, Radiohead's old label, reissued the band's first three albums in expanded editions in March 2009, featuring bonus discs of B-sides and live material. *Pitchfork* states: "Almost everything Radiohead put to tape professionally between 1992 and 1997 is represented here. New fans won't have to scrounge around for elusive B-sides and show footage on YouTube, which is a good thing. But still, it's hard to look at these reissues as anything other than a cash-grab for EMI/Capitol—an old media company that got dumped by their most forward-thinking band."[59] The label had also released a "best of" CD in 2008 that *Pitchfork* posited was the label's way of reminding listeners of the band's older, more accessible material, in which EMI/Capitol had a financial stake—in contrast to the then-recent *In Rainbows* release, which the band issued on their own.[60] EMI/Capitol reissued the band's next three albums in August 2009 after a series of twelve Radiohead vinyl EPs earlier, in April.[61] This reaction by a band's old label after the band jumps ship, releasing the back catalog owned by the label as a greatest-hits compilation, is not an uncommon one as more artists have begun fighting for the rights to their own work and setting up their own labels. Radiohead's "new direction" of releasing their material in digital format for free and outside the reach of the traditional record industry could be a reaction to their old label's continued plundering of their older material. Colin Greenwood noted in an interview with *Pitchfork* that "It would be really nice to be able to put out releases that wouldn't be conditional upon an album format, and just put out music in different ways."[62]

The process begun by Radiohead when they entered the studio for what would become *Kid A* and *Amnesiac*, after the three-year post–*OK Computer* hiatus, began a period of resistance that continues to this day. The band's philosophy can be traced all the way back to the "Creep" tour, which wore them down as they tried to promote one immensely popular single, but the *OK Computer* tour documented in *Meeting People Is Easy* marked a turning point in the band's relationship with the record industry. Although *The Bends* and *OK Computer* were still rooted in traditional ways of thinking, as each featured several singles, the band soon radically refashioned not only their sound but their approach to their own career with *Kid A* and its lack of singles. With *Amnesiac* and *Hail to the Thief*, the band kept the new sound but returned to at least a semblance of conventional promotion (though not going as far as the "children's TV appearances" that Yorke had joked about). At the same time, however, they looked for ways to transform the industry while still working within it, holding tours in conventional places but featuring unconventional products alongside the expected ones. After another long break, during which the band explored different musical directions (Yorke with *The Eraser* and Jonny Greenwood with *Bodysong* and *There Will Be Blood*), they interspersed studio work with playing new material live. This process resulted in enough material to form a new album, but Radiohead instead found a way to release the material outside the record industry, as a digital download for which their fans could choose the price. This set capitalism on its ear, by forcing the individual consumer to set his or her own rate, bypassing the traditionally conceptualized "market" as the arbiter of value.

Valuing a good for oneself forces the listener to approach the artwork as the commodity rather than the reverse. It is the curse of the capitalist system: the artist tries to rise above commodification but is forced to navigate within it in order to make a living. Turning the system upside down, by virtue of forcing their fans to set a price, Radiohead focused the attention on the product as a good to be exchanged for capital. Traditionally, albums all cost almost the same price, a price based on the physical format of the record, tape, or CD, corresponding in no way to an evaluation of the contents as art. Paintings vary in price, but albums by Beethoven and Taylor Swift, like paperbacks by Charles Dickens and Nora Roberts, cost about the same. By allowing listeners to set the price, Radiohead suggested a system where the content and context, rather than format, are what is valued and priced, while also obliterating the market value of the listener as a factor—you don't have be above a certain income bracket to obtain this music. In the process, the band commodified itself by foregrounding the means of production (posting pictures from the studio on their website is another way of focusing attention). A cynical way of looking at this process would be saying that the band is only "giving away" the good in order to bypass the cut given to the record industry; by selling the product themselves, the band eliminates the middleman, but they also force other artists as well as their labels to examine future means of record production and promotion. With iTunes and other download services gaining in popularity, it is possible that the album as something tangible was on its way out in 2007 anyway, so Radiohead's *In Rainbows* simply furthered the digital revolution that was already in progress. It remains to be seen how the band will promote itself in the future, but EMI/Capitol's rejoinder—the reissuing of all the band's older material—serves as a reminder that at least the major labels still see this older style of product as a viable commodity. Perhaps Radiohead's digital downloads are the way of the future, and labels like EMI/Capitol are the true "dinosaurs roaming the earth" as well as the "thief" being sarcastically hailed in the band's last release for that label.

Radiohead's fans have taken their resistant marketing strategy even further than the band, seeing solutions where there are no riddles to solve. It is interesting to note that fans still seem to want conventional album-length releases, at least in the form of the EP; although they are happy to receive individual tracks through digital download, they still crave the longer-form commodity. The band recognizes that packaging is still important with the shorter-length mp3 format, releasing artwork that it instructs listeners how to consume even as it purports to encourage them to use it in any way they like. In commodifying its music in new and unusual ways (placing greater value on the rarity of the free download), the band also commodifies its "cover" artwork, granting it the same status. The artwork for "My Twisted Words" encourages the process of open-ended interpretation, even if it is a visual one, that the band first appealed to on *Kid A* and *Amnesiac*. Listeners can now choose their own interpretation not only of the music, but even of the artwork that accompanies it. Rather than being a liberation from the confines of capitalism, however, this is simply another way of encasing the listener in the labyrinth that surrounds Radiohead. The free downloads are just another pretty toy to distract listeners from the perils of the modern world that continue to enslave them. In the end, Radiohead may be the "dollars and cents," but the listener willingly buys into the myth.

Note on Musical Examples

1. See Walter Everett, "Making Sense of Rock's Tonal Systems," *Music Theory Online* 10:4 (2004), http://mto.societymusictheory.org/issues/mto.04.10.4/mto.04.10.4.w_everett_frames.html (accessed 5 December 2009), for a compelling discussion of the various tonal systems used in popular music; an exploration of these systems is beyond the scope of this book.

2. Everett notes the possible V–I relationship for "Everything" in the single key of F major in "Making Sense," Fig. 9.

3. See Walter Everett's *The Beatles as Musicians:* Revolver *through the* Anthology (Oxford: Oxford University Press, 1999); and John Covach's *What's That Sound? An Introduction to Rock and Its History* (New York: W. W. Norton, 2006).

4. Mark Spicer, "(Ac)cumulative Form in Pop-Rock Music," *Twentieth-Century Music* 1:1 (2004): 30.

5. Ibid.

6. Timothy S. Hughes, "Groove and Flow: Six Analytical Essays on the Music of Stevie Wonder" (Ph.D. diss., University of Washington, 2003), 14.

7. Richard Middleton, *Studying Popular Music* (Bristol, Pa.: Open University Press, 1990), 138.

Introduction

1. Theodor Adorno with Max Horkheimer, *The Dialectic of Enlightenment,* trans. Edmund Jephcott (Stanford, Calif.: Stanford University Press, 2002 [1944]).

2. Frederic Jameson, "The Cultural Logic of Late Capitalism," in *Rethinking Architecture: A Reader in Cultural Theory,* ed. Neil Leach (London: Routledge, 1997), 227.

3. Interview with Nancy Price, *Consumable Online* (1 September 1997), quoted in Martin Clarke, *Hysterical and Useless* (London: Plexus, 2003), 21. See http://www.westnet.com/consumable/1997/09.01/intradio.html (accessed 5 December 2009) for the full text of the interview.

4. See http://news.bbc.co.uk/1/hi/entertainment/music/3725075.stm (accessed 5 December 2009).

5. Dai Griffiths, "Public Schoolboy Music: Debating Radiohead," in *The Music and Art of Radiohead*, ed. Joseph Tate (Aldershot, U.K.: Ashgate, 2005), 162.

6. William Stone, *Radiohead: Green Plastic Wateringcan* (London: UFO Music Ltd., 1996), 19.

7. Ibid., 37.

8. James Doheny, *Radiohead: Back to Save the Universe: The Stories Behind Every Song* (New York: Thunder's Mouth Press, 2002), 142.

9. Quoted in Clarke, *Hysterical and Useless*, 56.

10. Stone, *Green Plastic Wateringcan*, 41, 45, and 27.

11. Clarke, *Hysterical and Useless*, 100, 75, and 71.

12. Quoted in ibid., 92 and 96.

13. Stone, *Green Plastic Wateringcan*, 51.

14. Quoted in Clarke, *Hysterical and Useless*, 98.

15. Stone, *Green Plastic Wateringcan*, 57.

16. Doheny, *Back to Save the Universe*, 140. See http://www.grammy.com/GRAMMY_Awards/Winners/ (accessed 5 December 2009).

17. Mac Randall, *Exit Music: The Radiohead Story* (New York: Random House, 2000), 69–70.

18. Griffiths, "Public Schoolboy Music," 163–65.

19. See Jerry Lucky, *The Progressive Rock Files* (Burlington, Ontario: Collector's Guide Publishing, 1998), quoted in *Progressive Rock Reconsidered*, ed. Kevin Holm-Hudson (New York: Routledge, 2002), 3; and Allan F. Moore, *Rock: The Primary Text; Developing a Musicology of Rock* (Buckingham, Pa.: Open University Press, 1993).

20. Private communication, 6 August 2009.

21. Bill Martin, *Listening to the Future: The Time of Progressive Rock* (Chicago and La Salle, Ill.: Open Court, 1998), 121.

22. Edward C. Macan, *Rocking the Classics: English Progressive Rock and the Counterculture* (New York: Oxford University Press, 1996), 26.

23. Quoted in Clarke, *Hysterical and Useless*, 71.

24. Kevin Holm-Hudson, "'Worked Out Within the Grooves': The Sound and Structure of *Dark Side of the Moon*," in *Speak to Me: The Legacy of Pink Floyd's* The Dark Side of the Moon, ed. Russell Reising (London: Ashgate, 2006), 69–86; and Holm-Hudson, *Progressive Rock Reconsidered*, 16.

25. See Greg Hainge, "To(rt)uring the Minotaur: Radiohead, Pop, Unnatural Couplings, and Mainstream Subversion," in *The Music and Art of Radiohead*, ed. Joseph Tate (Aldershot, U.K.: Ashgate, 2005), 64–68, 74–78.

26. Clarke, *Hysterical and Useless*, 127–28.

27. *Q* magazine, special edition, "Pink Floyd & the Story of Prog Rock," 1:5 (2005): 111.

28. Chuck Klosterman, "The Rock Lexicon," *Spin* 21:5 (May 2005): 61. See also John J. Sheinbaum, "Progressive Rock and the Inversion of Musical Values," in *Progressive Rock Reconsidered*, 21–42; and John Covach, "Progressive Rock, 'Close to the Edge,' and the Boundaries of Style," in *Understanding Rock: Essays in Musical Analysis*, ed. Covach and Graeme M. Boone (New York: Oxford University Press, 1997).

29. Clarke, *Hysterical and Useless*, 127–28.

30. Mark Spicer, "(Ac)cumulative Form," 33n13.

31. Allan F. Moore and Anwar Ibrahim, "'Sounds Like Teen Spirit': Identifying Radiohead's Idiolect," in *The Music and Art of Radiohead*, 152.

32. *Q* magazine, 1:5 (2005): 135.

33. Roy Shuker, *Key Concepts in Popular Music* (London and New York: Routledge, 1998).

34. See Fred Maus, "Music as Drama," *Music Theory Spectrum* 10 (1988): 56–73; and Edward T. Cone, *The Composer's Voice* (Berkeley: University of California Press, 1974), for more on the idea of musical agents.

35. Quoted in David O. Montgomery, "The Rock Concept Album: Context and Analysis" (Ph.D. diss., University of Toronto, 2002), 17.

36. See Marianne Tatom Letts, "Sky of Blue, Sea of Green: A Semiotic Reading of the Film *Yellow Submarine*," *Popular Music* 27:1 (2008): 1–14, for a discussion of this hero's journey.

37. See Jody Rosen, "Positively 47th Street: Twyla Tharp Brings Bob Dylan to Broadway," *Slate*, 27 October 2006, http://www.slate.com/id/2152251/ (accessed 6 December 2009).

38. David Buckley, "Album," in *Grove Music Online. Oxford Music Online*, http://www.oxfordmusiconline.com/subscriber/article/grove/music/47210 (accessed 20 February 2010).

39. Donald Clarke, *The Penguin Encyclopedia of Popular Music* (London: Penguin, 1989), 273; quoted in Montgomery, "The Rock Concept Album," 7.

40. Macan, *Rocking the Classics*, 20.

41. Bill Martin, *Music of Yes: Structure and Vision in Progressive Rock* (Chicago and La Salle, Ill.: Open Court, 1996), 22.

42. Paul Stump, *The Music's All That Matters: A History of Progressive Rock* (London: Quartet Books, 1997), 158; quoted in Montgomery, "The Rock Concept Album," 13.

43. William J. Schafer, *Rock Music: Where It's Been, What It Means, Where It's Going* (Minneapolis: Augsburg Publishing, 1972), 103; quoted in Montgomery, "The Rock Concept Album," 14.

44. Montgomery, "The Rock Concept Album," 23.

45. See Marianne Tatom Letts, "Who Sells Out: Petra Haden in the Age of Mechanical Reproduction," *IASPM@Journal* 1:2 (2010), for a discussion of a reworking of *The Who Sell Out*.

46. Allan F. Moore, *The Beatles: Sgt. Pepper's Lonely Hearts Club Band* (Cambridge: Cambridge University Press, 1997), 65 and 71.

47. Macan, *Rocking the Classics*, 58.

48. Schafer, *Rock Music*, 108, quoted in Montgomery, "The Rock Concept Album," 15.

49. Shuker, *Key Concepts in Popular Music*, 6.

50. Allan F. Moore, *Rock: The Primary Text*, 84.

51. Shuker, *Key Concepts in Popular Music*, 5.

52. James Borders, "Form and the Concept Album: Aspects of Modernism in Frank Zappa's Early Releases," *Perspectives of New Music* 39 (2001): 125.

53. Susan Youens, "Song cycle," in *Grove Music Online. Oxford Music Online*, http://www.oxfordmusiconline.com/subscriber/article/grove/music/26208 (accessed 20 February 2010).

54. Mark Spicer, "Large-Scale Strategy and Compositional Design in the Early Music of Genesis," in *Expression in Pop-Rock Music: A Collection of Critical and Analytical Essays*, ed. Walter Everett (New York: Routledge, 2008), 313–44.

55. Peter Kaminsky, "The Popular Album as Song Cycle: Paul Simon's *Still Crazy After All These Years*," *College Music Symposium* 32 (1992): 38–54. Kaminsky notes that "[r]egardless of whether we are addressing 'high' or 'low' musical culture, the understanding of a multi-movement work as a whole remains a complex and elusive thing" (54).

56. Shaugn O'Donnell, "'On the Path': Tracing Tonal Coherence in *Dark Side of the Moon*," and Holm-Hudson, "'Worked Out Within the Grooves,'" both in *Speak to Me*, ed. Reising.

57. Shuker, *Key Concepts in Popular Music*, 5.

58. John Rockwell, "Rock opera," in *Grove Music Online. Oxford Music Online*, http://www.oxfordmusiconline.com/subscriber/article/grove/music/O008572 (accessed 20 February 2010).

59. Richard Middleton et al., "Pop," section III, "North America," in *Grove Music Online. Oxford Music Online*, http://www.oxfordmusiconline.com/subscriber/article/grove/music/46845 (accessed 20 February 2010). See Holm-Hudson, "'Worked Out Within the Grooves,'" for a discussion of the structure and importance of *What's Going On*.

60. Montgomery, "The Rock Concept Album," 14.

61. Moore, *Rock: The Primary Text*, 82.

62. Moore, *The Beatles*, 73.

63. Martin, *Listening to the Future*, 41.

64. Macan, *Rocking the Classics*, 13.

65. Ibid., 26.

66. Rockwell, "Rock opera."

67. Moore, *Rock: The Primary Text*, 82.

68. Ibid., 86.

69. Alan Parsons, quoted in Holm-Hudson, "'Worked Out Within the Grooves.'"

70. http://www.allmusic.com/cg/amg.dll?p=amg&sql=33:qlavqj5roj6a (accessed 6 December 2009).

71. Quoted in Doheny, *Back to Save the Universe*, 111; original interview in *Mojo*.

2. Back to Save the Universe

1. See http://www.listsofbests.com/list/49928 (accessed 6 December 2009); http://news.bbc.co.uk/go/pr/fr/-/2/hi/entertainment/4110278.stm (accessed 6 December 2009).

2. *Rolling Stone*, 24 December 2009–7 January 2010, http://www.rollingstone.com/news/story/31248017/100_best_albums_of_the_decade/42/ (accessed 18 March 2010).

3. Doheny, *Back to Save the Universe*, 78.

4. Ibid.

5. Nadine Hubbs, "The Imagination of Pop-Rock Criticism," in *Expression in Pop-Rock Music: A Collection of Critical and Analytical Essays*, ed. Walter Everett (New York: Routledge, 2008), 225–26.

6. Ibid., 226.

7. Macan, *Rocking the Classics*, 40.

8. Clarke, *Hysterical and Useless*, 107.

9. Moore and Ibrahim, "Identifying Radiohead's Idiolect," 139.

10. Griffiths, *OK Computer* (New York and London: Continuum International Publishing Group, 2004), 38.

11. Ibid., 59, 85, and 96.

12. Moore and Ibrahim, "Identifying Radiohead's Idiolect," 144–45.

13. Quoted in Clarke, *Hysterical and Useless*, 125.

14. Delingpole, "James Delingpole's Rock Records of the Year." *Sunday Telegraph*, 27 December 1997, quoted in Doheny, *Back to Save the Universe*, 59. See also http://www.telegraph.co.uk/culture/4711342/Records-of-the-year.html (accessed 6 December 2009).

15. Griffiths, *OK Computer*, 114.

16. Alex Ross, "The Searchers: Radiohead's Unquiet Revolution," *New Yorker* (20 and 27 August 2001): 115.

17. Doheny, *Back to Save the Universe*, 82.

18. See Tate, "Introduction," *The Music and Art of Radiohead*, 1; Selway quote taken from Ross, "The Searchers," 115.

19. Clarke, *Hysterical and Useless*, 128.

20. Randall, *Exit Music*, 205–206, 208, 211–12.

21. Ross, "The Searchers," 115.

22. Stone, *Green Plastic Wateringcan*, 63.

23. Clarke, *Hysterical and Useless*, 117.

24. Doheny, *Back to Save the Universe*, 84.

25. Clarke, *Hysterical and Useless*, 141.

26. See http://www.radiohead.com/tourdates/6may_tampa.html (accessed 6 December 2009) for a description of "green initiatives" offered by the band and tour promoters.

27. Clarke, *Hysterical and Useless*, 142.

28. Stone, *Green Plastic Wateringcan*, 60.

29. See http://en.wikipedia.org/wiki/Radiohead_discography#Singles (accessed 6 December 2009); Borow, "The Difference Engine," *Spin* (November 2000): 111ff, quoted in Erin Harde, "Radiohead and the Negation of Gender," 53; and *Uncut* (August 2001): 58. Selway quoted in Hainge, "To(rt)uring the Minotaur," 63.

30. Ross, "The Searchers," 112.

31. Doheny, *Back to Save the Universe*, 84.

32. Hainge, "To(rt)uring the Minotaur," 70.

33. Harde, "Radiohead and the Negation of Gender," 52.

34. Stone, *Green Plastic Wateringcan*, 8.

35. EMD/Capitol, directed by Grant Gee.

36. Doheny, *Back to Save the Universe*, 143.

37. See http://news.bbc.co.uk/2/hi/entertainment/968437.stm (accessed 6 December 2009).

38. Examples of this varied reaction from fans could be seen in the discussion on the Radiohead message board on America Online at the time.

39. Quoted in Clarke, *Hysterical and Useless*, 148.

40. Reviews quoted from http://www.metacritic.com/music/artists/radiohead/kida (accessed 6 December 2009).

41. Simon Reynolds, *Spin* review, quoted in Footman, *Radiohead: A Visual Documentary* (Surrey, U.K.: Chrome Dreams, 2002), 73.

42. Douglas Wolk, "Like Our New Direction?" *Village Voice*, 3 October 2000, http://www.villagevoice.com/issues/0040/wolk.php (accessed 6 December 2009).

43. In Andy Battaglia et al., "Radiohead's *Kid A*." *Salon*, 25 October 2000, http://www.salon.com/ent/music/feature/2000/10/25/radiohead/index.html (accessed 6 December 2009). The *Salon* article presents four critics debating the merits of *Kid A*.

44. Wolk, "Like Our New Direction?"

45. Footman, *Radiohead: A Visual Documentary*, 73.

46. Curtis White, "Kid Adorno," in *The Music and Art of Radiohead*, 13.

47. Quoted in Clarke, *Hysterical and Useless*, 148.

48. http://www.metacritic.com/music/artists/radiohead/kida (accessed 6 December 2009). See also *Resonance* no. 28:62.

49. http://www.allmusic.com/cg/amg.dll?p=amg&sql=10:yzapqjkqojaa (accessed 6 December 2009).

50. David Fricke, *Rolling Stone* review, quoted in Footman, *Radiohead: A Visual Documentary*, 73.

51. Andrew Goodwin, "Radiohead's *Kid A*," in Battaglia et al.

52. Nick Hornby, "Beyond the Pale," *New Yorker* (30 October 2000), http://bmxmusic.com/articles/articles/excerpt_from_beyond_the_pale.htm (accessed 6 December 2009).

53. Footman, *Radiohead: A Visual Documentary*, 73.

54. See Joseph Tate, "Radiohead's Antivideos: Works of Art in the Age of Electronic Reproduction," in *The Music and Art of Radiohead*, 103–17.

55. Clarke, *Hysterical and Useless*, 99.

56. See Richard Menta, "Did Napster Take Radiohead's New Album to Number 1?," MP3newswire.net (28 October 2000), quoted in Davis Schneiderman, "'We Got Heads on Sticks/You Got Ventriloquists': Radiohead and the Improbability of Resistance," in *The Music and Art of Radiohead*, 25.

57. Clarke, *Hysterical and Useless*, 145.

58. See http://www.radiohead.com/archive.html (accessed 6 December 2009).

59. See http://www.waste.uk.com/RadioheadLinks.html (accessed 6 December 2009).

60. See Hainge, "To(rt)uring the Minotaur," 64–68, 74–78.

61. Martin, *Listening to the Future*, 211.

62. Clarke, *Hysterical and Useless*, 97.

63. Ibid., 146.

64. Ross, "The Searchers," 115.

65. Macan links the "Gnostic" trait to progressive rock; thanks to Kevin Holm-Hudson for this insight.

3. Everything in Its Right Place

1. Harde, "Radiohead and the Negation of Gender," 52–61.

2. Carys Wyn Jones, "The Aura of Authenticity: Perceptions of Honesty, Sincerity, and Truth in 'Creep' and 'Kid A,'" in *The Music and Art of Radiohead*, 45. Jones ultimately concludes that "if the measure of authenticity is to be understood as the extent to which a song is an honest expression of the artist's self, 'Kid A' could be seen to succeed far more than 'Creep,' operating on a far more complex and reflexive plane" (46). She is referring here to the song "Kid A," but the analogy could be extended to the full album.

3. Moore and Ibrahim, "Identifying Radiohead's Idiolect," 145.

4. Cone, *The Composer's Voice*, 13; see also David Brackett, *Interpreting Popular Music* (Cambridge: Cambridge University Press, 1995); and Mikhail Bakhtin, *The Dialogic Imagination: Four Essays*, ed. Michael Holquist, trans. Caryl Emerson and Michael Holquist (Austin: University of Texas Press, 1988).

5. Kevin J. H. Dettmar, "Foreword," *The Music and Art of Radiohead*, xv.

6. Jacques Attali, *Noise: The Political Economy of Music* (Minneapolis: University of Minnesota Press, 1985), 34.

7. Dettmar, "Foreword," xvii and xviii. See also Jones, "The Aura of Authenticity," 38–51.

8. On the internet, quoted in Doheny, *Back to Save the Universe*, 92–93. The 1990s brought a proliferation of "unplugged" acoustic (though amplified and recorded) performances, which were conducted to illustrate a given band's authenticity. Nirvana frontman Kurt Cobain committed

suicide a few months after his band appeared on MTV's *Unplugged* (filmed 13 November 1993; aired 16 December 1993), almost as though the "real" were too much to cope with (Cobain made an unsuccessful suicide attempt on 4 March 1994 and succeeded on 5 April 1994). See Steve Dougherty, "No Way Out," *People* 41(15), 25 April 1994, http://www.people.com/people/archive/article/0,,20107919,00.html (accessed 6 December 2009).

9. See Slavoj Žižek, *Looking Awry: An Introduction to Jacques Lacan through Popular Culture* (Cambridge, Mass.: MIT Press, 1991), which discusses the "grey and formless mist" of the Lacanian real in Robert Heinlein's 1942 story *The Unpleasant Profession of Jonathan Hoag* (13–15).

10. Doheny, *Back to Save the Universe*, 78 and 110. This marks a contrast with earlier concept albums, in which the track order was often unified in performance before the album was even recorded.

11. Ross has noted Radiohead's use of pivot tones as early as "Creep." Whereas composers of the Romantic period used pivot chords to ease the transition to a new key, Radiohead's use of pedal and pivot tones lends their songs "a looser, roomier kind of harmony than the standard I–IV–V–I, and it gives the songs a distinct personality. It also helps sell records: whether playing guitar rock or sampling spaced-out electronica, Radiohead affix their signature." "The Searchers," http://www.newyorker.com/archive/2001/08/20/010820fa_FACT1?currentPage=all (accessed 6 December 2009).

12. *Kid A* musical score produced by Anna Joyce (Miami, Fla.: Warner Bros. Publications, 2001).

13. Moore, *The Beatles*, x. Lori Burns has written about the inadequacies of the transcribed score in attempting to replicate performance; see her "Meaning in a Popular Song: The Representation of Masochistic Desire in Sarah McLachlan's 'Ice,'" in *Engaging Music: Essays in Musical Analysis*, ed. Deborah Stein (New York: Oxford University Press, 2005), 141n16; and Burns and Mélisse Lafrance, *Disruptive Divas: Feminism, Identity & Popular Music* (New York and London: Routledge, 2002).

14. See definitions of these terms in the preface to this book and in Walter Everett, "Pitch Down the Middle," in *Expression in Pop-Rock Music: A Collection of Critical and Analytical Essays* (New York: Routledge, 2008), 112–13.

15. This marks a contrast with *Dark Side of the Moon*, which O'Donnell says "generates a continual sense of forward motion" through the "prolongation of an extended melodic arch." "'On the Path,'" in *Speak to Me*.

16. As mentioned in the preface, Walter Everett noted the possible V–I relationship for "Everything" in the single key of F major in his "Making Sense of Rock's Tonal Systems." Kevin Holm-Hudson noted in private communication (29 October 2009) that the progression could also be interpreted as "subsumed within an F major (modally mixed) tonic."

17. Footman, *Radiohead: A Visual Documentary*, 70.

18. http://www.followmearound.com/everything_in_its_right_place.php (accessed 6 December 2009). See also David Fricke, "Radiohead: Making Music That Matters," quoted in Mark B. N. Hansen, "Deforming Rock: Radiohead's Plunge into the Sonic Continuum," in *The Music and Art of Radiohead*, 118.

19. Hansen, "Deforming Rock," 118.

20. See R. Murray Schafer's *The*

New Soundscape: A Handbook for the Modern Music Teacher (Don Mills, Ontario: BMI Canada, 1969) and The Tuning of the World (Philadelphia: University of Pennsylvania Press, 1980).

21. Doheny, Back to Save the Universe, 92.

22. Interview with The Wire, quoted in Doheny, Back to Save the Universe, 92.

23. This anti-corporate/-government stance is similar to the one expounded upon in Naomi Klein's No Logo: No Space, No Choice, No Jobs (New York: Picador USA, 2000) and reappears on the band's website and in subsequent albums. Radiohead's political leanings seemed to become more foregrounded on their post-Amnesiac release Hail to the Thief (2003).

24. Footman, Radiohead: A Visual Documentary, 70.

25. David Riesman, The Lonely Crowd: A Study of the Changing American Character (New Haven, Conn., and London: Yale University Press, 2001 [1950]), 241, 257; see also Robert Putnam, Bowling Alone: The Collapse and Revival of American Community (New York: Simon & Schuster, 2000).

26. Griffiths, OK Computer, 49.

27. Ross, "The Searchers," 115.

28. Spicer, "(Ac)cumulative Form," 33.

29. Footman, Radiohead: A Visual Documentary, 70.

30. http://www.followmearound .com/national_anthem.php (accessed 6 December 2009).

31. Susan McClary discusses the notion of trying to break free from a confining musical frame in her "Excess and Frame: The Musical Representation of Madwomen," in Feminine Endings (Minneapolis: University of Minnesota Press, 1991), 80–111. See also Marianne Tatom Letts, "Mining for 'Goldheart': A Sketch Study in Popu-

lar Music," Indiana Theory Review 21 (Spring/Fall 2000): 147–67, for a discussion of this concept in a Guided By Voices song.

32. This graph is not meant to be a strict Schenkerian interpretation of the song. See also Burns and Lafrance, Disruptive Divas, 42–46, for a summary and analysis of some of the issues surrounding Schenkerian graphs in popular music.

33. Attali, Noise, 85.

34. Tate, "Radiohead's Antivideos," 108.

35. Yorke's mention of the Liffey recalls James Joyce's Ulysses and highlights the possibility for multiple interpretive levels.

36. Footman, Radiohead: A Visual Documentary, 71.

37. Jones, "The Aura of Authenticity," 46.

38. Simon Reynolds, "Walking on Thin Ice," The Wire, no. 209 (July 2001): 32; quoted in Jones, "The Aura of Authenticity," 46.

39. http://www.followmearound .com/how_to_disappear_completely .php (accessed 7 December 2009).

40. Quoted in Clarke, Hysterical and Useless, 129 (original quote from a Rolling Stone interview).

41. Cone, The Composer's Voice, 35–36.

42. Clarke states that "Treefingers" "comes as close as Radiohead ever could to pure ambience, but . . . still acknowledges their musical foundations: resting on what seem to be synthesizers, the song is actually based on an elongated guitar sample." Hysterical and Useless, 149.

43. See Stanley Cavell, The World Viewed: Reflections on the Ontology of Film (New York: Viking Press, 1971), 160.

44. See Paul Griffiths, "Messiaen, Olivier (Eugène Prosper Charles)," in

Grove Music Online. Oxford Music Online, http://www.oxfordmusiconline
.com/subscriber/article/grove/music/
18497 (accessed 20 February 2010).

45. Radiohead waited two years be-
tween *Pablo Honey, The Bends,* and *OK
Computer,* and then two years again
between *Amnesiac* and *Hail to the
Thief,* and another four years before *In
Rainbows.*

46. It may be, of course, that Radiohead had both albums ready to go
before the release of *Kid A,* but the
perception is that the second album
represented a reaction to the initially
negative commercial reception of the
first.

47. See Hansen, "Deforming Rock,"
118, as well as *Meeting People Is Easy,*
in which the rabid adulation of the
crowds serves merely to alienate the
band from its audience.

48. Doheny, *Back to Save the Universe,* 97. Radiohead toured with what
they called the No Logo tent after
Amnesiac's release, publicizing the tour
by word of mouth over the internet in
an attempt at subverting the corporate
ticketing structure. *Back to Save the
Universe,* 108.

49. Klein, *No Logo,* 207.

4. Cut the Kids in Half

1. Clarke asserts that "Electioneer-
ing" had been influenced by Noam
Chomsky's *Manufacturing Consent:
The Political Economy of the Mass Me-
dia* (New York: Pantheon Books, 1988).
Hysterical and Useless, 113.

2. Montgomery, "The Rock Concept Album," 51 and 171.

3. George Martin, *Summer of Love:
The Making of* Sgt. Pepper (London:
Macmillan, 1994), 63; quoted in Montgomery, "The Rock Concept Album,"
21.

4. Thanks to Kevin Holm-Hudson
for these examples.

5. Doheny, *Back to Save the Universe,* 96.

6. Ibid., 97.

7. See George Orwell, *1984* (New
York: Harcourt, Brace and Company,
1949), in which the phrase "We are
the dead" is first said by O'Brien and
echoed later by Winston and Julia.
("We are the dead. Our only true life is
in the future.")

8. Middleton's definition of "hook,"
given in the preface to this book, comes
somewhat obliquely via Adorno's discussion of the "idea": "a relatively independent, memorable element within
a totality." Adorno, *Introduction to the
Sociology of Music,* trans. E. B. Ashton
(New York: Continuum, 1988 [1962]),
34–37; quoted in Middleton, *Studying
Popular Music,* 51.

9. Clarke describes "Fitter Happier" as "listing a two-minute litany of
platitudes to aim for in a perfect modern life—advert slogans, media myths,
lifestyle ideals and so on." *Hysterical
and Useless,* 121.

10. There is no equivalent pause on
Pablo Honey or *The Bends.* On *Amnesiac,* the instrumental "Hunting Bears"
(track nine) provides a break from the
lyrics, but it comes quite late in the
album, the third track from the end.
It occurs between what are arguably
the two most anxiety-producing tracks
on the album, "Dollars & Cents" and
"Like Spinning Plates."

11. Griffiths, *OK Computer,* 62.

12. *Amnesiac*'s "Pulk/Pull Revolving
Doors" is similar to "Fitter Happier" in
its lack of a melody to go with the lyrics. It occurs on track four, between the
placid "Pyramid Song" and "You and
Whose Army."

13. Both Doheny (*Back to Save the
Universe,* 75–78) and Griffiths (*OK
Computer,* 70–71) discuss "Climbing
Up the Walls" as a horror-movie piece.

14. Footman ties these "oohs" to

the "woo-woos" of the Rolling Stones' "Sympathy for the Devil." *Radiohead: A Visual Documentary*, 71.

15. "Idioteque" is built around an electronic composition by Paul Lansky, "mild und leise." See Lansky, "My Radiohead Adventure," in *The Music and Art of Radiohead*, 168–76.

16. Footman, *Radiohead: A Visual Documentary*, 72.

17. This is a contrast to *Amnesiac*'s "Morning Bell," in which the beat has been stripped away to provide only crashing chords. The beat is also stripped away in "Treefingers" and in *Amnesiac*'s "Hunting Bears."

18. Because "Morning Bell" was reworked for *Amnesiac* it is even more subject to multiple interpretations. *Amnesiac*'s version of "Morning Bell" is re-orchestrated, lending the song a different interpretation within that context. Hansen observes that because of the albums' order of release, the *Amnesiac* version derives its "true significance . . . if it is heard and analyzed after and in light of the *Kid A* version." "Deforming Rock," 137n5. A "hybrid" version of "Morning Bell" also exists on the *I Might Be Wrong* live recordings. See "Deforming Rock," 130–31, for further discussion of this "hybrid" version.

19. Radiohead's "Talk Show Host" does appear on *Romeo + Juliet*'s soundtrack.

20. Clarke, *Hysterical and Useless*, 120. See also Hubbs, "The Imagination of Pop-Rock Criticism," for a longer discussion of "Exit Music (for a Film)."

21. Posted on a Radiohead message board, quoted in Clarke, *Hysterical and Useless*, 145. Harde has linked "Kid A" to the "mass-produced, assembly-line Alpha children" of Aldous Huxley's *Brave New World*. "Radiohead and the Negation of Gender," 56.

22. Žižek, *Looking Awry*, 66 and 65.

23. Ibid., 65.

24. Ibid., 64.

25. Ibid.

26. Moore and Ibrahim, "Identifying Radiohead's Idiolect," 156n47.

5. After Years of Waiting, Nothing Came

1. Quoted in Clarke, *Hysterical and Useless*, 152.

2. Posted on Radiohead message board, 30 December 2000, http://acrushdtinbox.tripod.com/id12.html (accessed 7 December 2009).

3. Doheny, *Back to Save the Universe*, 110.

4. Moore and Ibrahim, "Identifying Radiohead's Idiolect," 145.

5. Doheny, *Back to Save the Universe*, 110.

6. David Fricke, "Radiohead Talk *Amnesiac*," *Rolling Stone*, no. 869 (24 May 2001), http://www.rollingstone .com/artists/radiohead/articles/story/ 5919396/radiohead_talk_amnesiac (accessed 7 December 2009).

7. "Gnosticism," *Catholic Encyclopedia*, http://www.newadvent.org/ cathen/06592a.htm (accessed 7 December 2009).

8. Tony Whetstone, Mark Cross, and Lauren Whetstone, "Inhibition, Contextual Segregation, and Subject Strategies in List Method Directed Forgetting," *Consciousness and Cognition* 5 (1996): 395–417.

9. See Susan L. Joslyn and Mark A. Oakes, "Directed Forgetting and Autobiographical Events," *Memory and Cognition* 33:4 (2005): 577–87.

10. Anne P. DePrince and Jennifer J. Freyd, "Forgetting Trauma Stimuli," *Psychological Science* 15:7 (2004): 488–92.

11. See Tony Whetstone and Mark D. Cross, "Control of Conscious Contents in Directed Forgetting and

Thought Suppression," *PSYCHE* 4:16 (November 1998), http://journalpsyche.org/ojs-2.2/index.php/psyche/article/viewFile/2452/2381, accessed 7 December 2009.

12. Posted on Radiohead message board, 30 December 2000. http://acrushdtinbox.tripod.com/id12.html (accessed 7 December 2009). Some listeners believed that the albums should have been cut down and released as a single unit. In private communication, one fan stated that *"Kid A and Amnesiac* were only half good each, so I combined the best songs for the single album I thought the two released albums should have been."

13. Ian Watson, "The Ballad of Thom Yorke," *Rolling Stone* (Australian edition), no. 589 (July 2001): 46; quoted in Hainge, "To(rt)uring the Minotaur," 72.

14. Quoted in *The Big Issue*, January 2001. http://acrushdtinbox.tripod.com/id12.html (accessed 7 December 2009).

15. R. J. Smith, "Sounds Like Music," *Village Voice*, 26 June 2001, http://www.villagevoice.com/issues/0126/rjsmith.php (accessed 7 December 2009).

16. David Fricke, "Radiohead Talk *Amnesiac.*"

17. Quoted in Clarke, *Hysterical and Useless*, 156.

18. Hainge points out that although Yorke's lyrics are easier to hear, they are not necessarily more comprehensible. "To(rt)uring the Minotaur," 77.

19. Donwood received a Grammy for Best Recording Package for *Amnesiac* in 2002. See http://www.rocksbackpages.com/article.html?ArticleID=4526 (accessed 7 December 2009).

20. See Hainge, "To(rt)uring the Minotaur," for more on this image in Radiohead's work.

21. Radiohead seems to be taking the "rock in opposition" movement a

step further, by turning the idea of refusing to compromise over art into a hollow art project. See http://www.squidco.com/rer/RIO.html (accessed 7 December 2009) for a discussion of Rock in Opposition (RIO) plus the text of the pamphlet distributed at the original RIO concert on 12 March 1978. On the website, Phil Zampino defines "rock in opposition" as "music that is difficult to pigeonhole, which embraces progressive rock, improvisation, folk forms and often extreme experimentation, drawing source [*sic*] from the musics of many cultures, and utilizing modern techniques and technologies." Thanks to Bryan Sale for this suggestion.

22. Stephen Dalton, "Anyone Can Play Guitar: Radiohead on Record," *Uncut* 51 (August 2001): 45, quoted in Hainge, "To(rt)uring the Minotaur," 72.

23. Alex Abramovich, "The Anti-Christs: Radiohead Defies Rock's Own, Personal Jesus Myth," *Slate*, 8 June 2001, http://slate.msn.com/?id=109743 (accessed 7 December 2009).

24. Watson, "The Ballad of Thom Yorke," 48, 50; quoted in Hainge, "To(rt)uring the Minotaur," 72 and 73.

25. Clarke, *Hysterical and Useless*, 153.

26. These lyrics recall the Beatles' "Only a Northern Song" (*Yellow Submarine*, 1969): "If you think the harmony is a little dark and out of key, you're correct, there's nobody there. It doesn't matter what chords I play, what words I say or time of day it is, and I told you there's no one there."

27. Griffiths uses the term "image trail" to describe categories of images found on the album *OK Computer* and particularly in "Fitter Happier." *OK Computer*, 85–87.

28. Spicer, "(Ac)cumulative Form," 33–34.

29. Doheny, *Back to Save the Universe*, 112.

30. Ibid.

31. Footman, *Radiohead: A Visual Documentary*, 72. Kevin Holm-Hudson points out that an even earlier Beatles "tribute" had come with "Karma Police," which alludes to John Lennon's "Instant Karma!" single (1970) in its title and uses the chorus chord progression from "Sexy Sadie" (*The Beatles*, 1968). It could also be argued that the use of heavy reverb on Yorke's voice in the coda of "Karma Police" is a nod to Lennon's use of reverb on songs like "#9 Dream" (*Walls and Bridges*, 1974). Private correspondence, 29 October 2009.

32. Hansen, "Deforming Rock," 126–27.

33. Footman notes that the line "and we all went to heaven in a little row boat" comes from "The Clapping Song," which was "recorded by Shirley Ellis in 1965 and covered by the Belle Stars 17 years later." *Radiohead: A Visual Documentary*, 78.

34. Ibid., 72.

35. Hansen, "Deforming Rock," 127.

36. Ibid., 128.

37. Doheny, *Back to Save the Universe*, 118.

38. Ibid.

39. RSS stands for Really Simple Syndication; users can subscribe to an RSS feed through a reader and receive updates when the site's content changes. See http://www.radiohead.com/deadairspace/ (accessed 7 December 2009).

40. Footman, *Radiohead: A Visual Documentary*, 78.

41. Doheny, *Back to Save the Universe*, 119.

42. This section could also be called bridge one, but the published guitar-tab score labels it as a pre-chorus. They are essentially the same thing.

43. This notion brings to mind the ending poem on the Moody Blues' *Days of Future Passed*: "Cold-hearted orb that rules the night . . . we decide which is right, and which is an illusion." The subject ultimately must decide for himself within the confines of the album, whereas the listener gets to decide for himself outside the album.

44. Footman, *Radiohead: A Visual Documentary*, 78.

45. Ibid.

6. I Might Be Wrong

1. This cannibalistic imagery returns in *Hail to the Thief*'s "We Suck Young Blood."

2. Doheny, *Back to Save the Universe*, 123–24.

3. Hansen, "Deforming Rock," 130.

4. Doheny, *Back to Save the Universe*, 123.

5. Ibid., 125.

6. Footman, *Radiohead: A Visual Documentary*, 79.

7. http://www.ateaseweb.com/songs/dollarsandcents.php (accessed 8 December 2009).

8. Chris Harvey, ed., *Amnesiac* musical score (London: International Music Publications, 2005).

9. Doheny, *Back to Save the Universe*, 126.

10. Hainge, "To(rt)uring the Minotaur," 76.

11. The image of a musical artist being hunted by fans is a common one in movies about popular music, including *The Big Broadcast* (1932), in which Bing Crosby is nearly ripped apart by fans, as well as the Beatles' escape from fans at the train station in *A Hard Day's Night*.

12. Footman notes that in "Like Spinning Plates" Radiohead moves from "singing about cannibalism [in 'Knives Out'], to doing it." *Radiohead: A Visual Documentary*, 79. Arguably,

the band had already moved into this type of cannibalism with "Morning Bell/Amnesiac." See also http://www.greenplasticwateringcans.com/lyrics/i will.php (accessed 18 March 2010).

13. A similar effect can be heard in the Who's "I'm Free" (*Tommy*), in which the beat is established by the guitar, bass, and drums before the singer makes his entrance and then is heard as syncopated due to the strength of the voice's articulation of the beat.

14. Footman, *Radiohead: A Visual Documentary*, 79.

15. Doheny, *Back to Save the Universe*, 128.

16. Clarke, *Hysterical and Useless*, 97.

17. Footman, *Radiohead: A Visual Documentary*, 80; Doheny, *Back to Save the Universe*, 108.

18. Doheny, *Back to Save the Universe*, 116–17.

19. Hainge, "To(rt)uring the Minotaur," 73–74.

20. Quoted in Doheny, *Back to Save the Universe*, 133; original in Reynolds, "Walking on Thin Ice."

21. Tate, "Introduction," 3.

22. Tate notes that W.A.S.T.E. is named after "the underground postal system in Thomas Pynchon's *The Crying of Lot 49* [1966]." "*Hail to the Thief*: A Rhyzomatic Map in Fragments," in *The Music and Art of Radiohead*, 195n3.

23. Doheny, *Back to Save the Universe*, 132.

24. Hansen, "Deforming Rock," 131.

25. http://www.greenplastic.com/lyrics/truelovewaits.php (accessed 8 December 2009).

26. http://www.setlist.fm/stats/radiohead-bd6bd12.html (accessed 8 December 2009).

27. http://www.greenplastic.com/lyrics/truelovewaits.php (accessed 8 December 2009).

28. http://www.ateaseweb.com/songs/truelovewaits.php (accessed 8 December 2009).

29. http://www.greenplastic.com/lyrics/truelovewaits.php (accessed 8 December 2009); http://www.ateaseweb.com/songs/truelovewaits.php (accessed 8 December 2009).

30. http://www.greenplastic.com/lyrics/truelovewaits.php (accessed 8 December 2009).

7. We Are the Dollars and Cents

1. Interview with the Dutch magazine *OOR*, quoted in Tate, "*Hail to the Thief*," 194.

2. Quoted in Moore and Ibrahim, "Identifying Radiohead's Idiolect," 139.

3. Moore and Ibrahim, "Identifying Radiohead's Idiolect," 139. See also Danny Eccleston, *Q* magazine, Radiohead Special Edition, EMAP Metro Limited: 34–35; Jake Kennedy, *Record Collector* (November 2000): 33; Gareth Grundy, *Q* magazine, Radiohead Special Edition, 122; David Cheal and Andrew Perry, "Radiohead: Are They Still the Best?," *Daily Telegraph* (5 June 2003): 21.

4. Tate, "*Hail to the Thief*," 177–97.

5. Schneiderman, "Radiohead and the Improbability of Resistance," 22.

6. Quoted in Lisa Leblanc, "'Ice Age Coming': Apocalypse, the Sublime, and the Paintings of Stanley Donwood" (2005), in *The Music and Art of Radiohead*, 100. Leblanc discusses how Donwood has worked with the band since *The Bends* to create "an iconographic language" that "provid[es] a strong visual analog to the music" (85).

7. The band considered naming the album after the subtitle to "There There"—"The Bony King of Nowhere"—but the title was deemed "too prog." *Q* magazine, quoted in Tate, "*Hail to the Thief*," 189.

8. Capitol Records website, quoted in Tate, "*Hail to the Thief*," 196n6.

9. Clarke, *Hysterical and Useless*, 164.

10. Tate, "Hail to the Thief," 182.

11. Ibid., 185. Tate refers to Žižek's *On Belief* (Routledge: London and New York, 2001).

12. Tate, "Hail to the Thief," 191.

13. Klosterman, "Meeting Thom Is Easy," *Spin* 19:7 (July 2003): 62–70; quoted in Tate, "Hail to the Thief," 192.

14. Tate, "Hail to the Thief," 194.

15. Tate describes a marketing campaign for *Hail to the Thief* in which flyers with lyrics from "We Suck Young Blood" were posted around Los Angeles. The toll-free number included was for the "Hail to the Thief hotline, a voicemail labyrinth in which callers can easily be lost but can also hear songs from the album." "Hail to the Thief," 187–88.

16. Dettmar, "Foreword," xix.

17. Jon Pareles, "Pay What You Want for This Article," *New York Times*, 9 December 2007, http://www.nytimes.com/2007/12/09/arts/music/09pare.html?pagewanted=1 (accessed 8 December 2009).

18. Ann Powers, "Thom Yorke, Free Agent," 28 June 2006, *Los Angeles Times*, http://www.ateaseweb.com/2006/06/28/la-times-interview-thom-yorke-free-agent/ (accessed 8 December 2009).

19. Stanley Donwood interview with Colette Meacher, "Got It Covered," *Latest Art*, 2006, http://latest-art.co.uk/features/?id=4 (accessed 8 December 2009).

20. Ibid.

21. Radiohead At Ease, http://www.ateaseweb.com/2006/07/20/the-eraser-charts-at-number-2-in-usa/ (accessed 8 December 2009).

22. Powers, "Thom Yorke, Free Agent."

23. Louis Pattison, "Thom Yorke: The Eraser," *New Musical Express*, 7 July 2006, http://www.nme.com/reviews/thom-yorke/7973 (accessed 8 December 2009).

24. Powers, "Thom Yorke, Free Agent."

25. Rob Sheffield, *The Eraser*: Thom Yorke: Review, *Rolling Stone*, 26 June 2006, http://www.rollingstone.com/reviews/album/10621185/review/10681006/the_eraser (accessed 8 December 2009).

26. Powers, "Thom Yorke, Free Agent."

27. Sheffield, *The Eraser*.

28. David Fricke, "Radiohead's Thom Yorke on Going Solo," *Rolling Stone*, 1 June 2006, http://www.rollingstone.com/news/story/10464376/radioheads_thom_yorke_on_going_solo/ (accessed 8 December 2009).

29. Fricke, "Radiohead's Thom Yorke on Going Solo."

30. Sheffield, *The Eraser*.

31. Powers, "Thom Yorke, Free Agent."

32. Fricke, "Radiohead's Thom Yorke on Going Solo."

33. Josh Tyrangiel, "Radiohead Says: Pay What You Want," *Time*, 1 October 2007, http://www.time.com/time/arts/article/0,8599,1666973,00.html (accessed 8 December 2009).

34. "Radiohead Reveal *In Rainbows* Download Details, We Anxiously Salivate into Our Keyboards," *Rolling Stone*, 9 October 2007, http://www.rollingstone.com/rockdaily/index.php/2007/10/09/radiohead-reveal-in-rainbows-download-details-we-anxiously-salivate-into-our-keyboards/ (accessed 8 December 2009).

35. Pareles, "Pay What You Want."

36. Ibid.

37. See "Radiohead Cryptically Post New Song Lyrics, Make Sudoku Seem Irrelevant," *Rolling Stone*, 21 Sep-

tember 2007, http://www.rollingstone
.com/rockdaily/index.php/2007/09/21/
radiohead-cryptically-post-new-song-
lyrics-make-sudoku-seem-irrelevant/
(accessed 8 December 2009); "Radiohead Post More Cryptic Messages, We
Break Out Our Decoder Rings," *Rolling Stone*, 26 September 2007, http://
www.rollingstone.com/rockdaily/index
.php/2007/09/26/radiohead-post-more-
cryptic-messages-we-break-out-our-
decoder-rings/ (accessed 8 December
2009). See http://www.citizeninsane.eu/
images/wormbuffetcode.png for an image of the code with its key (accessed 8
December 2009).

38. Pareles, "Pay What You Want."

39. See http://www.radiohead.com/
deadairspace/index.php?c=292 (accessed 8 December 2009).

40. "New Radiohead Album Com-
ing Out October 10th," *Rolling Stone*,
30 September 2007, http://www
.rollingstone.com/rockdaily/index
.php/2007/09/30/new-radiohead-album-
coming-out-october-10th/ (accessed 8
December 2009).

41. "Radiohead's *In Rainbows*:
Track-by-Track Preview," *Rolling Stone*,
1 October 2007, http://www.rollingstone
.com/news/story/16654550/radioheads_
in_rainbows_trackbytrack_preview (accessed 8 December 2009).

42. Ryan Dombal, interview with
Colin Greenwood, *Pitchfork*, 28 March
2008, http://pitchfork.com/features/
interviews/7489-radiohead/ (accessed 8
December 2009).

43. Tyrangiel, "Radiohead Says: Pay
What You Want."

44. "Radiohead Reveal How Successful *In Rainbows* Download Really
Was," *New Musical Express*, 15 October
2008, http://www.nme.com/news/radio
head/40444 (accessed 8 December
2009).

45. Ibid.

46. See Robert Andrews, "Radiohead
Downloaders Preferred Illegal P2P to
Legal Free," *Guardian*, 1 August 2008,
http://www.guardian.co.uk/media/
pda/2008/aug/01/radioheaddownloaders
preferre (accessed 8 December 2009);
Ben Rogerson, "Radiohead Beaten
by BitTorrent," 4 August 2008, http://
www.musicradar.com/news/guitars/
radiohead-beaten-by-bittorrent-168026
(accessed 8 December 2009).

47. Ben Rogerson, "Radiohead
In Rainbows Download Stats Made
Public," 15 October 2008, http://
www.musicradar.com/news/guitars/
radiohead-in-rainbows-download-stats-
made-public-177472 (accessed 8 December 2009).

48. Lars Brandle, "Radiohead in
Direct-Licensing Deal for New CD,"
Billboard, 9 October 2007, http://web
.archive.org/web/20080214170133/http://
billboard.com/bbcom/news/article_
display.jsp?vnu_content_id=1003655864
(accessed 8 December 2009).

49. Pareles, "Pay What You Want."

50. Pattison, "Thom Yorke: The
Eraser."

51. Tyrangiel, "Radiohead Says: Pay
What You Want."

52. Andrew Lindsay, "Radiohead
Begin Recording New Album,"18 May
2009, http://stereokill.net/2009/05/18/
radiohead-begin-recording-new-album/
(accessed 8 December 2009).

53. See "Private Harry Patch," *Telegraph*, 25 July 2009, http://www
.telegraph.co.uk/news/obituaries/
military-obituaries/army-obituaries/
5907316/Private-Harry-Patch.html (accessed 8 December 2009); and http://
www.radiohead.com/deadairspace/
index.php?a=495 (accessed 8 December
2009).

54. "Radiohead Artist Reveals Secret
In Rainbows Cover Art," *New Musical
Express*, 24 October 2007, http://www

.nme.com/news/radiohead/32012 (accessed 8 December 2009).

55. Ashleigh Wilson, "Composer Pulls Some Old Strings," *Australian*, 14 August 2009, http://www.theaustralian.news.com.au/story/0,25197,25925014-16947,00.html (accessed 8 December 2009).

56. See "Is a New Radiohead EP on Its Way?," 13 August 2009, http://www.ateaseweb.com/2009/08/13/is-a-new-radiohead-ep-on-its-way/; and "Radiohead's *Wall of Ice* EP: More Clues," http://www.ateaseweb.com/2009/08/14/radioheads-wall-of-ice-ep-more-clues/ (both accessed 8 December 2009).

57. http://xkcd.com/86/ (accessed 8 December 2009).

58. http://www.contagiousmagazine.com/2009/08/radiohead.php (accessed 11 December 2009).

59. Ryan Dombal, "Radiohead's First Three Albums Reissued and Expanded," *Pitchfork*, 14 January 2009, http://pitchfork.com/news/34391-radioheads-first-three-albums-reissued-and-expanded/ (accessed 8 December 2009).

60. Scott Plagenhoef, review of *Radiohead: The Best Of*, in *Pitchfork*, 5 June 2008, http://pitchfork.com/reviews/albums/11686-the-best-ofthe-best-of-special-edition/ (accessed 8 December 2009).

61. "Radiohead Reissuing Expanded Collectors Edition Albums," *SMN News*, 11 August 2009, http://www.smnnews.com/2009/08/11/radiohead-reissuing-expanded-collectors-edition-albums/ (accessed 8 December 2009).

62. Dombal, interview with Colin Greenwood.

"100 Best Albums of the Decade."
2009–2010. *Rolling Stone*, 24 December–7 January. http://www.rolling
stone.com/news/story/31248017/100_
best_albums_of_the_decade/42.

Abramovich, Alex. 2001. "The Anti-Christs: Radiohead Defies Rock's Own, Personal Jesus Myth." *Slate*, 8 June, http://slate.msn.com/?id=109743.

Adorno, Theodor. 1988 [1962]. *Introduction to the Sociology of Music*, trans. E. B. Ashton. New York: Continuum.

Adorno, Theodor, with Max Horkheimer. 2002 [1944]. *The Dialectic of Enlightenment*, trans. Edmund Jephcott. Stanford, Calif.: Stanford University Press.

Andrews, Robert. 2008. "Radiohead Downloaders Preferred Illegal P2P to Legal Free." *Guardian*, 1 August, http://www.guardian.co.uk/media/pda/2008/aug/01/radioheaddown
loaderspreferre.

Attali, Jacques. 1985. *Noise: The Political Economy of Music*. Minneapolis: University of Minnesota Press.

Bakhtin, Mikhail. 1988. *The Dialogic Imagination: Four Essays*, ed. Michael Holquist, trans. Caryl Emerson and Michael Holquist. Austin: University of Texas Press.

Battaglia, Andy, Michelle Goldberg, Andrew Goodwin, and Joe Heim. 2000. "Radiohead's *Kid A*." *Salon*, 25 October, http://www.salon.com/ent/music/feature/2000/10/25/radiohead/index.html.

Borders, James. 2001. "Form and the Concept Album: Aspects of Modernism in Frank Zappa's Early Releases." *Perspectives of New Music* 39: 119–61.

Brackett, David. 1995. *Interpreting Popular Music*. Cambridge: Cambridge University Press.

Brandle, Lars. 2007. "Radiohead in Direct-Licensing Deal for New CD." *Billboard*, 9 October, http://web
.archive.org/web/20080214170133/
http://billboard.com/bbcom/news/
article_display.jsp?vnu_content_id=
1003655864.

Buckley, David. "Album," in *Grove Music Online, Oxford Music Online*, http://www.oxfordmusiconline.com/
subscriber/article/grove/music/47210.

Burns, Lori. 2005. "Meaning in a Popular Song: The Representation of Masochistic Desire in Sarah McLachlan's 'Ice.'" In *Engaging Music: Essays in Musical Analysis*, ed. Deborah Stein. New York: Oxford University Press.

Burns, Lori, and Mélisse Lafrance. 2002. *Disruptive Divas: Feminism, Identity & Popular Music*. New York and London: Routledge.

Cavell, Stanley. 1971. *The World Viewed: Reflections on the Ontology of Film*. New York: Viking Press.

Clarke, Donald. 1989. *The Penguin Encyclopedia of Popular Music*. London: Penguin.

Clarke, Martin. 2003. *Hysterical and Useless*. London: Plexus.

Cone, Edward T. 1974. *The Composer's Voice*. Berkeley: University of California Press.

Covach, John. 1997. "Progressive Rock, 'Close to the Edge,' and the Boundaries of Style." In Covach and Graeme M. Boone, eds., *Understanding Rock: Essays in Musical Analysis*. New York: Oxford University Press.

———. 2006. *What's That Sound? An Introduction to Rock and Its History*. New York: W. W. Norton.

Delingpole, James. 1997. "James Delingpole's Rock Records of the Year." *Sunday Telegraph*, 27 December, http://www.telegraph.co.uk/culture/4711342/Records-of-the-year.html.

DePrince, Anne P., and Jennifer J. Freyd. 2004. "Forgetting Trauma Stimuli." *Psychological Science* 15:7: 488–92.

Dettmar, Kevin J. H. 2005. "Foreword." In *The Music and Art of Radiohead*, ed. Joseph Tate. Aldershot, U.K.: Ashgate, xiv–xx.

Doheny, James. 2002. *Radiohead: Back to Save the Universe: The Stories Behind Every Song*. New York: Thunder's Mouth Press.

Dombal, Ryan. 2008. Interview with Colin Greenwood, *Pitchfork*, 28 March, http://pitchfork.com/features/interviews/7489-radiohead/.

———. 2009. "Radiohead's First Three Albums Reissued and Expanded." *Pitchfork*, 14 January, http://pitchfork.com/news/34391-radioheads-first-three-albums-reissued-and-expanded/.

Dougherty, Steve. 1994. "No Way Out." *People* 41(15), 25 April, http://www.people.com/people/archive/article/0,,20107919,00.html.

Everett, Walter. 1999. *The Beatles as Musicians: Revolver through the Anthology*. Oxford: Oxford University Press.

———. "Making Sense of Rock's Tonal Systems." 2004. *Music Theory Online* 10:4, http://mto.societymusictheory.org/issues/mto.04.10.4/mto.04.10.4.w_everett_frames.html.

———, ed. 2008. *Expression in Pop-Rock Music: A Collection of Critical and Analytical Essays*. New York: Routledge.

———. 2008 [1999]. "Pitch Down the Middle." In *Expression in Pop-Rock Music: A Collection of Critical and Analytical Essays*, ed. Walter Everett. New York: Routledge, 111–74.

Footman, Tim. 2002. *Radiohead: A Visual Documentary*. Surrey, U.K.: Chrome Dreams.

Fricke, David. 2001. "Radiohead Talk *Amnesiac*." *Rolling Stone*, no. 869 (24 May), http://www.rollingstone.com/artists/radiohead/articles/story/5919396/radiohead_talk_amnesiac.

———. 2006. "Radiohead's Thom Yorke on Going Solo." *Rolling Stone*, 1 June, http://www.rollingstone.com/news/story/10464376/radioheads_thom_yorke_on_going_solo/.

Gee, Grant, dir. 1998. *Meeting People Is Easy*. EMD/Capitol video.

Griffiths, Dai. 2004. *OK Computer*. New York: Continuum International Publishing Group.

——. 2005. "Public Schoolboy Music: Debating Radiohead." In *The Music and Art of Radiohead*, ed. Joseph Tate. Aldershot, U.K.: Ashgate, 159–67.

Griffiths, Paul. "Messiaen, Olivier (Eugène Prosper Charles)." In *Grove Music Online, Oxford Music Online*, http://www.oxfordmusiconline.com/subscriber/article/grove/music/18497.

Hainge, Greg. 2005. "To(rt)uring the Minotaur: Radiohead, Pop, Unnatural Couplings, and Mainstream Subversion." In *The Music and Art of Radiohead*, ed. Joseph Tate. Aldershot, U.K.: Ashgate, 62–84.

Hansen, Mark B. N. 2005. "Deforming Rock: Radiohead's Plunge into the Sonic Continuum." In *The Music and Art of Radiohead*, ed. Joseph Tate. Aldershot, U.K.: Ashgate, 118–38.

Harde, Erin. 2005. "Radiohead and the Negation of Gender." In *The Music and Art of Radiohead*, ed. Joseph Tate. Aldershot, U.K.: Ashgate, 52–61.

Harvey, Chris, ed. 2005. *Amnesiac* musical score. London: International Music Publications.

Holm-Hudson, Kevin, ed. 2002. *Progressive Rock Reconsidered*. New York: Routledge.

——. 2006. "'Worked Out Within the Grooves': The Sound and Structure of *Dark Side of the Moon*." In *Speak to Me: The Legacy of Pink Floyd's The Dark Side of the Moon*, ed. Russell Reising. London: Ashgate, 69–86.

Hornby, Nick. 2000. "Beyond the Pale." *New Yorker* (30 October); accessed at http://bmxmusic.com/articles/articles/excerpt_from_beyond_the_pale.htm.

Hubbs, Nadine. 2008 [1999]. "The Imagination of Pop-Rock Criticism." In *Expression in Pop-Rock Music: A Collection of Critical and Analytical*

Essays, ed. Walter Everett. New York: Routledge, 215–37.

Hughes, Timothy S. 2003. "Groove and Flow: Six Analytical Essays on the Music of Stevie Wonder." Ph.D. diss., University of Washington.

Huxley, Aldous. 1932. *Brave New World*. London: Chatto & Windus.

Jameson, Frederic. 1997. "The Cultural Logic of Late Capitalism." In *Rethinking Architecture: A Reader in Cultural Theory*, ed. Neil Leach. London: Routledge.

Jones, Carys Wyn. 2005. "The Aura of Authenticity: Perceptions of Honesty, Sincerity, and Truth in 'Creep' and 'Kid A.'" In *The Music and Art of Radiohead*, ed. Joseph Tate. Aldershot, U.K.: Ashgate, 38–51.

Joslyn, Susan L., and Mark A. Oakes. 2005. "Directed Forgetting and Autobiographical Events." *Memory and Cognition* 33:4:577–87.

Joyce, Anna, prod. 2001. *Kid A* musical score. Miami, Fla.: Warner Bros. Publications.

Kaminsky, Peter. 1992. "The Popular Album as Song Cycle: Paul Simon's *Still Crazy After All These Years*." *College Music Symposium* 32:38–54.

Klein, Naomi. 2000. *No Logo: No Space, No Choice, No Jobs*. New York: Picador USA.

Klosterman, Chuck. 2003. "Meeting Thom Is Easy." *Spin* 19:7 (July): 62–70.

——. 2005. "The Rock Lexicon." *Spin* 21:5 (May): 61.

Kostka, Stefan, and Dorothy Payne. 2008. *Tonal Harmony*, 6th ed. New York: McGraw-Hill.

Lansky, Paul. 2005. "My Radiohead Adventure." In *The Music and Art of Radiohead*, ed. Joseph Tate. Aldershot, U.K.: Ashgate, 168–76.

Leblanc, Lisa. 2005. "'Ice Age Coming': Apocalypse, the Sublime, and the Paintings of Stanley Donwood." In

The Music and Art of Radiohead, ed. Joseph Tate. Aldershot, U.K.: Ashgate, 85–102.

Letts, Marianne Tatom. 2000. "Mining for 'Goldheart': A Sketch Study in Popular Music." *Indiana Theory Review* 21 (Spring/Fall): 147–67.

———. 2008. "Sky of Blue, Sea of Green: A Semiotic Reading of the Film *Yellow Submarine*." *Popular Music* 27(1): 1–14.

———. 2010. "Who Sells Out: Petra Haden in the Age of Mechanical Reproduction." *IASPM@Journal* 1:2.

Lindsay, Andrew. 2009. "Radiohead Begin Recording New Album." 18 May, http://stereokill.net/2009/05/18/radiohead-begin-recording-new-album/.

Lucky, Jerry. 1998. *The Progressive Rock Files*. Burlington, Ontario: Collector's Guide Publishing.

Macan, Edward C. 1996. *Rocking the Classics: English Progressive Rock and the Counterculture*. New York: Oxford University Press.

Martin, Bill. 1996. *Music of Yes: Structure and Vision in Progressive Rock*. Chicago and La Salle, Ill.: Open Court.

———. 1998. *Listening to the Future: The Time of Progressive Rock*. Chicago and La Salle, Ill.: Open Court.

Martin, George. 1994. *Summer of Love: The Making of* Sgt. Pepper. London: Macmillan.

Maus, Fred. 1988. "Music as Drama." *Music Theory Spectrum* 10: 56–73.

McClary, Susan. 1991. "Excess and Frame: The Musical Representation of Madwomen." In *Feminine Endings*. Minneapolis: University of Minnesota Press, 80–111.

Meacher, Colette. 2006. "Got It Covered." *Latest Art*, http://latest-art.co.uk/features/?id=4.

Menta, Richard. 2000. "Did Napster Take Radiohead's New Album to Number 1?" MP3newswire.net (28 October).

Middleton, Richard. 1990. *Studying Popular Music*. Bristol, Pa.: Open University Press.

Middleton, Richard, et al. "Pop," section III, "North America." In *Grove Music Online, Oxford Music Online*, http://www.oxfordmusiconline.com/subscriber/article/grove/music/46845.

Montgomery, David O. 2002. "The Rock Concept Album: Context and Analysis." Ph.D. diss., University of Toronto.

Moore, Allan F. 1993. *Rock: The Primary Text; Developing a Musicology of Rock*. Buckingham, Pa.: Open University Press.

———. 1997. *The Beatles: Sgt. Pepper's Lonely Hearts Club Band*. Cambridge: Cambridge University Press.

Moore, Allan F., and Anwar Ibrahim. 2005. "'Sounds Like Teen Spirit': Identifying Radiohead's Idiolect." In *The Music and Art of Radiohead*, ed. Joseph Tate. Aldershot, U.K.: Ashgate, 139–58.

"New Radiohead Album Coming Out October 10th." 2007. *Rolling Stone*, 30 September, http://www.rollingstone.com/rockdaily/index.php/2007/09/30/new-radiohead-album-coming-out-october-10th/.

O'Donnell, Shaugn. 2006. "'On the Path': Tracing Tonal Coherence in *Dark Side of the Moon*." In *Speak to Me: The Legacy of Pink Floyd's* The Dark Side of the Moon, ed. Russell Reising. London: Ashgate.

Orwell, George. 1949. *1984*. New York: Harcourt, Brace and Company.

Pareles, Jon. 2007. "Pay What You Want for This Article." *New York Times*, 9 December, http://www.nytimes.com/2007/12/09/arts/music/09pare.html?pagewanted=1.

Pattison, Louis. 2006. "Thom Yorke: The Eraser." *New Musical Express*,

7 July, http://www.nme.com/reviews/thom-yorke/7973.

Plagenhoef, Scott. 2008. Review of *Radiohead: The Best Of*. *Pitchfork*, 5 June, http://pitchfork.com/reviews/albums/11686-the-best-ofthe-best-of-special-edition/.

Powers, Ann. 2006. "Thom Yorke, Free Agent." *Los Angeles Times*, 28 June, http://www.ateaseweb.com/2006/06/28/la-times-interview-thom-yorke-free-agent/.

"Private Harry Patch," *Telegraph*. 2009. 25 July, http://www.telegraph.co.uk/news/obituaries/military-obituaries/army-obituaries/5907316/Private-Harry-Patch.html.

Putnam, Robert. 2000. *Bowling Alone: The Collapse and Revival of American Community*. New York: Simon & Schuster, 2000.

"Radiohead Artist Reveals Secret *In Rainbows* Cover Art." 2007. *New Musical Express*, 24 October, http://www.nme.com/news/radiohead/32012.

"Radiohead Cryptically Post New Song Lyrics, Make Sudoku Seem Irrelevant." 2007. *Rolling Stone*, 21 September, http://www.rollingstone.com/rockdaily/index.php/2007/09/21/radiohead-cryptically-post-new-song-lyrics-make-sudoku-seem-irrelevant/.

"Radiohead Post More Cryptic Messages, We Break Out Our Decoder Rings." 2007. *Rolling Stone*, 26 September, http://www.rollingstone.com/rockdaily/index.php/2007/09/26/radiohead-post-more-cryptic-messages-we-break-out-our-decoder-rings/.

"Radiohead Reissuing Expanded Collectors Edition Albums." 2009. *SMN News*, 11 August, http://www.smnnews.com/2009/08/11/radiohead-reissuing-expanded-collectors-edition-albums/.

"Radiohead Reveal How Successful *In Rainbows* Download Really Was."

2008. *New Musical Express*, 15 October, http://www.nme.com/news/radiohead/40444.

"Radiohead Reveal *In Rainbows* Download Details, We Anxiously Salivate into Our Keyboards." 2007. *Rolling Stone*, 9 October, http://www.rollingstone.com/rockdaily/index.php/2007/10/09/radiohead-reveal-in-rainbows-download-details-we-anxiously-salivate-into-our-keyboards/.

"Radiohead's *In Rainbows*: Track-by-Track Preview." 2007. *Rolling Stone*, 1 October, http://www.rollingstone.com/news/story/16654550/radioheads_in_rainbows_trackbytrack_preview.

Randall, Mac. 2000. *Exit Music: The Radiohead Story*. New York: Random House.

Reynolds, Simon. 2001. "Walking on Thin Ice." In *Wire*, no. 209 (July): 26–33.

Riesman, David. 2001 [1950]. *The Lonely Crowd: A Study of the Changing American Character*. New Haven, Conn.: Yale University Press.

Rockwell, John. "Rock opera." In *Grove Music Online, Oxford Music Online*, http://www.oxfordmusiconline.com/subsriber/article/grove/music/O008572.

Rogerson, Ben. 2008. "Radiohead Beaten by BitTorrent." 4 August, http://www.musicradar.com/news/guitars/radiohead-beaten-by-bittorrent-168026.

———. 2008. "Radiohead *In Rainbows* Download Stats Made Public." 15 October, http://www.musicradar.com/news/guitars/radiohead-in-rainbows-download-stats-made-public-177472.

Rosen, Jody. 2006. "Positively 47th Street: Twyla Tharp Brings Bob Dylan to Broadway." *Slate* (27 October), http://www.slate.com/id/2152251/.

Ross, Alex. 2001. "The Searchers: Radiohead's Unquiet Revolution." *New Yorker* (20 and 27 August): 112–23.

Schafer, R. Murray. 1969. *The New Soundscape: A Handbook for the Modern Music Teacher.* Don Mills, Ontario: BMI Canada.

———. 1980. *The Tuning of the World.* Philadelphia: University of Pennsylvania Press.

Schafer, William J. 1972. *Rock Music: Where It's Been, What It Means, Where It's Going.* Minneapolis: Augsburg Publishing.

Schneiderman, Davis. 2005. "'We Got Heads on Sticks/You Got Ventriloquists': Radiohead and the Improbability of Resistance." In *The Music and Art of Radiohead*, ed. Joseph Tate. Aldershot, U.K.: Ashgate, 15–37.

Sheffield, Rob. 2006. "*The Eraser*: Thom Yorke: Review." *Rolling Stone*, 26 June, http://www.rolling stone.com/reviews/album/10621185/ review/10681006/the_eraser.

Sheinbaum, John J. 2002. "Progressive Rock and the Inversion of Musical Values." In *Progressive Rock Reconsidered*, ed. Kevin Holm-Hudson. New York: Routledge, 21–42.

Shuker, Roy. 1998. *Key Concepts in Popular Music.* London and New York: Routledge.

Smith, R. J. 2001. "Sounds Like Music." *Village Voice*, 26 June. http://www .villagevoice.com/issues/0126/rjsmith .php.

Spicer, Mark. 2008 [1999]. "Large-Scale Strategy and Compositional Design in the Early Music of Genesis." In *Expression in Pop-Rock Music: A Collection of Critical and Analytical Essays*, ed. Walter Everett. New York: Routledge, 313–44.

———. 2004. "(Ac)cumulative Form in Pop-Rock Music." *Twentieth-Century Music* 1:1: 29–64.

Stone, William. 1996. *Radiohead: Green Plastic Wateringcan.* London: UFO Music Ltd.

Stump, Paul. 1997. *The Music's All That Matters: A History of Progressive Rock.* London: Quartet Books.

Tate, Joseph, ed. 2005. *The Music and Art of Radiohead.* Aldershot, U.K.: Ashgate.

———. 2005. "Introduction." In *The Music and Art of Radiohead*, ed. Joseph Tate. Aldershot, U.K.: Ashgate, 1–8.

———. 2005. "Radiohead's Antivideos: Works of Art in the Age of Electronic Reproduction." In *The Music and Art of Radiohead*, ed. Joseph Tate. Aldershot, U.K.: Ashgate, 103–17.

———. 2005. "*Hail to the Thief*: A Rhyzomatic Map in Fragments." In *The Music and Art of Radiohead*, ed. Joseph Tate. Aldershot, U.K.: Ashgate, 177–95.

Tyrangiel, Josh. 2007. "Radiohead Says: Pay What You Want." *Time*, 1 October, http://www.time.com/time/arts/ article/0,8599,1666973,00.html.

Whetstone, Tony, Mark Cross, and Lauren Whetstone. 1996. "Inhibition, Contextual Segregation, and Subject Strategies in List Method Directed Forgetting." *Consciousness and Cognition* 5:395–417.

Whetstone, Tony, and Mark D. Cross. 1998. "Control of Conscious Contents in Directed Forgetting and Thought Suppression." *PSYCHE* 4:16, November, http://journalpsyche .org/ojs-2.2/index.php/psyche/article/ viewFile/2452/2381.

White, Curtis. 2005. "Kid Adorno." In *The Music and Art of Radiohead*, ed. Joseph Tate. Aldershot, U.K.: Ashgate, 9–14.

Wilson, Ashleigh. 2009. "Composer Pulls Some Old Strings." *Australian*, 14 August, http://www.theaustralian

.news.com.au/story/0,25197,25925014-16947,00.html.

Wolk, Douglas. 2000. "Like Our New Direction?" *Village Voice*, 3 October. http://www.villagevoice.com/issues/0040/wolk.php.

Youens, Susan. "Song cycle." In *Grove Music Online, Oxford Music Online*, http://www.oxfordmusiconline.com/subscriber/article/grove/music/26208.

Žižek, Slavoj. 1991. *Looking Awry: An Introduction to Jacques Lacan through Popular Culture*. Cambridge, Mass.: MIT Press.

1993 *Pablo Honey* (Capitol CDP 0777 7 81409 2 4)

1995 *The Bends* (Capitol CDP 7243 8 29626 2 5)

1997 *OK Computer* (Capitol CDP 7243 8 55229 2 5)

2000 *Kid A* (Capitol CDP 7243 5 27753 2 3)

2001 *Amnesiac* (Capitol CDP 7243 5 32764 2 3)

2001 *I Might Be Wrong: Live Recordings*
      (Capitol CDP 7243 5 36616 2 5)

2003 *Hail to the Thief* (Capitol CDP 7243 5 84543 2 1)

2006 *The Eraser* (Thom Yorke, XL Recordings XLCD200)

2007 *In Rainbows* (Xurbia Xendless Limited CDS X X001)

INDEX

Page numbers in italics refer to illustrations and tables.

MARIANNE TATOM LETTS is an independent scholar who holds music degrees from the University of North Texas and the University of Texas at Austin. Her publications include articles on the Beatles' film *Yellow Submarine*, the indie band Guided By Voices, the a cappella artist Petra Haden, and John Cameron Mitchell's film *Shortbus*. She lives in Seattle, where she enjoys calling and playing clarinet for contra, Scandinavian, and English country dances.